Geographies of Violence

SOCIETY AND SPACE SERIES

The *Society and Space* series explores the fascinating relationship between the spatial and the social. Each title draws on a range of modern and historical theories to offer important insights into the key cultural and political topics of our times, including migration, globalisation, race, gender, sexuality and technology. These stimulating and provocative books combine high intellectual standards with contemporary appeal for students of politics, international relations, sociology, philosophy, and human geography.

Series Editor: Professor Stuart Elden, University of Warwick

Geographies of Violence

Killing Space, Killing Time

Marcus A. Doel

SAGE

Los Angeles | London | New Delhi
Singapore | Washington DC | Melbourne

SAGE

Los Angeles | London | New Delhi
Singapore | Washington DC | Melbourne

SAGE Publications Ltd
1 Oliver's Yard
55 City Road
London EC1Y 1SP

SAGE Publications Inc.
2455 Teller Road
Thousand Oaks, California 91320

SAGE Publications India Pvt Ltd
B 1/I 1 Mohan Cooperative Industrial Area
Mathura Road
New Delhi 110 044

SAGE Publications Asia-Pacific Pte Ltd
3 Church Street
#10-04 Samsung Hub
Singapore 049483

© Marcus Doel 2017

First published 2017

Editor: Robert Rojek
Editorial assistant: Matthew Oldfield
Production editor: Katherine Haw
Copyeditor: Camille Bramall
Indexer: Marcus Doel
Marketing manager: Susheel Gokarakonda
Cover design: Wendy Scott
Typeset by: C&M Digitals (P) Ltd, Chennai, India
Printed by CPI Group (UK) Ltd, Croydon, CR0 4YY

Library of Congress Control Number: 2016958237

British Library Cataloguing in Publication data

A catalogue record for this book is available from the British Library

ISBN 978-1-4739-3768-0
ISBN 978-1-4739-3769-7 (pbk)

At SAGE we take sustainability seriously. Most of our products are printed in the UK using FSC papers and boards. When we print overseas we ensure sustainable papers are used as measured by the PREPS grading system. We undertake an annual audit to monitor our sustainability.

Contents

About the Author

Marcus Doel is Professor of Human Geography at Swansea University in Wales, where he is also the Deputy Pro-Vice-Chancellor for Research and Innovation, and the Co-Director of the Centre for Urban Theory. Marcus is an alumnus of the University of Bristol, and held positions at Liverpool John Moores University and Loughborough University in England prior to his move to Swansea University in 2000. He is the author of *Poststructuralist Geographies: The Diabolical Art of Spatial Science* (Rowman and Littlefield, Edinburgh University Press), the co-author of *Writing the Rural: Five Cultural Geographies* (Sage), and the co-editor of *Jean Baudrillard: Fatal Theories* (Routledge), *Moving Pictures/ Stopping Places: Hotels and Motels on Film* (Lexington Books), and *The Consumption Reader* (Routledge) amongst other works. Marcus has written and lectured widely on critical human geography, social and spatial theory, and post-structuralism, and he has published over 100 articles and book chapters in these and related fields.

The Joy of Killing

Should the history of geography be X-rated?

David Livingstone, 1992: 1

For us, the mirror of history, the continuity of history is shattered.

Jean Baudrillard, 2010a: 72

Jean-Luc Godard once quipped that a film should have a beginning, a middle, and an end – but not necessarily in that order. Violence, however, has neither beginning nor end and it certainly needs no introduction. You have been a victim, perpetrator, and bystander of violence ever since you squatted in your mother's womb: assaulted day and night by pounding innards; lashing out in the dark at the viscera all around; securing an escape by any means necessary – a labour of love, perhaps – only to scream, cry, and holler thereafter; and enduring severance from your Siamese twin, the accursed afterbirth, which was almost certainly either incinerated as medical waste or else syphoned off for the pharmaceutical and cosmetics industries. You were born amid faeces and urine, as St Augustine memorably put it. You are an agent, instrument, and product of violence. You are horrified through and through, like a plasticized cadaver or petrified trunk. Suffice to say that each individual harbours a unique genealogy of violence; that the 'trouble with being born' and the 'temptation to exist', to borrow fine phrases coined by Emil Cioran (2012a, 2012b), is that you are a horror – a horror from the off; a horror before anything 'happens' to you out there in the world into which you were thrown – dissevered, dividuated, denuded, and deshelled (Sloterdijk, 2011). And your destiny is to die from exposure to that world, as Lars von Trier demonstrates so adeptly in his film, *Antichrist* (2009).

The kernel of our mission, then, is horror – the horror of you, your existence, and your exposure to the world. You are saturated with violence and immersed in violence. It is your life-blood and death wish. So, I have no intention of introducing you to the violent geographies that are coming. You will encounter them soon enough. You have been encountering them all of your life. They are striking. Handsome even – like Death (Gracq, 2013). Some, such as Terror, are very close. Others, like droning specks over Waziristan, 'from a long way off look like flies' (Jorge Luis Borges, quoted in Foucault, 1974: xv). So, while innumerable violent geographies wait to be reacquainted with you, I wager that they are 'chatting madly … in an impersonation of gaiety', like bride-seeking zombies are wont to do: 'Beautiful day!' 'Certainly is!' 'Bought a new coat!' 'You did!' 'Yes, bought a new coat, this coat I'm wearing, I think it's very fine!' (Barthelme, 2003: 345). Or rather, these geographies of violence should be striking. For I also wager that so much of the violence and the horror that courses through you and your world no longer touches you at all. You have become wraithlike – a ghastly figure cut out of the horror; a ghostly figure cut off from the horror. Not all of the horror, to be sure, but most of it. Granted, you have your mortal wounds and mental scars, like everyone else: an identity, perhaps; a sorry saga, no doubt. But let's not dwell on that. Not now, at least.

Setting the pleasantries aside, then, dear reader, my aim is to bring you back from the land of the living dead, not by giving you a grand tour of the geographies of violence and their sublime ruins that stretch as far as the eye can see – a genteel 'show-and-tell' conducive to a cosy exchange of opinions or God forfend a heated debate – but rather by striking you anew with them. I want to hit you in the face and the stomach with the violence and the horror that is you and your world. So, dear reader, beware of what's coming. The horrors in this shattered mirror are closer than they appear! Consequently, I have a host of them reserved for you, from womblike torture chambers and humane killing machines to char-grilled cities and corpse mines. And in lieu of an introduction, and to add insult to injury, there will be a few 'savage welcomes' along the way: complete with howling guards, barking dogs, and excremental assaults. I will also – for the most part – dispense with the unpleasant business of appearing reasonable and argumentative, and the tiresome bother of trading opinions, especially with the tedious banter that hails from the Right. This world self-evidently deserves to perish and desires to perish. It is going forward, ever worstward, in word and in deed, fortified by the deliriums of sustainability and resilience. 'Another world' is not only possible (such low expectations!), it is inevitable. The end of the world is indeed nigh, but rest assured that it is only *this* world that is destined to perish. That should make us smile – like the Cheshire Cat, perhaps; or an enlightened torturer, even.

Now, having dispensed with the introductions, and settled into the gay chatter of violence, we are all but ready to strike out into the midst of the horror. So much violence awaits us: earthquakes and airquakes, asphyxiation booths and barbed-wire enclosures, heretic hunts and cat massacres, fumigators and firestorms, death marches and slaughterhouses, ghost cities and lethal labour, slander and iconoclasm, timetables and tele-vision, desk killers and cannibal bankers, life unworthy of life and the gift of death – not to mention 'the often catastrophic consequences of the smooth functioning of our … systems' (Žižek, 2009: 1) and the 'contemporary landscapes of terror, fear and political violence' (Gregory and Pred, 2007: 2) with which we are all too familiar. But before so doing, suffice to say that whilst we will be moving 'ever worstwards' in accordance with the spirit of our age – *'Progress!' 'Going forward!' 'Into eternity!'* – I would caution against reading too much into this hysterical 'line of flight'. For while it is true that we will encounter a sequence of violent geographies, beginning with 'the best' and ending with 'the worst', the line that skewers them is neither logical, nor causal, nor geographical, nor historical. The line is a mere contrivance. The sequence could obviously have been skewered otherwise. Reshuffled and remixed to infinity and beyond. And therein lies the essence of what I am after: to hit you with a constellation of violence; a constellation that can obviously be folded, unfolded, and refolded in many ways. Gilles Deleuze (1994) called it an 'explication' (from the Latin, *explicare*, to fold out). Deleuze and Félix Guattari (1988) called it a 'plateau', a 'rhizome' or 'origami', Manuel DeLanda (1997) a 'nonlinear history', and Michel Foucault (1972: 10) a 'space of dispersion'. Accordingly, what I am after is 'a hinge-logic, a hinge-style', as Jean-François Lyotard (1990a: 123) expressed it, so that we can 'put ourselves there where the disparate itself holds together, without wounding the dis-jointure, the dispersion, or the difference' (Derrida, 1994: 29). Violent conjunctures and disjunctures – such is the world.

So, as you strike out into the field of violence that lies ahead – peppered with mantraps, entanglements, and improvised explosive devices – I have sought to accompany your travails with a remix of the constellation that will amplify the resonance and maximize the shock. My guerrilla strategy chimes with Walter Benjamin's (2002: 460) 'literary montage', which was another explosive technique designed to awaken the living dead of modernity. 'In the fields with which we are concerned, knowledge comes only in lightning flashes', he said. 'The text is the long roll of thunder that follows' (Benjamin, 2002: 456). Consequently, the constellation to come is made up entirely of fragments that have been wrenched from their previous contexts, skewered by countless lightning rods, with reference and sense spilling out from these mutilated morsels in all directions. The work is an exquisite corpse (*cadavre exquis*). 'This text induces by agglutinating rather than demonstrating, by coupling and decoupling, gluing and ungluing rather than by exhibiting the continuous, and analogical, instructive, suffocating necessity of a discursive rhetoric' (Derrida, 1986: 75). And since I prefer noise to music, dissonance to harmony, disorder to order, cut-ups to stitch-ups, and the chaosmos to the cosmos, the resonances that resound throughout this ungodly constellation of labyrinthine echo chambers are entirely attuned to my deviant tastes. Pop geography: just repetitive beats and a passion for extreme tempos that risks smearing everything into a frightful drone. So, with a drum roll rather than a fanfare, let our violent encounters begin.

The Best of All Possible Violence

The Frightful Fallout from the Great Lisbon Earthquake

The true Evil is the very gaze which sees evil all around itself.

Hegel, quoted in Žižek, Santner and Reinhard, 2005: 139

Our taste for violence is as ardent as ever. My fondest example is a housewife recalling her first use of a food processor. 'Crushing food with lightning rapidity seems brutal and shocking', she recalls. 'I see hard nuts, apples, lemon peel cut to pieces and transformed into an unrecognizable mass. ... Something inside me rebels against this bringing of food into line' (quoted in Wildt, 1995: 31). Her distaste for the miniature slaughterhouse placed at her disposal is palpable. And yet, she continues, 'once I had tried it out a few times my hostility changed to honest admiration'.

Although unleashing ferocious violence on innocent vegetables is hardly a moral outrage, it nicely illustrates how violence has been industrialized and domesticated: from the ritual cruelty shared between lovers (teasing, taunting, belittling) to the calculated exploitation of mass-murder machines. Our culture has not become accustomed to all violence, to be sure; but enough violence, nonetheless: more than enough, perhaps. For just as millions of tabletop slaughterhouses rip through the flesh of soft fruit, millions of financial transactions tear through the fabric of the world: everything from deforestation and strip mining to ghost cities and suburban sprawl (Ewing, 2016; Leslie, 2013). Neighbourhoods, conurbations, and landscapes are shredded by capitalist development in an ever-intensifying maelstrom of violence: 'from its relentless and insatiable pressure for growth and progress; ... its pitiless destruction of everything and everyone it cannot use ... and its capacity to exploit crisis and chaos as a springboard for still more development, to feed itself on its own self-destruction' (Berman, 1999: 138–9). Capitalism is a carnival of cannibalism (Baudrillard, 2010b), some of which is spectacularly dramatized, especially in times of 'crisis', but most of which takes the form of an 'attritional lethality' (Nixon, 2011) that nibbles away at the face of the Earth – as if the planet itself had been taken to Room 101 in the Ministry of Love (Orwell, 2000). 'Landscapes could be classified in terms of how easily they can be nibbled, BITTEN', suggests Lyotard (1989a: 214). Walter Benjamin (1985) famously drew inspiration from Paul Klee's painting, *Angelus Novus* (1920), to convey this nightmarish storm of gnawing violence:

> Where we perceive a chain of events, he sees one single catastrophe that keeps piling wreckage upon wreckage and hurls it in front of his feet. The angel would like to ... make whole what has been smashed. But a storm is blowing from Paradise. ... This storm irresistibly propels him into the future to which his back is turned, while the pile of debris before him grows skyward. This storm is what we call progress. (Benjamin, 1985: 257–8)

Before entering the slaughterhouses of modernity and the ruins of capitalist development, I want to consider another key instance of divine violence: the Lisbon earthquake of 1755, which shook Europe's newly acquired spirit of philosophical optimism (*that all was for the best*) and its renewed confidence in human reason (*daring to know*), leaving 'those who lived through it feeling *conceptually* devastated' (Neiman, 2004: 239). We remain subject to the aftershocks of a shattered optimism and a wrecked Enlightenment, aftershocks that continue to reverberate around the world.

Optimism – in the sense of the optimal, *the best possible*, rather than the merely 'hopeful', which, once soured, becomes 'cruel optimism' (Berlant, 2011) – sought to explain how a thoroughly good, all-knowing, and all-powerful God could allow evil to flourish in His world, and the explanation boiled down to an optimal calculation that only a divinity could make: not simply that the occurrence of evil contributes to the greater good (sacrifice and silver linings), but rather that these specific evils are necessary for the greatest possible good to occur (optimization). God chose *these* evils because they are *the best* evils for His world. For an optimist, then, whatever happens is not only an integral part of a 'divine plan', it is essential to the unfolding of 'the best possible world'. Disease, war, famine, and suchlike all turn out to have been for the best. Similarly, with storms, floods, droughts, and so on. What was so shocking about the Lisbon earthquake, however, was that it demolished one of the most religious and modern cities on Earth. Indeed, the Lisbon of 1755 was a powerful imperial city in the grip of a construction boom. In the reign of King João V (1706–50), around 500 tons of gold had been brought to Lisbon from Portugal's most lucrative colony, Brazil, along with other plundered riches, including diamonds, sugar, tobacco, coffee, and slaves. '"Riches do not profit in the day of wrath," warned Proverbs, and on All Saints' 1755 they didn't', comments Nicholas Shrady (2009: 111), 'like a biblical day of reckoning, most of what the city and its inhabitants had coveted was reduced to rubble'. At least 60,000 people were killed, and 12,000 buildings destroyed, by the earthquake, tsunami, and wildfires. Such devastation shocked God-fearing folk, not least because 'one in six of Lisbon's adult population was a *religioso*', notes Edward Paice (2008: 10). 'With more than 500 monasteries and convents and countless churches, the Portugal of this era came to be memorably described as "more priest-ridden than any other country in the world, with the possible exception of Tibet"' (Paice, 2008: 10, quoting Charles Davison, 1936). Whether this 'urbicide' expressed God's wrath or the optimal unfolding of the world, people feared what lay in store for other, less pious, places.

The Lisbon of 1755 was on the cutting edge of modernity. Like many other European cities, Lisbon became a repository for extraordinary wealth plundered from a worldwide empire. The suffering of millions of distant others was transmogrified into monumental architecture and lavish interiors. And yet Lisbon remained in the grip of monarchy and church, whose despotic tendencies were a fetter on the Enlightenment spirit of entrusting human reason with the power to take command of the brave new world of modernity. The Portuguese Inquisition, established in 1536 by Pope Paul III at the request of King João III, was still combating heresy in the 1750s through 'torture, show trials, and ghastly public *autos-da-fé*' (Shrady, 2009: 89) – those ritual 'acts of faith' by way of which evildoers performed public penance through suffering, such as being flayed, hung or burnt at the stake; acts that could even seize the dead. For example, 'the execution of suicides ... was usually done by dragging their corpses through the street' (Friedland, 2012: 188). Secular versions of the *auto-da-fé* continued well beyond the eighteenth century, not least in the form of public executions and exemplary punishments; although with the death of God, and the abandonment of Man to the 'here and now', at least the dead were spared the indignity of postmortem execution as their souls were cast beyond the reach of power. Death no longer necessarily signified the transition from one authority to another (from an earthly sovereign to a Heavenly Father), but rather 'the moment when the individual escapes all power, falls back on himself and retreats ... into his own privacy' (Foucault, 2004: 248). Nevertheless, cadavers would continue to be exploited for all manner of purposes, from dissection to crash tests (Roach, 2004).

Lisbon, then, was a Janus-faced city in 1755, and optimism bridged the gulf between faith and reason. The city glanced forward to the blossoming of modernity by gingerly 'daring to know' (as Immanuel Kant belatedly put it when answering the question 'What is Enlightenment?' in 1784), thereby risking the wrath of God for usurping His prerogative; whilst also harking back to the foundations of the monarchy and church that still had to be secured at all costs: faith, devotion, and servitude to God and His representatives on Earth, enforced through the law-preserving violence of the Inquisition, and the long-standing institutions of a 'persecuting society' originally designed to control heretics, lepers, and Jews (Moore, 1990). Trying to reconcile faith with reason was always a risky undertaking, and the Inquisition was well versed in the suppression of such heresy: from idiosyncratic ravings to rival doctrines. Even proving the necessity of God by way of doubt was to put Him on trial. Indeed, the seventeenth century's toying with 'doubt' (which offered a foretaste of 'critical' and 'revolutionary' thinking), exemplified by René Descartes, would lead Karl Marx and Friedrich Engels to declare in their *Communist Manifesto* (1848): 'All that is solid melts into air, all that is holy is profaned, and man is at last compelled to face with sober senses his real conditions of life.' Accordingly, empowering human reason, daring to know, and raising doubt all flirted with heresy and invited the wrath of God and the state. Enlightenment thinking was primarily a clandestine and scurrilous affair in the eighteenth century, doggedly pursued by the police and censors. The iconic 'Light of Reason' tended to illuminate not the upper echelons of society (enlightening despotism from above), but the filth of 'Grub Street', often in the guise of pornography and slander (Darnton, 1996).

Faith and reason have always been blood-soaked terms, and would become even more so in the 'Age of Revolution' (1789–1848) and the 'Age of Empire' (1875–1914), to use Eric Hobsbawm's (1962, 1994) periodization. The enlightened doctrine of optimism (from the Latin '*optimum*', meaning 'best'), which was most famously associated with Leibniz's (1985) claim in 1710 that God had created 'the best of all possible worlds', sought to reconcile faith and reason. For Leibniz, there was no contradiction between the notion that God is omnibenevolent, omnipotent, and omniscient, and the fact that suffering, misfortune, and evil exist in His world. God has chosen *this* world precisely because it is the best of *all* possible worlds. This combination of good and evil is optimal, and each instance of minimalist evil contributes to the greater good. Accordingly, what we regard as inexplicable suffering, misfortune, or evil from our all-too-human perspective is necessary for the realization of all that is good. Optimism is essentially a philosophy of silver linings in which 'evil is a rational manifestation of God's grandeur and forms a requisite part in the most complex fulfillment of a providential plan' (Yolton et al., 1995: 382).

Optimism was the perfect mentality for Janus-faced Lisbon, with its 'embarrassment of riches' garnered from landscapes of horror on the one hand and its pious devotion to church and state on the other hand. 'Armed with a portentous faith and a treasury swollen with Brazilian gold', writes Shrady (2009: 107), King João V 'went on a building frenzy for the glory of God and his own majesty', the most lavish part of which was a vast monastery-cum-palace at Mafra. From 1715 to 1735, the project occupied 50,000 workers, 'had nearly a thousand rooms, from gilt-filled royal chambers to spartan monks' cells', and cost an astronomical figure (£4 million), entirely 'financed by the infernal, slave-driven mines of Brazil' (Shrady, 2009: 108). And then, on All Saints' Day 1755, an earthquake laid the priest-ridden and slave-driven city of Lisbon to waste.

'By the time the first English refugees returned home religious shock-waves generated by the earthquake had spread throughout the northern hemisphere', contends Edward Paice (2008: 163). Religious and scientific orthodoxy obviously agreed that God spoke through 'natural' disasters. While 'the role of science was to ascertain the exact means by which his speech had been articulated' (Paice, 2008: 216), the role of religion was to interpret God's speech: 'what was His message? And to whom exactly was it addressed?' (Paice, 2008: 164).

Many Protestants averse to Catholicism, such as the Methodist preacher John Wesley, insisted that God's wrath was directed at the barbaric Inquisitions of Spain, Portugal, and Rome. By contrast, the Catholic Church attributed the disaster to the sinfulness of the people, even though 'many people were killed as they crowded into their churches' while the red-light district emerged largely unscathed (O'Hara, 2010: 38) and 'hundreds of criminals ... made their escape from the fallen prisons' (Hamblyn, 2009: 44). Despite the ruination of much of Lisbon's inquisitorial infrastructure – including the Palace of the Inquisition itself, two of its prisons, and its torture chambers – the Catholic Church concluded that it needed to be more, rather than less, zealous in its persecution of heretics, a response that Voltaire (François-Marie Arouet) satirized in his best-selling underground novella, *Candide, or Optimism*: 'After the earthquake, which had destroyed three-quarters of Lisbon, the sages of that country could think of no more effective means of averting further destruction than to give the people a fine *auto-da-fé*' (Voltaire, 2005: 15). *Candide* was published in 1759 – in the midst of the Seven Years War (1756–63), which was the last major conflict involving all of the great European powers prior to the French Revolution (1789). It was also published under a pseudonym (Dr Ralph), and as a faux translation (ostensibly from German), to misdirect the religious and secular authorities. (Arouet had adopted the *nom de plume* Voltaire in 1718, after a spell in the Bastille for composing satirical verses that defamed the Duke of Orléans, Regent of France.)

If the disaster was occasioned by the vices of Lisbon's population, then what did God have in store for rapacious London and debauched Paris? As a precaution, King George II decreed 6 February 1756 as a day of fasting and penance throughout Britain. After all, even the French were 'shocked by "the extraordinary licentiousness that reigns openly in London"' (White, 2012: 347). But not every monarch was so god-fearing and credulous. The court of King Louis XV at Versailles 'seems to have regarded the disaster as a source of morbid amusement' (Shrady, 2009: 46). Jittery Britain also offered unprecedented aid, sending six ships laden with food, construction materials, and gold and silver coins. Meanwhile, Spain sent four wagonloads of gold coins, and Hamburg sent four shiploads of timber and clothing. Richard Hamblyn (2009: xviii) considers the Lisbon quake to have been 'the first modern disaster, establishing the protocols of international humanitarian response', while Shrady attributes this newfound generosity to the growing interdependencies of the

European powers. Eighteenth-century Europe was already binding itself into one incestuous world, and Lisbon was its third busiest port.

While Europe was fixated on the meaning of the Lisbon earthquake, it remained oblivious to the devastation of other places, including Albufeira, Cádis, Cascais, Faro, Lagos, Sanlúcar, and Setúbal, and had been largely indifferent to other destructive quakes, such as Lima in 1746, and Port au Prince in 1751. Indeed, Lisbon itself had endured many earthquakes, 'including severe ones in 1597, 1598, 1699 and 1724' (Hamblyn, 2009: 12). As always, some people and places are presumed to matter to all, while others count for next to nothing. The suffering of the latter does not yield grievable lives, says Judith Butler (2004, 2009). Such is the intertwined 'asymmetry of suffering' and 'asymmetry of compassion' (Klein, 2002: 166 and 168, respectively) that reveals the existence of not one but two worlds (at least), despite all of the guff about globalization, the global village, and one-worldism. The world *as such* 'does not really exist', insists Alain Badiou (2008: 60). 'What exists is a false and closed world, artificially kept separate from general humanity by incessant violence.' This is why the Occident's encounter with the New World was so terrifying and diabolical – not only for those Amerindians exterminated and enslaved in their millions, and the millions of Africans subsequently swept up by the transatlantic slave trade to feed the sugar, tobacco, and cotton plantations' insatiable demand for labour, but also for those god-fearing Europeans who came face to face with the material existence of what should have remained void. It is also why Arizona's Sonoran Desert (which braces the US–Mexico border) and the Mediterranean Sea (buttressing Europe against incursions from North Africa and the Middle East) have become key sites for the enforcement of lethal border control in the twenty-first century. Thousands have died in these and similar deathscapes, through drowning, dehydration, hypothermia, etc. (De León, 2015; IOM, 2014; Rubio-Goldsmith et al., 2016). The death marches and death voyages have continued, under policies with poetic names such as *Prevention Through Deterrence* (est. 1994), the US Border Patrol's on-going strategy, which has 'pushed unauthorized migration away from population centers and funneled it into more remote and hazardous border regions. This policy has had the unintended consequence of increasing the number of fatalities along the border, as unauthorized migrants attempt to cross over the inhospitable Arizona desert' (Haddal, 2010: 13–14). The optimization of such policies has made them more lethal, precipitating efforts to ameliorate the suffering, such as the US Border Safety Initiative (with its water stations, panic poles, and rescue teams for 'distressed aliens'), Italy's short-lived 'Operation Mare Nostrum', the European Union's (EU) Frontex-led 'Operation Triton' (named after the Greek God who weaponized the oceans), and the European Border Surveillance System (Eurosur), all of which deliver militarized humanitarianism and humane militarism. Behind the veil of optimism, which spares the blushes of good people the world over, lies a wasteland where all of the residual evils are dumped.

The screening off from one another of the interconnected worlds of slave-driven colonial horror on the one hand and priest-ridden metropolitan civility on the other is exemplified by the 'rubber terror' of the Congo Free State under King Leopold II of Belgium, a century or so after the Lisbon quake. In the late 1890s, Edmund Morel worked for a Liverpool-based shipping company that carried all cargo to and from the Free State via Antwerp. While vessels filled with valuable commodities (mainly rubber and ivory) came out of the Congo, they returned laden with military supplies, steamer parts, and little else. 'From what he saw at the wharf in Antwerp, and from studying his company's records in Liverpool, [Morel] deduced the existence – on another continent, thousands of miles away – of slavery' (Hochschild, 2006: 180). Between 1880 and 1920, as many as 10 million Congolese were murdered, worked to death, starved to death, or died from disease as Leopold's Congo became the most lucrative colony in Africa. Moreover, since the Congo was the king's personal property, it was not an affair of state (and therefore not subject to public scrutiny), but an investment vehicle for various companies (such as the Anglo-Belgian India Rubber and Exploration Co., and Société Anversoise du Commerce au Congo), backed by a mercenary gendarmerie (*Force Publique*), whose brutality became legendary once the veil of commercial secrecy was lifted by Morel (Hochschild, 2006). Like the 'Honourable East India Company' – a British joint-stock company backed by Royal Charter (1600) and vast private armies that effectively ruled India for 100 years (from the 1757 Battle of Plassey to the 1857 Indian Rebellion, after which the Crown assumed direct control of India), and which, once China had been broken open during the 'Opium Wars' (1839–42, and 1856–60), controlled half of the world's trade (Milligan, 1995; Robins, 2012) – the Congo Free State was a proving ground for regimes of optimal horror more commonly associated with totalitarianism and the mercenary armies of disaster capitalism's increasingly lucrative 'war on terror' (Scahill, 2008; Singer, 2008).

The screening off from view of the 'Congo Holocaust' was so effective that Leopold came to be seen as a great humanitarian for the vast expenditure this 'Builder King' lavished on the 'good people' of Belgium: parks, museums, galleries, and palaces. Meanwhile, Jeremy Black (2011: 226) wryly notes that Leopold's form of 'colonialism involved a degree of control that, while not slavery, was scarcely freedom'. Thereafter, the adventure of capitalism experimented with countless ways of enforcing 'slavery by another name', as Douglas Blackmon (2008) phrased it when referring to the re-enslavement of African Americans through involuntary servitude from the Civil War to the Second World War, such as California's 'Golden Gulag', the wider 'Prison Industrial Complex', and the 'global war prison' (Gilmore, 2007; Gilmore and Gilmore, 2008; Gregory, 2006, 2007). The US contains barely one twentieth of the world's population, but holds a quarter of its prison population. It enjoys – by a considerable margin – the highest per capita rate of imprisonment of any country on earth. The re-emergence of 'precarity' as a key component of the neoliberal regime of accumulation and mode of social regulation is only the latest variant of wage slavery (Standing, 2011).

On an even greater scale than the Congolese Holocaust, Tzvetan Todorov (1992) estimates that as the Spanish colonized the Americas, the indigenous population collapsed from 80 million to 10 million, most dying from disease and starvation attributable to colonization, and the rest from massacres and slave labour. 'None of the great massacres of the twentieth century can be compared to this hectatomb', he declares (Todorov, 1992: 133). Moreover, Todorov emphasizes the modern character of this sixteenth-century annihilation. The age-old desire for gold was no longer just one passion amongst others (alongside prestige, obligation, purgation, pleasure, etc.). It had become *the* passion subsuming all others, pursued with unprecedented ferocity. Furthermore, this monomania accords with the subsequent acceleration of capital accumulation, and the obliteration of all obstacles that stood in its way; the use of famine as a weapon of mass destruction (Conquest, 1986; Davis, 2002; Dikötter, 2011), or *'terror by starvation'*, as Gregori Maximoff (1940: 45) memorably called it; and the disposability of prisoners of war (Steinbacher, 2004). For example, from 1933 to 1945, the Nazi *Schutzstaffel* (SS) constructed an ever-shifting concentration-camp system (*Konzentrationslager* – KL or KZ for short), comprising 27 main camps and over 1,100 satellite camps, primarily for forced and lethal labour. The KL held millions of prisoners, most of whom died. The SS brought optimized evil into the heart of Europe, and revelled in the worst of all possible worlds. Optimism has remained indelibly stained with horror ever since.

KL labour perfectly illustrates horror at work, the spectre of which stalks capitalism (Cederström and Fleming, 2012), not least because dead labour (capital) feeds off living labour (work), as if it were a vampire or cannibal (Carver, 1998; Neocleous, 2003; Sutherland, 2011). Whereas capital consumes labour in its thirst for profit, and fattens itself by devouring the flesh and brains of others, 'labor in the camp was a means of oppression, an instrument of terror. It was meant to humiliate, to torment, to break the power of the inmates to resist, to drain and destroy them' (Sofsky, 1997: 21). Indeed, camp labour took its place alongside mass shootings, gas chambers, disease, and starvation as 'one of the principal instruments of annihilation' (Cavarero, 2011: 37). While regimes of 'convict labour', 'slave labour', and even 'wage labour' entail at least some effort to sustain people's capacity to work, regimes of 'lethal labour' consume them directly. 'The economy of the concentration camps was an economy of waste, the squandering of human labor power' (Sofsky, 1997: 21). These people were not regarded as valuable lives 'sacrificed' to an insatiable war economy, but worthless lives to be 'wasted' pure and simple. Indeed, 'the Germans' invocation of "work" was not necessarily or primarily referring to productive labor, "work" for Jews having been understood … for what it was: just another means of slaughter' (Goldhagen, 1997: 369). At Buchenwald, for instance, 'work consisted of carrying sacks of wet salt back and forth', and starvation diets made it fatal. It is worth recalling that the so-called 'work ethic' emerged in prisons as a disciplinary technique for moral instruction – breaking rocks, digging earth, hauling logs – rather than as a productive technique to be exploited. It is also worth noting that the movement of people can also be murderous, such as the Bataan death march (1942) and the Armenian death caravans (1915–16). As the Ottoman Empire was emptied of its Armenian population, those that were not immediately massacred were herded towards the Syrian Desert.

> Only a quarter of all deportees survived the hundreds of miles and weeks of walking. ... The Ottoman government had made no provisions for the feeding and the housing of the hundreds of thousands of Armenian deportees on the road. On the contrary, local authorities went to great lengths to make travel an ordeal from which there was little chance of survival. ... At remote sites along the routes ... the killing units slaughtered the Armenians with sword and bayonet. (Adalian, 1997: 44–5)

In the autumn of 1941, on the outskirts of the small Polish town of Oświęcim (Auschwitz), near a recently established concentration camp for Polish political prisoners, the Nazi SS began to construct a gigantic concentration camp at the village of Brzezinka (Birkenau). Heinrich Himmler 'wanted to intern tens of thousands of Soviet prisoners of war here and engage them in forced labour. There were plans for a "prisoner of war camp" for 50,000 inmates, which could later be enlarged first to 150,000, and later to 200,000 prisoners', writes Sybille Steinbacher (2004: 89). With the German invasion of Russia in the previous summer, 'the supply of Soviet prisoners of war was initially thought to be inexhaustible [and so] hundreds of thousands of them were thus abandoned to starvation. Of a total of 5.7 million Soviet prisoners of war, 3.3 million died', she continues (Steinbacher, 2004: 94), and of those, 'two-thirds never left the occupied territories and remained under the supervision of the Wehrmacht' (Mazower, 2009: 161). By winter, as the German advance faltered and the Red Army pushed back, 'it became clear that Soviet prisoners of war were not going to be supplying the massive numbers of workers expected', and so Auschwitz–Birkenau 'was transformed ... into an extermination camp'. At least 870,000 Jews were murdered according to Nikolaus Wachsmann's (2015) estimate, along with at least 230,000 others, thereby aligning the camp with the five other extermination centres that killed at least 2 million more Jews between them: the other hybrid KL concentration and extermination camp at Majdanek; the three *Aktion Reinhard* camps dedicated to extermination at Belzec, Sobibor, and Treblinka; and the death camp at Chelmno. All of these built on the involuntary 'euthanasia' *Aktion T-4* programme that imposed 'mercy deaths' on those mentally ill and physically disabled patients in German medical institutions who were deemed 'useless eaters', 'burdensome', and 'lives unworthy of life' (Friedlander, 1995; Gallagher, 1997). Naturally, T-4 doctors preached the optimism of the *Aktion*. The purgation of 'lives unworthy of life' was for the greater good. Indeed, the Nazis' optimism knew no bounds: worldwide racial purgation would yield the best of all possible worlds – a world 'free' and 'clean' of the Jews (*Judenfrei*). 'In Auschwitz, Chelmno, and the three *Aktion Reinhard* death camps, the Germans gassed the overwhelming majority of the almost exclusively Jewish victims upon arrival. In Majdanek, they gassed or shot 40 per cent' (Goldhagen, 1997: 293), with the rest dying primarily from starvation-induced exhaustion and disease.

In addition to those killed in the camps, at least 1.5 million Jews were killed on the spot, mostly in mass shootings undertaken by SS death squads (*Einsatzgruppen*) and Police Battalions, which accompanied the Wehrmacht advance into the Soviet Union. They all 'understood that this ... was not to be a war of military conquest, but one in which the opponents ... were to be vanquished utterly, destroyed, obliterated from the face of the earth' (Goldhagen, 1997: 149). Hundreds of thousands more died through lethal labour, starvation, epidemics in the ghettoes – 'those German holding tanks for Jews consigned to extermination' (Goldhagen, 1997: 149) – and death marches, which 'were not means of transport; the marching transports were means of death' (Goldhagen, 1997: 367). Some of the trains that transported Jews to the ghettoes, transit camps, and extermination camps also functioned as 'death trains' (Browning, 2001; Gigliotti, 2010).

Given that the Nazis could exterminate millions of people using little more than paramilitary death squads, Daniel Goldhagen (1997: 10) challenges the notion 'that without gas chambers, modern means of transportation, and efficient bureaucracies, the Germans would have been unable to kill millions of Jews'. Indeed, the Armenian and Rwandan genocides, which claimed over 2 million lives between them, were essentially low-technology affairs: 'death caravans' (death marches) for the former – 'organized like an ambulatory extermination camp' (Cavarero, 2011: 33) – and machete attacks for the latter; and all the while shooting and raping (Balakian, 2005; Hatzfeld, 2005). Moreover, at the January 1942 meeting in Wannsee to coordinate the so-called 'Final Solution to the Jewish Question', the concentration-camp system was conspicuously absent:

> Within days of the Wannsee conference, however, SS leaders changed their tune. The trigger, it seems, was their final acceptance that the grandiose settlement plans in the east would never be realized with Soviet POWs. ... The SS now looked for replacements and soon found them: instead of Soviet soldiers, Jews would build the gigantic settlements. (Wachsmann, 2015: 295)

Wachsmann (2015) estimates that 2.3 million people passed through the SS concentration-camp system between its inception in 1933 and its cessation in 1945, of whom at least 1.7 million died. Meanwhile, Anne Applebaum (2004) estimates that between the 1920s and 1950s, almost 29 million passed through the Soviet Gulag. This was a vast system of 'corrective labour camps', 'labour colonies', and prisons, that comprised 476 camps with around 2.5 million inmates at its fullest extent in the early 1950s, and numerous 'special settlements' and 'colonization villages', with around 1.8 million 'special settlers' at its peak in 1931. The Gulag was created for the express purpose of liquidating much of the peasantry (the so-called 'dekulakization' and 'collectivization' of farming) and in so doing provided a vast pool of labour for the USSR's most inhospitable regions (Khlevniuk, 2004; Viola, 2007). In the decade of the Stalinist Purges and the Great Terror, the 1930s, there were at least 2 million deaths in custody, around a third of which were accomplished by firing squad (Getty and Naumov, 2010). 'Estimates of the number of Stalin's victims over his twenty-five-year reign, from 1928 to 1953, vary widely, but 20 million is now considered the minimum' (Brent, 2008: 3). Maximoff (1940) coined a pair of chilling phrases to convey the emergence under Lenin of this two-fold regime of extermination through shooting and 'state slavery'. He called the former the 'wet guillotine' and the latter the 'dry guillotine' – the physical annihilation of people 'by handing out long prison sentences, by exiling them to baneful places, to break their morale by making them living corpses' (Maximoff, 1940: 129). Likewise, the Nazi regime's move away from the mass murder of Jews by shooting squads (*Einsatzgruppen*) to their mass murder in death factories is another example of the shift from a 'wet' to a 'dry' guillotine. 'Between Auschwitz and the Gulag, there was no difference in kind' (Vidal-Naquet, 1996: 153). The best of all possible worlds would have the worst of all possible evils for its foundations.

Scarcely anyone now gives much credence to the notion that the horrors of the nineteenth and twentieth centuries were expressions of either God's wrath or His optimism. In 1755, however, few were prepared to countenance the possibility that God had not singled out Lisbon for destruction. And yet, a more enlightened view about the catastrophe was beginning to occur to some doubting Thomases: that 'this was a natural disaster, without malice, direction or purpose' (O'Hara, 2010: 39). For although hardly anyone was ready to embrace the earth-shattering realization that we inhabit a godless world, in which nothing is permitted or proscribed, the Lisbon quake undoubtedly 'shook the confidence of many Enlightenment thinkers in providence and the essential goodness of God. ... The earthquake undermined faith in a rational God, and precipitated a backlash against Enlightenment optimism' (O'Hara, 2010: 39). Voltaire powerfully articulated this backlash in a letter to his banker, Jean Robert Tronchin, in November 1755:

> This is indeed a cruel piece of natural philosophy! We shall find it difficult to explain ... such fearful disasters *in the best of all possible worlds* – when a hundred thousand ants, our neighbours, are crushed to death in seconds in one of our ant-heaps. ... What will the preachers say now – especially if the Palace of the Inquisition is left standing! I flatter myself that those reverend fathers, the Inquisitors, have been crushed just like everyone else; which ought to teach men not to persecute men: for, while a few sanctimonious hypocrites are burning a few fanatics, the earth opens up and swallows them all. (Voltaire, 2005: 128, note 3)

Voltaire argued that 'optimism was a cruel deceit for human sufferers' (Yolton et al., 1995: 382), and his satirical novella, *Candide, or Optimism* (1759), was a scathing parody. Candide lives in an Eden-like paradise and is indoctrinated with optimism by his tutor, Pangloss. Once ousted from paradise, however, Candide gradually becomes disillusioned with optimism as he witnesses all manner of catastrophes. In Lisbon's harbour, a storm destroys their boat. A sailor makes no effort to save a drowning man, and Pangloss explains that the harbour was created so that the man might drown. When they reach Lisbon, an earthquake and tsunami kill tens of thousands. The sailor starts looting, and Pangloss lectures Candide on the optimism of the situation. Subsequently, Pangloss discusses his optimism with Inquisitors, leading to him and Candide being arrested as heretics. Candide is flogged, and Pangloss miraculously survives a hanging. Eventually, Candide concludes that nothing turned out for the best – 'the ultimate reason of things is unknown and unknowable' (Hampson, 1990: 92). When the earth, sea or air quake, there is nothing to understand or explain. There is no solution – least of all a Final Solution – to the horror of the world.

While shaken optimists and anxious moralists agonized over the meaning and significance of the quake, those accustomed to the Grand Tour simply embraced the ruined landscape, which, unlike the sublime ruins of Ancient civilizations, 'was far more immediate and sinister because it lacked the patina of age' (Shrady, 2009: 166). Lisbon's ruins 'produced only horror' (Shrady, 2009: 167). Such horror echoes down the centuries. For example, it echoes in the wake of San Francisco's 1906 earthquake and firestorm, 'one of history's biggest urban infernos before aerial warfare' (Solnit, 2009: 13), which some regarded as yet another expression of God's wrath. 'All along the path of the earthquake, priests seized upon this act of nature to warn that damnation was at hand' (Thomas and Morgan Witts, 1971: 217–18; cf. Solnit, 2009). Likewise with contemporary quakes (Gergan, 2017). Lisbon's horror also echoes in the postindustrial ruins of cities such as Detroit (Marchand and Meffre, 2010; Moore, 2010), a city destroyed by the violence of finance capitalism, which may yet prove to have the best possible ruins if the metastatic urban sprawl gives way to a sublime 're-wilding' and 'pastoralization' through plant recolonization and urban agriculture (Gallagher, 2010). And it also echoes in the wake of the Allies' Second World War area-bombing campaign (1942–5), which consumed cities such as Dresden and Hamburg in hurricane-force firestorms (Addison and Crang, 2006; Lowe, 2007; Taylor, 2004). If the '1944 proposal … for the post-war "pastoralization" of Germany by the removal of all its heavy industry had ever been implemented, how long would it have taken for woodland to cover the mountains of ruins all over the country?' (Sebald, 2003: 40–1).

By a cruel twist of fate, much of the ruination wrought by the slow violence of finance capitalism has been consumed in its turn by the slow-motion conflagration unleashed by the 'best of all possible' arsonists: from legions of landlords who made the rational calculation that building-insurance fraud was more lucrative than residential lettings, to spatial scientists working for the RAND corporation who optimized New York City's Fire Department, with the result that 'Jimmy Carter, Ronald Reagan, and Mother Teresa came to marvel at the spectacular ruins and wonder just how it was that the richest city in the world could burn down' (Flood, 2010: 277). At the peak of the destruction, 1970–80, 'roughly 600,000 people's homes were lost to fire and abandonment' (Flood, 2010: 18). Some census tracts in the South Bronx lost more than 97 per cent of their buildings, and many others lost more than half. Detroit has recently been at the forefront of postmodernity's creeping firestorms (LeDuff, 2013), just as New Orleans has been at the forefront of its creeping floods (Brinkley, 2006; Cooper and Block, 2006; Dyson, 2006; Giroux, 2006).

In the aftermath of the Lisbon earthquake, the Portuguese Court considered relocating to Brazil but chose instead to rebuild Lisbon, embracing enlightened 'conceptions of monumental town planning' (Yolton et al., 1995: 291), including seismic-resistant buildings, standardized construction techniques, and comprehensive sanitation (Shrady, 2009). Modernity was badly shaken by the quake but back on track, although without the optimized stabilizers of faith and reason. If there was going to be a world in which all turned out for the best, then it would have to be *forced* into existence by human action. So, we can anticipate much more horror to come. The 'Age of Revolution' (1789–1848) is only a few twists and turns ahead, and a different class of heretic will find itself seeking salvation through secular *autos-da-fé*: strung up from lamp posts and beheaded by Saint Guillotine.

Ironically, Portugal was an early beneficiary of revolutionary zeal. As the Napoleonic Wars raged (1803–15), 'something remarkable was happening, unparalleled in the history of European colonialism' (Wilcken, 2004: 3). In 1807, King João VI, and 10,000 of his subjects, fled Lisbon for Rio de Janeiro, leaving Portugal to be picked over by the other European powers. 'The seat of the Portuguese Empire, cast adrift from the Continent, had come to rest in the New World' (Wilcken, 2004: 3). Having endured the Inquisition, the wrath of God, and ferocious warfare, perhaps all had been for the best after all. Or perhaps not: 'The gold mines long exhausted, the colony had fallen back on its traditional role – as a slave-driven factory farm for Europe. Rio was then the largest slave market town in the Americas', writes Patrick Wilcken (2004: 4). In Brazil, 'the regent's ministers and advisers were forced to contemplate the effects of their policies and, worse still, to live amongst their own colonial handiwork. The shock was mutual.'

Across the nineteenth and twentieth centuries, optimism was largely kept at bay. The twentieth century in particular was a century of *extremes* (Hobsbawm, 1995) rather than optima, of *fractures* rather than integrals, and of *antagonisms* rather than reconciliations: 'the omnipresence of scission', says Alain Badiou (2007: 38). 'The passion of the [twentieth] century is the real, but the real as antagonism.' The twentieth century was above all the century of geno-cide, extermination, and annihilation – of Herero, Nama, Armenians, Kulaks, Jews, Slavs, Tutsi, Bosniaks, and many others (Levene, 2013a, 2013b; Totten, Parsons and Charny, 1997). If there is any optimizing to be done, then it is for maximum efficiency and asymmetry, in an attempt to extinguish all resistance (Caygill, 2013). The historical geography of 'manhunting' (heretic hunts, witch hunts, Jew hunts, jihadi hunts, etc. of both men and women) is a perfect illus-tration (Chamayou, 2012; Gaskill, 2010; Maxwell-Stuart, 2003; Scarre and Callow, 2001), especially when it is interlaced with the historical geography of barbed wire (Krell, 2002; Netz, 2009; Razac, 2002). Tens of millions of people were killed in the twentieth century as if they were animals, prey, or pests – rounded up, hunted down, fumigated, and incinerated.

With the fall of the Berlin Wall, collapse of the Soviet Union, and capitula-tion of 'communist' and 'socialist' states to capitalism, in the 1990s it seemed as though optimism had returned in a blaze of glory. As the millennium stag-gered to a close, capitalism imagined itself to be globally triumphant, with nothing standing in the way of its unfettered 'globalization' – not even the archaic revival of ethnically and religiously charged civil wars in the Congo, Rwanda, Sierra Leone, Yugoslavia, and elsewhere, which it regarded as merely parochial anachronisms harking back to feuds from yesteryear; and certainly not the spluttering of the biosphere as it started to choke on the ash clouds of three centuries' worth of industrial activity, which it regarded as a new investment frontier crying out for capital-intensive and financialized solutions: weather derivatives, catastrophe bonds, carbon trading, etc. At long last, then, everything was poised to revolve around 'You' – politics, eco-nomics, culture, religion, and even the future of the climate and the planet. Francis Fukuyama was the most vocal in proclaiming the optimistic Good News. We have arrived at *The End of History*, he declared (Fukuyama, 1993), thanks to the victorious and virtuous Holy Trinity of consumer capitalism, liberal democracy, and Enlightened individualism. There was seemingly noth-ing left to challenge the Empire of Capital and its New World Order – except, perhaps, for an anachronistic blast from the past, such as religious fundamen-talism, violent extremism, or a suicide pact between the climate and the biosphere. Welcome to the twenty-first century, which sees only Capitalism or Barbarism ahead. In *Specters of Marx*, Jacques Derrida (1994) advances a wonderful riposte to Fukuyama's neo-evangelistic and optimistic tone. Everything is far from the best in the Empire of Capital (Hardt and Negri, 2001; Harvey, 2010, 2014; Wood, 2005), and silver linings are conspicuously absent from the 'catastrophic convergence' of so many environmental, climatic, and social disasters (Parenti, 2011). By way of example, Derrida (1994: 81) lists ten of the most obvious 'plagues' of the 'new world order', which include inter-ethnic wars, nuclear weapons, and phantom states (drug cartels, the mafia, etc.).

Our world is clearly far from being the best. Indeed, I am tempted to say that if it is making progress, then its progress is 'ever worstward' into the 'utmost dim', as Samuel Beckett put it in *Worstward Ho!* 'So leastward on. So long as dim still. Dim undimmed. Or dimmed to dimmer still. To dimmost dim. Leastmost in dimmost dim. Utmost dim. Leastmost in utmost dim. Unworsenable worst' (Beckett, 2009: 108). So many genocides. So many Gulags. So many death factories. So many incinerated cities. And the promise of so much worse to come. Now that God is dead, and it is the turn of zombie capitalism to run amok over the face of the Earth, we are perhaps left with the *worst* of all possible worlds: a world of *optimal* evil, of *optimized* evil – not *pure* evil or *absolute* evil; but the *lesser* evil, the *leastmost* evil, the *calculated* evil; an evil that is precisely tailored by the 'invisible hand' of optimization to the measure of the situation. Hereinafter, modernity promises *just enough* violence and *just enough* horror. Such is the judicious reasoning of the strongest. Accordingly, Eyal Weizman suggests that we should memorialize this optimal evil:

> in the form of the digits 6-6-5 built of concrete blocks, and installed like the Hollywood sign. ... This number, one less than the number of the beast – that of the devil and of total evil – might capture the essence of our humanitarian present obsessed with the calculations and calibrations that seek to moderate, ever so slightly, the evils that it has largely caused itself. (Weizman, 2011a: 6)

Leibniz conceived of God as perpetually optimizing the combination of good and evil as if He were an econometrician 'solving a minimum problem in the calculus of variations' (Weizman, 2011a: 2). Optima are always balanced calculations – of positive and negative variances – and yet the fiendish twist for the calculus of the optimal evil is that the positive and negative variances are no longer cast as 'good' and 'evil', but rather as 'lesser' and 'greater' evils. The 'lesser' evil only appears to be relatively good in the mirror of the 'greater' evil (and vice versa). This is a truly diabolical twist, since the goodly are always *forced* to choose the 'lesser evil' to counter the 'greater evil', and they are always forced to choose *evil*. No wonder, then, that 'those who choose the lesser evil forget very quickly that they chose evil' (Arendt, 2003: 37). And the goodlier their intentions, the faster they loosen the 'lesser' and the quicker they forget their investment in evil. Given that the goodly *must* do evil, how can they do evil *well*? How can they undertake the *best* of all possible evils? Michael Ignatieff (2004) argues that when liberal democracies seek to prevent greater evils by resorting to lesser evils (coercive interrogation, torture, extrajudicial killings, human-rights violations, etc.), then it 'imposes an obligation on government[s] to justify such measures publicly, to submit them to judicial review, and to circumscribe them with sunset clauses so that they do not become permanent'; and he insists that 'exceptions do not destroy the rule but save it, provided that they are temporary, publicly justified, and deployed only as a last resort' (Ignatieff, 2004: viii). The law is called upon to circumscribe and govern its own suspension, like a slipped clutch that expends energy but without applying force. When the 'greater' evil tends towards pure evil, then the 'lesser' evil can correspondingly expand to approach asymptotically pure evil itself. Such is the logic that can rationalize the goodly recourse to internment camps, detention centres, terror bombing, and the weaponization of life itself. And when the goodly combat evildoers, they are frequently tempted to treat the latter as if they were beasts or rogues (Chomsky, 2005; Derrida, 2005). 'When a hypocritical imperialism combats its enemies in the name of human rights and treats its enemies like beasts, ... it is waging not a war but ... a state terrorism' (Derrida, 2011: 74).

The logic of the lesser evil is well suited to the imperatives that now govern the military–industrial–humanitarian complex. Optimal violence – optimized violence – is efficient and effective violence. It can be modulated and leveraged over time and space in a measured response to the ups and downs of the situation as it unfolds. Such is the supple logic of a 'society of control' (Deleuze, 1992). Similarly, international humanitarian law also accords with the logic of the lesser evil. Its principle of *proportionality*, which aims to avoid 'excessive' violence and 'undue' suffering, is perfectly attuned to the principle of *optimal* violence. Indeed, there is nothing new about limiting excessive violence, which in so doing legitimates all forms of violence that are not excessive: 'by delineating categories of "illegitimate violence," the rules and regulations of war implicitly and explicitly construct what is legitimate violence' (Bourke, 2014: 79). Curtailing violence to suit the minimalist needs of the occasion was enshrined in the English Bill of Rights in 1689: *'excessive bail ought not to be required, nor excessive fines imposed, nor cruel and unusual punishments inflicted'* (my emphasis). This snug tailoring of violence was also woven into the Eighth Amendment to the US Constitution in 1791 (Bessler, 2013). What is new today is that the military and humanitarian convergence upon the miserly energetics of optimal violence is modulated by 'increasingly sophisticated technologies for minimizing the number of "necessary" corpses, [and] the search for "the best of all possible worlds" started giving ground to the present neo-Panglossian pessimism of the "least of all possible evils"' (Weizman, 2011a: 3). This modulation allows the optimal quantity and quality of violence to be continuously applied to sustain the desired objective indefinitely – whether that be the suppression of a marginalized community's capacity to riot in the rotting fringes of cities like London and Paris, or the 'splintered occupation' of territories such as the West Bank and Gaza Strip (Ophir, Givoni, and Hanafi, 2009; Segal and Weizman, 2003; Weizman, 2007, 2012). The ebb and flow of optimal violence would enable the perfect siege – in places such as the Arizona Desert, the Mediterranean Sea, the West Bank, and the Gaza Strip. Accordingly, Weizman (2011a: 6) argues that 'Gaza – where the system of humanitarian government is now most brutally exercised – is the proper noun for the horror of our humanitarian present.' That enduring obscenity is symptomatic of our worstward drift into the utmost dim, whilst beaming with undiminished optimism, even if the latter has turned increasingly cynical and cruel, and strayed far from equilibrium on countless occasions (DeLanda, 1997). Still, it could be worse, I suppose. We might have lived long, long ago, when things were dimmer still.

(2)

Once Upon a Time, Long, Long Ago

The Cesspits of the Enlightenment

And in truth, there is no such thing as reason; it exists only in bits and pieces.

Gilles Deleuze, 1997: 82

While the eighteenth century is often dubbed the 'Age of Enlightenment', we have begun to see that this is a misnomer. 'To equate the Enlightenment with the totality of Western thought in the eighteenth century is to get it badly wrong', cautions Robert Darnton (2003: 6). 'By viewing it as a concerted campaign on the part of a self-conscious group of intellectuals, one can reduce it to its proper proportions.' Although a certain Enlightenment spirit may have suffused parts of Europe by century's end, the continent remained largely unenlightened. Ignorance, superstition, and unreason held sway – just as with all the power of church and state at their disposal they still do today. Accordingly, Darnton proposes a 'deflation' of the Enlightenment. 'It was a concrete historical phenomenon, which can be located in time and pinned down in space' (Darnton, 2003: 4). Like the first, faltering attempts to illuminate the nighttime streets of Paris by lantern in the seventeenth century, the dim light of reason was more of a symbolic force than an actual accomplishment. It would take two more centuries for the European urban nightscape to be fully colonized be the luminary forces of law and order (the cold, harsh, and penetrative light of police surveillance: gas light, and then electric light, and more recently cameras), which formed a secure shell within which the capitalist 'world interior' of festivity, seduction, and play could flourish (the warm caress of commercial lighting draped an enchanting aura over things, especially commodities, much to the monomaniacal delight of entranced consumers ever since) (Olalquiaga, 1999; Schivelbusch, 1988; Sloterdijk, 2014). In the eighteenth century, even in cities such as Paris, 'policing' was mainly concerned with 'the ordering of public space' in terms of its material fabric, and all manner of regulations to 'keep the citizens fed, healthy and safe' (Zamoyski, 2014: 22–3). Policing in the pervasive and repressive sense that we have come to know it only really blossomed in the late twentieth century, when personal intimacy completed its migration into the commercial world of quotidian telecommunication and thereby fully exposed itself to the state's apparatuses of algorithmic control. Even today, the cold light of reason remains eclipsed by the soft light of seduction and the harsh light of surveillance.

Despite its diminution and dimness, the Enlightenment left many traces. It was a transatlantic and cosmopolitan 'Republic of Letters', and its exponents, the so-called *philosophes*, generated a huge volume of texts – most of which circulated through the pan-European 'literary underground' beneath the noses of those charged with suppressing sedition and heresy; frequently in slanderous, irreligious, and pornographic forms; and often through the media channels of the regime itself. 'French-language journals published outside the country but distributed inside it made a mockery of royal censorship', writes James Leith (1991: 34), just at the moment when 'public opinion rather than the royal will was becoming the basis of legitimacy'. This gave added impetus to the extension of police operations into the surveillance of 'public opinion', and its suppression if it endangered 'public safety', a task that was easier said than done.

Although the Enlightenment had established itself in many major cities (including Amsterdam, Berlin, Edinburgh, Lisbon, London, and Milan), Paris – the nascent 'City of Light' (*La Ville Lumière*) – was 'the capital of the Republic of Letters', because that was 'where the movement came together and defined itself as a cause' (Darnton, 2003: 6). And although the Enlightenment came to be associated with a radical undertaking (reason rather than despotism, liberty rather than tyranny, freedom rather than servitude, and cosmopolitanism rather than sectarianism), the *philosophes* drew on a common stock of well-established notions. 'What, then, set the *philosophes* apart?' asks Darnton (2003: 5). 'Commitment to a cause. *Engagement*. The *philosophe* ... put his ideas to use, to persuade, propagandize, and change the world around him.' The *philosophes* were reformers rather than revolutionaries, seeking to graft reason onto monarchy to produce a hybrid form of 'enlightened despotism' or 'benevolent absolutism'. So, while the *philosophes* 'were marked as a group by persecution, just enough to dramatize their daring and not enough to deter them from undertaking more', suggests Darnton (2003: 5), it is important to realize that most were well ensconced in the elite: aristocrats, clerics, lawyers, professionals, and students. 'Despite the leveling tendency inherent in their faith in reason, they aimed to take over the commanding heights of culture and to enlighten from above', argues Darnton (2003: 5). They sought 'the conquest of salons and academies, journals and theatres, Masonic lodges and key cafés, where they could win the rich and powerful to their cause and even gain access, by the back doors and boudoirs, to the throne. They reached a broad public among the middle classes, but they drew a line above the peasantry' (Darnton, 2003: 5). Little wonder, then, that in the wake of the French Revolution many regarded the *philosophes* with deep suspicion. For example, Maximilien Robespierre warned that 'philosophical enlightenment, however desirable it may be, had made common cause with despotism and could in no way be considered the forerunner of the Revolution' (Huet, 1997: 22).

While dim, then, the Enlightenment left traces courtesy of the licit and illicit publishing industry, but they remain bound up with the elite. So, what of the dimmer still? What of those excluded from the Republic of Letters and the enlightened ranks of the *philosophes*? What of the illiterati who made up the vast bulk of the population, especially in the countryside? These were the great mass of peasants, and the emerging army of wage labourers, as well as the utmost dim: an ever-expanding 'floating population' driven out of close-knit communities by famine, enclosure, and suchlike, and cast adrift in an increasingly inhospitable continent that regarded them as 'dangerous classes' of 'masterless men', necessitating new forms of 'disciplinary' control – poorhouses, workhouses, hospitals, and other spaces of confinement. For example, when the American Revolutionary War (1775–83) halted the mass deportation of British convicts to the New World, decommissioned ships were pressed into service as a stopgap measure to provide additional capacity for a dangerously overcrowded prison system, 'with hundreds of male convicts aboard each one. They slept in fetters, meagerly fed, continually prey to fever and kept at heavy labour from dawn to dusk' (Rees, 2001: 69). These floating prisons were the ur-form of the concentration and internment camps that would plague the twentieth century.

Darnton sifts through what remains of the Republic of Letters, but the 'mental universe of ordinary people' – their *mentalité* – 'seems to be irretrievably lost. It is so difficult, if not impossible, to locate the common man in the eighteenth century that it seems foolish to search for his cosmology' (Darnton, 1984: xvi and 9, respectively). One will, however, find traces of the unenlightened mass of peasants, labourers, and vagabonds in church and state registers, and some of their words and deeds will resound in court records and Inquisition transcripts. (Parenthetically, social scientists would do well to note that the Inquisition introduced verbatim transcripts – including the sighs and screams elicited from the tortured body – so that Rome, the Empire's 'centre of calculation', could identify and discipline Inquisitors who departed from the prescribed Inquistorial practices.)

Official records contain traces of common folk, but they are over-determined by the perspective of the elites who composed them. To circumvent this problem, Darnton adopted an inspired solution: listening to the stock of 'folk tales' that have been handed down through the centuries by word of mouth. Folk tales, fairy tales, and nursery rhymes are neither timeless nor placeless. Darnton focuses on those that hail from eighteenth-century France, including Bluebeard, Cinderella, Little Red Riding Hood, Puss in Boots, and Sleeping Beauty. However, the versions with which we are familiar were recast to suit the peculiar sensibility of the Parisian elite, most famously by Charles Perrault, in his 1697 collection *Tales and Stories of the Past with Morals*, many of which were given a subsequent makeover in Germany by the Brothers Grimm over a century later (1812–57). In the late seventeenth century 'a new fashion for fairy-tale originated, it seems, with story-telling in the salons', notes Christopher Betts (in Perrault, 2010: xiii). 'The usual explanation is that the dazzling achievements of Louis XIV's early reign were fading into decline, and that in a decade marked also by a series of national disasters (royal deaths, military defeat, spreading poverty, famine) escapist literature was popular' (Betts, in Perrault, 2010: xiii–xiv). So, while the *philosophes* came to wallow in the slanderous filth (*libelles*) that illicitly flowed through 'Grub Street', the aristocracy came to enjoy the comforting dreamworld of morality tales. This literary partition of the ruling classes was mirrored by the proliferation of 'coffeehouses' to rouse the workaholic mind and entrepreneurial spirit of the nascent bourgeoisie, and also of 'chocolate houses' and 'chocolate parlours' to relax the languid body and sleepy soul of the ensconced aristocracy. 'If coffee virtually shook drinkers awake for the workday that lay ahead, chocolate was meant to create an intermediary state between lying down and sitting up', notes Wolfgang Schivelbusch (1993: 91). 'Illustrations of the period nicely portray this ideal of an idle class's morning-long awakening to the rigors of studied leisure.' After the Revolution, fairy tales and hot chocolate would suffer an ignoble debasement. 'The former status drink of the *ancien régime* had sunk to the world of women and children' (Schivelbusch, 1993: 93). They have remained bedtime favourites ever since.

The bourgeois recasting of the peasant folk tales by Perrault and others turned them into 'morality tales' – edifying stories designed to teach children that happy endings come to those who successfully negotiate life-threatening trials and tribulations with courage and virtue. Perrault crafted 'good' tales for the 'good people' of the *ancien régime*. He 'wrote prolifically in praise … of Louis XIV and his achievements, from the mottos on commemorative medals to panegyrics on military victories', notes Betts (in Perrault, 2010: xi), playing his part 'in a concerted effort to promote the prestige of the king'. Little wonder, then, that Perrault's morality tales are fit only for the bourgeoisie. For instance, in his version of Puss in Boots, its first moral 'could have been written with himself in mind'. Puss, the master cat, 'exemplifies the royalist meritocracy which was gradually acquiring power' (Betts, in Perrault, 2010: xi).

Darnton draws upon folk tales from the peasant oral tradition collected by Paul Delarue and Marie-Louise Teneze (*Le conte populaire français*, 1976). Rather than edifying morality tales or escapist literature, these versions convey 'a terrifying irrationality that seems out of place in the Age of Reason' (Darnton, 1984: 13). 'Far from veiling their message with symbols, the storytellers of eighteenth-century France portrayed a world of raw and naked brutality' (Darnton, 1984: 15). The peasant tales evoke a nightmarish world of sexual violence and incest, mutilation and murder, child abduction and abandonment, poverty, plague, and famine, pacts with the Devil, and a constant struggle to stay alive. These tales tend to be located in one of two key settings: first, households and villages, which are characterized by gruelling labour, nasty neighbours, and the punishment of those who consume without working, with a particular focus on women and daughters; and, second, open roads, which are characterized by the miseries of dispossession (no land, no work, no food) that force people to roam, scavenge, beg, and steal, with a particular focus on men and sons. And far removed from the escapism and morality of the bourgeois tales for the 'good people' of Paris and Versailles, the peasant tales served two key functions. First, they provided a vernacular account of how the world works. 'Without preaching or drawing morals, French folktales demonstrate that the world is harsh and dangerous' (Darnton, 1984: 53). Such a world has no room for optimism and Enlightenment. 'However edifying some folktale characters may be in their behavior, they inhabit a world that seems arbitrary and amoral. ... There is neither rhyme nor reason in such a universe. Disaster strikes fortuitously. Like the Black Death, it cannot be predicted or explained, it must simply be endured' (Darnton, 1984: 53–4). For example, Little Red Riding Hood gets eaten by the wolf in more than half of the 35 different versions collected by Delarue and Teneze. There is no indication that she ever deserves to be eaten or could have avoided being eaten. She has not transgressed any moral boundary associated with the household or community, unlike the versions offered by Perrault and the Brothers Grimm. Being eaten was simply her fate.

Second, the tales advance a coping strategy for such a fickle world. 'As no discernible morality governs the world in general, good behavior does not determine success in the village or on the road' (Darnton, 1984: 54). Instead, the strategies most likely to succeed are mistrust (especially of family and neighbours), roguery, and cunning, which Darnton calls tricksterism. Importantly, the trickster does not turn the world upside down, just his or her own situation, social standing, and material condition. This is a reactive strategy suited to an oppressed peasantry. The trickster is not opposed to the ruling elites, but to numbskulls. 'Numbskulls represent the antithesis of tricksterism; they epitomize the sin of simplicity, a deadly sin, because naïveté in a world of confidence men is an invitation to disaster' (Darnton, 1984: 56). So, although the tales may overturn the social order for a short time, they do not overthrow it. There is no prospect of revolution. People merely swap places within the prevailing order of things – but only if they are devious and lucky. Humiliation is the limit of social disruption: the privileged fooled and ridiculed. Mistrust and cunning enabled adept tricksters to survive, and even thrive, within a world whose coldness and cruelty was stacked against them.

The burst of laughter enjoyed at someone else's expense is a form of symbolic violence that is not limited to the tricksterism of eighteenth-century peasants. It is also associated with the savage wit of courtly slander, which could ruin the reputation of those who depended upon patronage and prestige, and the festive cruelty of nascent class struggle. The capacity of wit to advance a 'good' cause in the *ancien régime*, particularly when enlightened wit crossed swords with courtly wit, is beautifully explored in Patrice Leconte's film, *Ridicule* (1996). Darnton's account of what he calls 'the great cat massacre' in a Parisian printing workshop in the late 1730s is a perfect example of savage wit. Like other forms of artisanal manufacturing, print shops were far from being the harmonious working environments often associated with pre-industrial production. 'Some even portray the workshop as a kind of extended family in which master and journeymen labored at the same tasks, ate at the same table, and sometimes slept under the same roof' (Darnton, 1984: 79). By the 1730s, a small oligarchy of large printing houses had emerged in Paris, making it increasingly unlikely for a skilled and long-serving printer (a journeyman) to rise through the ranks to become a master. Although the personification of capital was still decades away, the print-shop masters had already become a class apart. 'The master ... ate different food, kept different hours, and talked a different language. His wife and daughters ... kept pets. Clearly, the bourgeois belonged to a different subculture – one which meant above all that he did not work' (Darnton, 1984: 82). Such idlers would soon be recast as entrepreneurs, dispensing the gift of work (as employers) whilst accepting the burden of risk (as investors). The carnival of capitalism has idolized these noble savages ever since.

The skilled printers were not only losing touch with the masters, they were also being displaced by under-qualified and much cheaper labourers, the *alloués*, whose 'degradation stood out in their name: they were *à louer* (for hire), not *compagnons* (journeymen) of the master' (Darnton, 1984: 80). The *alloués* personified the tendency for work to be turned from a partnership into a commodity, and for the worker to be bought (or left to rot) at the master's convenience; not so much as property, like a slave, which would at least bring with it the burdens as well as the benefits of ownership, but as something merely to use for a while, like a prostitute, in exchange for nothing more than a sum of money: wages. 'The hiring and firing went on at such a fierce pace that the work force was rarely the same from one week to the next' (Darnton, 1984: 80). In the 1730s, then, the Parisian print shops were the ur-form of today's so-called 'precariat' – that great mass of precariously employed workers who are perpetually held at the disposal of a predatory capitalism whose mercy is less and less forthcoming. And then as now, those placed at the whim of capital are invariably cast as 'dangerous classes' and 'revolting subjects' in need of surveillance and suppression (Shoemaker, 2004; Standing, 2011; Tyler, 2013).

Darnton's account of the cat massacre is taken from the memoir of Nicolas Contat, who was a print-shop apprentice at the time. In stark contrast to the bourgeois comforts of the master and his family, which included the strange new fashion of keeping cats as pets, the apprentices lived in miserable conditions. The apprentices devised a ruse to strike back at the master by contriving a witch hunt. For while keeping pet cats was a novelty enjoyed by the bourgeoisie, the long-standing association between cats and witchcraft still held sway. Diabolical nighttime activities, such as witches' Sabbaths, were typically accompanied by the meowing of cats. 'To protect yourself from sorcery by cats there was one, classic remedy: maim it. Cut its tail, clip its ears, smash one of its legs, tear or burn its fur, and you would break its malevolent power' (Darnton, 1984: 93–4). In the dead of night, one of the apprentices, Léveillé, set about meowing to frighten the master into thinking that the household and print shop had been cursed. 'Our sniper succeeds so well that the whole neighborhood is alarmed. The word spreads that there is witchcraft afoot' (Contat, quoted in Darnton, 1984: 103). As the apprentices anticipated, the superstitious master was pan-icked into launching a cat massacre. Naturally, the workers were instructed to spare the mistress's beloved pet cat, 'the grey', and, obviously, this was the first to be killed. 'The men produce terror on the rooftops. Seized by panic, the cats throw themselves into the sacks. Some are killed on the spot. Others are con-demned to be hanged for the amusement of the entire printing shop' (Contat, quoted in Darnton, 1984: 103).

The killing of the mistress's cat was a symbolic attack, with all of the familial and sexual violence that such an attack entailed. In killing the mistress's cat, the workers were effectively accusing her of being a witch and a whore. Moreover, the cat massacre was not only a symbolic attack on the master and mistress. It was also a joyful event. 'The torture of animals, especially cats, was a popular amusement throughout early modern Europe' (Darnton, 1984: 90). In fact, 'once you start looking you see people torturing animals everywhere'. Some animals are good for eating, some for working, some for hunting, some for petting, some for witching, and some for suffering. And it is worth noting that as late as the end of the nineteenth century, animals had better legal protection from cruelty than British women, prompting one 'earnest Englishwoman' to write to *The Times* in April 1872 to enquire: 'are women animals?' (quoted in Bourke, 2011: 1). For while law-makers remained incredulous that women should be regarded as men's equals, perhaps they would be prepared to elevate women to the status of animals. In fact, the age-old legal status of women – and children – as property (and therefore placed at the sovereign disposal of their owners, typically fathers and husbands) is still being unwound today, especially in relation to hereditable entitlements and domestic violence.

Before being rebranded as pets by the ascendant bourgeoisie, cats were mainly good for killing. In the case of the cat massacre, the workers killed them in a parodic *auto-da-fé*. They 'staged a mock trial, complete with guards, a confessor, and a public executioner. After pronouncing the animals guilty and administering last rites, they strung them up on an improvised gallows' (Darnton, 1984: 77). For Contat, the massacre was the funniest incident in his entire career, and one that he and his colleagues re-enacted repeatedly to amuse themselves. It was a delicious '"theatre of violence" improvised in the work place, in the street, and on the rooftops ... the burlesquing of other ceremonies, such as trials and chari-varis' (Darnton, 1984: 100). Half a century later, in 1789, Parisian streets would again resound to an improvised 'theatre of violence', only now it would be the accursed familiars of the *ancien régime* dangling from ready-made gallows: the agents of despotism and tyranny, rather than the cats of witchcraft and sorcery, strung up from lamp posts. Yet the cat massacre was not even a vicarious revolution (acting out on animals what they dare not act out on the bourgeoisie). It was an act of insubordination rather than of insurrection. Its success was measured by the raucous laughter that echoed through the streets, and not by the overturning of the *ancien régime*. 'The workers pushed their symbolic horseplay to ... the point at which the killing of cats would turn into an open rebellion. ... The boundaries within which this jesting had to be contained suggest the limits to working-class militancy' (Darnton, 1984: 101).

When the Revolution came in 1789, animals once again played a significant role: not bourgeois pets, but aristocratic menageries, and in particular the one at Versailles. Enlightened thinkers had already condemned these spectacles for their elitism, extravagance, and conquest of nature. The most famous Enlightenment publication, the monumental *Encyclopédie ou Dictionnaire raisonné des sciences, des arts et des métiers*, insisted that 'at a time when people have no bread, the menageries must be destroyed; it would be shameful to feed beasts at great expense when men die of hunger all around' (quoted in Baratay and Hardouin-Fugier, 2002: 73). In 1792, revolutionaries abolished 'this symbol of tyranny, handing monkeys, stags and birds over to skinners. The plan was to install a stud farm ... to substitute the menagerie's useless beasts with a breeding ground that would benefit agriculture, transport and the army' (Baratay and Hardouin-Fugier, 2002: 74). The plan mutated into the transformation of the botanical gardens in Paris into a natural history museum. It incorporated a few exotic animals that remained in the Versailles menagerie (including a lion and a zebra), as well as performing animals that had previously been exhibited in the streets of Paris and which the revolutionary police now regarded as a catalyst for mob violence.

> Changing the nature of the stock of animals itself would differentiate the new establishment from the monarchy and its hunter instincts. This could be achieved by a reduction in the ferocious species that exemplified devastating cruelty, supported the belief that nature sanctioned the rule of force, and illustrated and legitimized tyranny. Docile animals were to be favoured instead, placed under the banner of public utility and functioning in essence as an allegory for the hardworking citizenry. (Baratay and Hardouin-Fugier, 2002: 75)

Following its long-awaited opening in 1860, *Le Jardin zoologique d'acclimatation* 'averaged about a quarter million visitors per year, held about five thousand animals ... and usually managed to meet costs' (Osborne, 1995: 40). The opening of this zoo in the same decade as the opening of the new slaughterhouse complex at La Villette perfectly illustrates modernity's ambivalent treatment of animals – some as spectacles, some as meat, some as workers, some as specimens, some as pets, etc. 'The institution was closed during the Franco-Prussian War and the Commune of 1870–1, when it became home to 130,000 sheep and

20,000 cattle destined to feed a starving Paris', notes Michael Osborne (1995: 40–1). Some of its 'animals became evacuees and rode the rails to Belgian zoos at Antwerp and Brussels. Those that remained, enough to fill thirty-five railway cars and sixty carriages, went to the museum menagerie, where most died, or were killed for food' (Osborne, 1995: 41). Meanwhile, a vast, rail-fed cattle market, slaughterhouse, and butchery complex had opened just a couple of years before, in 1867, on the northeastern outskirts of Paris, at La Villette, dubbed the 'City of Blood'. It was both a major killing compound and a key tourist attraction. As with the Paris Morgue, a popular form of mass entertainment in the nineteenth century, which attracted up to 150,000 visitors a day for the most popular corpses, the spectacle of death has cast a long shadow over modernity, not least in terms of 'dark tourism', which consumes everything from cemeteries and battlefields to death camps and killing fields (Hooper and Lennon, 2017; Schwartz, 1999; Sion, 2014).

> The Morgue is a show that anyone can afford. … There are connoisseurs who go out of their way not to miss one of these spectacles of death. When the slabs are empty, people go out disappointed, robbed, muttering under their breath. When the slabs are well filled, and when there is a fine display of human flesh, the visitors crowd in, getting a cheap thrill, horrified, joking, applauding or whistling, as in the theatre, and go away contented. (Zola, 2004: 73)

The burst of laughter enjoyed at someone else's expense was a form of symbolic violence in eighteenth-century France that was not only shared by the 'trickster-ism' of long-suffering peasants and the 'theatre of cruelty' of increasingly alienated workers, it was also shared by the savage wit of courtly and enlight-ened slander. In the *ancien régime*, politics was not a popular affair, least of all a matter for the so-called 'court of public opinion'. Strictly speaking, the people – even the educated classes – were not entitled to hold an opinion on matters of state, just as they were not entitled to hold an opinion on matters of faith. On the contrary, the political was the sovereign's prerogative, limited to the monarch and his or her advisors, whose deliberations were state secrets. 'When the revo-lutionaries looked back at the history of the press' under the *ancien régime*, 'they saw nothing but newslessness before 1789' (Darnton, 2003: 33). The official media did not seek to manipulate 'public opinion' or 'manufacture consent' (Chomsky, 1988). Newspapers, journals, and gazettes were not supposed to address 'politics at all, except in the form of official pronouncements on court life. All printed matter had to be cleared through a baroque bureaucracy that included nearly two hundred censors, and the censors' decisions were enforced by a special branch of the police, the inspectors of the book trade' (Darnton, 2003: 33). As both literacy and the demand for information increased, however, a large and vibrant pan-European 'literary underground' emerged through which illicit news circulated, alongside other illicit material, such as religious heresy, political satire, Enlightenment philosophy, and pornographic slander, much of which repeated the same charge levelled against the entire *ancien régime*: it was riddled with vice and rotten to the core, and its tyranny and corruption weakened and debased the nation.

During the eighteenth century, 'the literature of libel gathered force and transformed itself into a full-scale indictment of the regime, even if it did not call for a revolution' (Darnton, 1996: 216). Libellous books claimed to expose in lurid detail the scandalous conduct of those in power, including the king, along with other key figures in the regime. These books were often written by French émigrés in relatively liberal cities, such as Amsterdam and London, and then distributed in France through the literary underground. *Libels* became a very popular genre, and many libellous books were best sellers. And like other scandalous works of the Enlightenment, the main consumers of this libellous literature were aristocrats, priests, professionals, and students (Darnton, 1979). 'From the beginning of the century to the end, libellers hammered at the same theme: despotism … . They built up a picture of monarchy riddled with the abuse of power' (Darnton, 2010b: 441). Censors and the police tried to suppress such literature, not only because destroying the reputation of rivals was a key weapon in court politics, but also because, by 1749, King Louis XV feared that the people had forsaken him. In practice, however, the censors and police were ill equipped to suppress such literature (Zamoyski, 2014).

Officially, then, the quotidian world of the *ancien régime* was supposed to remain silent when it came to issues that were a royal prerogative and a matter of state. In reality, however, everyday life was alive with all kinds of more or less disturbing opinions. 'Slander, libel, defamation, calumny, character assassination, mudslinging, scandalmongering, bad-mouthing, and billingsgate flourished as never before in eighteenth-century Paris' (Darnton, 2010b: 439). Darnton considers the *ancien régime* as an eighteenth-century 'information society', and focuses in particular on the multi-media circulation of politically sensitive knowledge in Paris in the 1750s. (Joan DeJean (2014) does something similar with respect to the 'siege of Paris' in 1649, during the civil war, when breaking news and propaganda were spread rapidly through the city via the mass production of engravings, pamphlets, periodicals, newspapers, and placards, as well as speeches, poems, and songs.) The Tree of Cracow, located in the Palais-Royal, was the nerve centre of a communication network that spanned such ordinary places as park benches, street corners, cafés, and salons, and which entailed a brisk trade in everything from court gossip and risqué jokes to slanderous poems and seditious songs. 'But ordinary hearsay did not satisfy Parisians with a powerful appetite for information', insists Darnton (2003: 27). They wanted true knowledge, which required them to filter

> the public noise in order to discover what was *really* happening. Sometimes
> they pooled their information and criticized it collectively by meeting in
> groups such as the famous salon of Mme. Doublet, known as the 'parish.'

Twenty-nine 'parishioners,' many of them well connected with the Parlement of Paris or the court ... gathered once a week in Mme. Doublet's apartment. (Darnton, 2003: 27)

The daily 'news' was gathered by one of Mme. Doublet's servants, 'who may qualify as the first "reporter" in the history of France' (Darnton (2003: 27). According to the surviving records of the police, who had the 'parish' under sustained surveillance, each morning Mme. Doublet's servant went 'from house to house asking, in the name of his mistress, "What's new?" The servant wrote the first entries for each day's news on the registers; the "parishioners" read through them, adding whatever other information they had gathered; and after a general vetting, the reports were copied and sent to select friends of Mme. Doublet' (Darnton, 2003: 28–9).

By 1750, just as Louis XV was getting very anxious about the souring of public opinion towards him, Mme. Doublet's 'parish' news, and other clandestine reports like it, were being reproduced by numerous print shops, and illicitly circulated to an ever-growing number of 'subscribers' around Paris and into the provinces. From 1777, these 'newsletters' began to be published as books, often becoming best sellers of the underground trade. This trade mushroomed in the years leading up to the Revolution, and it was a source of constant concern for the censors and the police. Since licit and illicit material flowed through the same media channels, and often merged with each other, the seemingly sharp distinction between them gave way to the more ambivalent distinction between the tolerable and intolerable. For example, the 28 volumes of the *Encyclopédie*, edited by Denis Diderot and Jean le Rond d'Alembert, and published and distributed illicitly between 1751 and 1772, 'caused a scandal and nearly went under; but by 1789 it had become the greatest best seller in the history of publishing' (Darnton, 2003: 10). Indeed, this pinnacle of the Enlightenment, which dared to criticize and satirize religious orthodoxy and absolutist monarchy, as well as scandalously placing sacred and profane subjects side by side, accompanied the pan-European 'recasting of autocratic power in the form of enlightened absolutism' as more and more 'sovereigns and ministers looked to the philosophers for guidance or legitimation' (Darnton, 2003: 10). Yet Enlightenment remained a delicate affair: 'all knowledge is a seizure of power, a challenge, a deed of the same stamp as a political revolution' (Huet, 1997: 15).

Just as the twentieth century had a soundtrack (Ross, 2012), so too did eighteenth-century France. 'Paris was suffused with songs' and 'the entire kingdom could be described as "an absolute monarchy tempered by songs"', since 'a catchy song could spread like wildfire' (Darnton, 2003: 54). The police were especially interested in 'hostile verses' directed against Louis XV. Yet with so many more or less dubious 'poems, songs, epigrams, rumors, jokes, and *bons mots* shuttling though the communication networks of the city' (Darnton, 2010a: 21), deciding which of them were tolerable and which were intolerable was something of an arbitrary affair. For example, an ode that referred to Louis XV as a monster 'belonged to a flood of hostile verse that coursed through the city during the first six months of 1749' (Darnton, 2003: 33). As the ode spread, the police 'organized a campaign to wipe it out', which 'triggered an extraordinary poetry hunt and manhunt' (Darnton, 2003: 33). The hunt crossed paths with other seditious songs, poems, and verses, and eventually petered out after 14 'quite ordinary and unthreatening Parisians' (Darnton, 2010a: 3) were imprisoned in the Bastille: students, priests, lawyers, notaries, and clerks; all from respectable professions, and most of whom were young and naive. From the evidence in the police files, they 'hardly seemed to understand their crime. Parisians had always sung disrespectful songs and recited naughty verse. ... Why had the Fourteen been plucked out of the crowd and made to suffer exemplary punishment? ... After several anxious months in prison, they were all exiled far away from Paris, ... their lives ... ruined' (Darnton, 2010a: 37). Here as elsewhere, state violence has a tendency to become automatic, consuming all manner of people who frequently have little or no comprehension of why their destiny is to suffer in the cold and calculated embrace of a repressive apparatus: from the extermination of entire categories of humanity, such as the Armenian *people* (Balakian, 2005), the Kulak *class* (Applebaum, 2004; Khlevniuk, 2004; Viola, 2007), and the Jewish *race* (Burleigh and Wippermann, 1991; Friedlander, 1995; Friedländer, 2007b; Gilbert, 1997; Wytwycky, 1980) to the destruction of particular individuals, such as the sixteenth-century miller who was burnt at the stake by the Inquisition for weird notions such as likening the genesis of the world to the curdling of milk: *out of the elemental chaos, a solid mass formed, and worm-like angels appeared, one of whom was God* (Ginzburg, 1992, my italics); or the condemned man in Franz Kafka's *In the Penal Colony* (1999).

Modernity has unleashed all manner of frightful apparatuses that have inscribed a cold and calculated violence directly into the flesh of the world, from the accursed slave trade (Rediker, 2008; Thomas, 1997; Walvin, 2011) and the brutal scramble for Africa and the Americas (Gilroy, 1993; Pakenham, 1991b; Todorov, 1992), to the recent butchery of cities such as Detroit and New York, and the creation of a 'planet of slums' (Berman, 1983; Davis, 2007b; LeDuff, 2013). We will return to cold and calculated violence in due course, but for the moment I want to set the scene by considering impassioned violence, which is exemplified by Rome's gladiatorial games and the Aztecs' human sacrifice.

$$\textbf{3}$$

Pre-industrial Mass Killing

The Gift of Death from Ancient Rome to the Aztec Empire

Every people, the proverb has it, loves its own form of violence.

Clifford Geertz, 2005: 84

In *The Cunning of History*, Richard Rubenstein (2001: 7) mentions how 'twentieth-century mass slaughter began in earnest with World War I. About 6,000 people were killed every day for over 1,500 days.' Martin Gilbert (1995: 541) adds that while '20,000 British soldiers were killed on the first day of the Battle of the Somme is often recalled with horror ... a similar number of soldiers were killed in every four-day period of the First World War'. What I find chilling about this slaughter is not the body count. After all, the God Worshippers' Taiping Heavenly Kingdom in China, led by Christ's sibling, Hong Xiuquan, mobilized over a million Chinese peasants against the ruling Manchu-led Qing dynasty. This 'Taiping Rebellion' (1851–64) left upwards of 20 million dead from warfare, famine, and disease, and was only defeated once Britain entered the fray in the early 1860s in order to defend the commercial advantages it had gained from the first Opium War. What I find chilling is Rubenstein's and Gilbert's phrasing, which echoes the nature of the slaughter: cold and mechanical – a steady accumulation of corpses. 'Once begun', writes David Thomson (1990: 548), 'war ran its remorseless course of insatiable demands for human sacrifice, discipline, organization, and ingenuity, until it became almost an end in itself.' I will shortly return to the logic of this industrial slaughter machine, which was fully 'explicated (unfolded)' in the Second World War. By mid-century, modernity had bequeathed to humanity a perfectly engineered, human-disassembly machine. For the moment, however, I want to consider two forms of mass killing that stand in stark contrast to these slaughter machines: the Roman games and Aztec sacrifice. This will set the scene for a profound slippage that marks the fundamental shift from the impassioned killing accomplished by the Romans and the Aztecs, amongst others, and the impassive killing administered by the decidedly chilly apparatuses of modernity in the wake of the Enlightenment: the humane slaughter of animals, the gentle execution of prisoners, and the granting of 'mercy deaths' to lives unworthy of life.

The Roman Republic (509–27 BC) thrived on warfare. 'In foreign wars, campaigns and battles spanning 150 years between 275 BC and 132 BC, the aristocratic élite led the republic to victory across the length and breadth of the Mediterranean' (Baker, 2007: 98). After merely half a century of conquest (219–167 BC), 'the Senate was able to abolish direct taxation in Italy, replacing it with the riches that the republic received in revenue from its provinces abroad' (Baker, 2007: 48). Rather than consolidate its power, however, the Republic was consumed by civil war, as rival factions struggled for supremacy. Octavian emerged victorious and, as 'saviour of Rome', he was proclaimed Emperor 'Augustus' by the Senate in 27 BC, effectively ending the Roman Republic and inaugurating the Roman Empire, which lasted until AD 1453.

At its height under Emperor Trajan (ca. AD 117), the Empire covered 5 million square kilometres of Europe, North Africa, and Asia Minor, strung out around the Mediterranean and the Black Sea – from Portugal in the west to Mesopotamia in the east, and Egypt in the south to Britain in the north. It contained 70–90 million people. Rome itself had a population of 1 million, most of whom were poor. Indeed, around the dawn of the first century AD, 'the Roman world in general and the city of Rome in particular were rapidly filling up with citizens of the lesser sort. ... This class did not have a voice except by resort to rioting and violence, reserved mostly for life-threatening crises such as food shortages' (Southern, 2001: 147). Countless slaves were set free (manumitted), frequently using an informal method that enabled their masters to avoid a hefty manumission tax. However, unlike the formal method, which entailed the expense of a magistrate as well as the tax, the informal approach did not entitle the erstwhile slaves to Roman citizenship and, crucially, the welfare protection that citizens enjoyed, such as the 'corn dole' (*cura annonae*). The latter originated as a gift of grain to the citizenry in order to garner their political support, although poor citizens soon came to rely on it, especially during famines. (By AD 2, more than 200,000 were entitled to the corn dole, while many more were in need of assistance but not entitled to it.) Huge numbers 'of ex-slaves were thrust into the wide world without the means to support themselves, nowhere specific to go, no employment, and lacking the advantage of citizenship' (Southern, 2001: 151). Rome had engendered a new and frightful phenomenon: a dangerous class of free people without citizenship. 'Between 17 BC and AD 4, the *Lex Junia*, the *Lex Fufia Caninia*, and the *Lex Aelia Sentia* were successively put into operation to try to stem the flow of manumissions, and to cater for those already freed by the informal processes' (Southern, 2001: 151). Eventually, in AD 212, Emperor Caracalla bestowed full citizenship on all free men in the Empire, although by then it was so overstretched that the privileges of citizenship were waning.

The Republic lasted five centuries, and the Empire spanned one-and-a-half millennia. Its Western part disintegrated in the fifth century AD, finally coming to an end in AD 476–80, with the deaths of Romulus Augustus and Julius Nepos. Its Eastern (Byzantine) side survived for another millennium, finally falling to the Ottoman Turks in AD 1453. The shift in the balance of power from the Western to the Eastern parts of the Empire was cemented as early as AD 324–30, when Emperor Constantine transferred the capital from Rome to Byzantium – the 'New Rome' – which was renamed Constantinople in his honour. (Once conquered by the Turks, Constantinople became the capital of the Ottoman Empire, and it was renamed Istanbul.) Just as astonishing as the transfer of power from West to East was the fact that within a decade of the most sustained suppression of the bothersome Christian cult, under Emperor Diocletian, who issued an edict in AD 303 'ordering churches to be destroyed, scriptures to be burnt, some Christians to be stripped of their offices and others to be made slaves' (Baker, 2007: 314), Christianity was decriminalized by Constantine in AD 313. This paved the way for the once-despised pacific cult of Christianity to become the official religion of the Roman world in AD 324. It is ironic that a 'slave morality' attuned to resentful yet docile victims, as Nietzsche (2003a) famously put it, would become the offensive religion of a fearsome state that would haunt Europe and world history to the present day: the Holy Roman Empire, which was founded around AD 800 by Charlemagne (Charles the Great, King of the Franks, and crowned Holy Roman Emperor by Pope Leo III) and effectively destroyed by Napoleon Bonaparte a millennium later in AD 1806, who appropriated the title 'King of Rome' for his son, Napoleon II. During its millennial existence, the Holy Roman Empire would forge the heart of Europe and lay the foundation for a 'persecuting society' that would flourish after AD 1200, not least through the establishment of the Inquisition in AD 1231 (Green, 2007; Moore, 1990; Murphy, 2013). It is ironic that the Latin Church should have adopted Roman methods, such as judicial torture and spectacular violence, for its own persecution of heretics and rivals. And once forged, the guardians of Europe would become all the more persecutory because the Empire remained forever 'flaccid' (Lyotard, 1989b: 48), no matter how much it fought to solidify its territory and cement its identity. (The Third Reich was perhaps the most deranged attempt to make a flaccid Europe turgid, primarily through the obsessive–compulsive cleansing of absolutely everyone and everything that was within reach of the regime. This is a salutary reminder that even a hardcore desire for impervious borders is the least of the problems for those on either side of a Wall – the Atlantic Wall, the Berlin Wall, the Pacific Wall, or even our very own Mediterranean Wall, Mexican Wall, and Separation Wall.)

The Romans excelled in warfare and domination, which was essential given that most of their 'wealth came from conquest' (Sennett, 1996: 96) rather than from production or trade. Conquered territories were plundered and forced to supply tributes to Rome, a venerable tradition that cities such as Chicago, Frankfurt, London, and New York continue to enjoy in our own Empire of Capital – except that financial services now spearhead the looting, with insurance and banking leading the way (Lapavitsas, 2013; Marazzi, 2010). 'Capital realizes a Roman idea of imperial expansion', claims Lyotard (1989b: 8). 'American presidents are emperors. Washington is Rome. The USA is Italy. And Europe is its Greece.' Goods tended to circulate through networks of patronage rather than commercial networks, which enabled factions of the Roman elite to vie for power, particularly through spectacular displays of conspicuous consumption to edify and entertain the citizenry. The Romans excelled not only in the violence needed to forge an empire and sustain the circulation of tributes; they also excelled in staging these spectacles of violence. 'Rome ... remains extraordinary for the scale and the method of its violence, and for applauding skill, artistry, and diligence in the punishment and destruction of creatures', notes Donald Kyle (2001: 1). They 'killed on an enormous scale, with efficiency, ingenuity, and delectation' (Kyle, 2001: 2). With its growing number of freed slaves without citizenship, and its mass of poor citizens, Rome was a socially unstable city in a dangerous world. The games invaginated this situation, dramatizing the power of Rome over a world shrunk to a manageable size. 'This theatre of cruelty was more than sadistic entertainment', argues Richard Sennett (1996: 98), since it 'accustomed people to the carnage necessary for imperial conquest'. The games were 'spectacular civics lessons in schools of death' (Kyle, 2001: 9). Gladiatorial games started in Rome in 264 BC, and spread thereafter throughout the Roman world, particularly under Augustus at the close of the first century BC.

Outside of warfare and public executions, 'the prime occasions for abundant human death were the *munera*, which were originally violent rites associated with funerals as duties or tributes owed to dead ancestors' (Kyle, 2001: 43). From the third century BC, the Romans 'greatly expanded these spectacles of death and changed their emphasis from private rites or necessary punishments into public entertainments' (Kyle, 2001: 2). They came to be associated with everything from military thanksgivings to the emperor cult. The most spectacular games took on a distinct form: animal hunts in the morning, ritual executions around midday, and gladiatorial combat in the afternoon; and they often involved a cast of hundreds of animals and people. In his *Res Gestae* (funerary inscription), Augustus recorded many of his accomplishments, including repeatedly giving money and grain to the plebs (commoners) of Rome – 'My largesse never reached fewer than 250,000 men' – as well as financing three major gladiatorial games during which 'some 10,000 men did battle to the death', and many other 'scenic shows', such as athletics and re-enactments (quoted in Eck, 2003: 139 and 142, respectively). The most celebrated games occurred in 17 BC. 'The Games of the Ages was a festival the likes of which no Roman had ever seen before, nor would ever see again' (Baker, 2007: 155). It entailed 'three days of visually spectacular sacrifices followed by seven days of chariot races, tragedies and comedies in Latin and Greek, plus stunning exhibitions of trick riders, animal hunting and mock battles' (Baker, 2007: 155). These games drew a line under the civil war that had torn the Republic apart over previous decades, and signalled the renewal of Rome under Augustus.

Gladiatorial games peaked under Trajan. 'In AD 107, as an entertainment and a celebration after his Dacian campaigns, Trajan held 23 days of games in which 11,000 animals were killed and 10,000 gladiators fought' (Kyle, 2001: 35). Most of those killed were animals and *noxii* (condemned convicts) rather than either gladiators (whose training was expensive and time consuming) or Christians (who were mostly irritants rather than fodder for the games). Trained gladiators were generally slaves, criminals, prisoners of war, and, from the first century AD, some former soldiers and even free men. Animals were often drawn from distant locations, such as Egypt, and frequently 'paraded like exotic prisoners of war' (Kyle, 2001: 43). During the late Republic, and especially during the imperial period, exotic animals came to the fore in animal hunts, often spending time on public display prior to the games. Rome 'adopted the custom of "royal hunts," of collecting and transporting large numbers of beasts, often unusual and foreign ones, to be displayed or usually killed as a demonstration of imperial power and territorial control' (Kyle, 2001: 43). Crocodiles, elephants, hippopotami, leopards, lions, and tigers were brought to Rome from Africa, for example.

'Spectacles played a major role in the festival calendar, the social life, and the public space of ancient Rome for over a millennium' (Kyle, 2001: 2). By dramatizing the military virtues of Rome, the games 'showed imperial power and control even over nature, and with the variety and multitude of species and races involved, the games were a microcosm of the territorial extent and imperial majesty of Rome' (Kyle, 2001: 9). The representational character of these spectacles is well illustrated by Julius Caesar's triumphant games in 46 BC, which included a battle in Rome's Circus Maximus 'between two opposing armies, in which five hundred foot-soldiers, twenty elephants, and thirty horseman engaged on each side. ... For the naval battle a pool was dug in the lesser Codeta and there was a contest of ships' (Kyle, 2001: 34). The games would also give rise to the monumental architecture of the amphitheatres, the most spectacular of which was the Flavian Amphitheatre (Colosseum) in Rome. Completed in AD 80 under Emperor Titus, it held over 50,000 spectators. At its inauguration, which lasted for 100 days, 9,000 animals were killed. Subsequent games typically lasted from five to 20 days, each with a wide variety of activities: chariot racing, animal hunts, wild-animal combat, gladiatorial combat, and ritual executions, including crucifixions, burnings at the stake, and beheadings.

Although the Romans elevated the mass killing of humans to a fine art, they did not kill indiscriminately. Rooted in a tradition of sacred violence, and steeped in the noble virtues of duty, obligation, and honour, they took pains to kill only those who either deserved to die or were destined to die; either because mortal combat was inherent to their nature (wild animals and gladiators) or because they had been condemned to death (convicts and Christians, although the latter were usually encouraged to recant, since judges preferred creating apostates rather than martyrs): 'victims were always seen as worthy of punishment. Their presence in the arena ... was taken as proof that their victimization was justified' (Kyle, 2001: 267). Given the huge demand for *noxii*, the legal system was manipulated to ensure that it 'gathered human fodder for the arena' (Kyle, 2001: 266). As always, the law produces the criminality that it desires and deserves.

The Roman spectacles of death gave rise to a problem that has also dogged modern forms of mass killing, starting with the Revolutionary recourse to the guillotine in the 1790s: corpse disposal. For the Romans, this was primarily a problem of quantity – hundreds of thousands of animal carcasses and human corpses that were considered to be both physical and spiritual pollutants; whereas for the French, it was essentially a problem of fear – thousands of accursed corpses that threatened the living. In the 1790s, 'the Parisian debates regarding their cemeteries were guided by one overwhelming desire: to be rid of the guillotined corpses' (Huet, 1997: 139). The number of guillotined corpses was tiny compared to ordinary burials from 'natural' deaths. Likewise for the Roman games: 'The total number of human and animal arena victims pales by comparison with the bulk from wars, pestilences, or simply the normal dead', notes Kyle (2001: 78–9). The number of guillotined corpses was also tiny when compared to the killings by pre-revolutionary and counter-revolutionary regimes. As Maximilien Robespierre astutely proclaimed: 'For how long will the rage of despots be called justice, and the people's justice be called barbarity or rebellion? How tender people are towards oppressors and how inexorable towards the oppressed!' (speech to the National Convention, 5 February 1794, quoted in Žižek, 2007: 115). Nevertheless, guillotined corpses provoked fear, much like the bodies of lepers and plague victims had since time immemorial. And just as disposing of hundreds of thousands of corpses and carcasses has taxed countless regimes from the Romans to the Nazis – not least because rivers such as the Tiber (Rome), the Seine (Paris), 'Bubble Creek' (Chicago), and the Sola and the Vistula (Auschwitz–Birkenau) could only take so much blood, bone, and ash – the moral problem posed by human corpses has been equally taxing. Invariably, those killed have had to be made either sacred or profane, so that the killing is either ritualized (acts of mercy, sacrifice, or redemption) or a matter of utter indifference (they die an animal, insectile, vegetal, or mineral death: slaughtered like beasts, fumigated like pests, eradicated like weeds, or smashed like rocks).

The gladiatorial games spanned the republican and imperial periods of Roman power, from the third century BC to the fourth century AD, when, in AD 325, Constantine outlawed them. What brought the games to an eventual end was neither the Christianization of the Roman Empire nor the waning of the public's appetite for spectacular violence, but rather the increasing inability of the elites to sustain such a hugely expensive and highly complex worldwide apparatus of death. For the Roman games depended not only on the desire of the masses and the imperatives of the empire, nor even on the supply of animals and humans to kill and be killed, but also on the willingness and ability of the ruling elites to compete amongst themselves for power and prestige via the escalating logic of endless one-upmanship that inflated the spectacles of death to monumental proportions, much like the 'pecuniary emulation' and 'conspicuous leisure' of the modern consumer society (Veblen, 2007), which are partly acted out in the amphitheatres of the commodity fetish: pleasure gardens, arcades, and department stores. As the games fell into desuetude, vestiges remained scattered across post-Roman Europe, such as the blood sports of coursing, dog fighting, and bear baiting. By and large, however, mass killing would return whence it came: plague, famine, disaster, and war.

While the Roman games came to obey an essentially imperial logic cut loose from its sacred moorings, the mass killings of the Aztecs remained faithful to their sacred roots. And while the games accustomed Romans to the violence necessary for territorial conquest and expropriation, such violence would have been anathema to the Aztecs of Mesoamerica (central Mexico and central America), who were bound together by kinship and reciprocity. Through the Triple Alliance of three city-states – Tenochtitlan (Mexico City), Texcoco, and Tlacopan – the Aztec Empire existed from the fourteenth century until it was conquered by the Spanish, led by Hernán Cortés, in the early 1520s, and decimated by the lethal diseases that the conquistadors brought with them. From a European perspective, warfare primarily concerned territory. European warfare gave birth to those diabolical Siamese twins known as the 'nation–state', with each twinset coming to expect not only its rightful portion of the good Earth for its exclusive habitation, but also additional 'living space' (*lebensraum*) into which it could grow organically as it heroically struggled for survival. Territories have been cut into the surface of the Earth by nation–state war machines ever since (Elden, 2013).

Pierre Clastres (1989: 195) asks of pre-conquest Amerindians: 'why would the men of these societies work and produce more, given that three or four hours of peaceful activity suffice to meet the needs of the group?' And again: 'What purpose would be served by the surplus thus accumulated?' His answer to these rhetorical questions is blistering: 'Men work more than their needs require only when forced.' There is only one reason to produce and accumulate an ever-expanding surplus: to enrich and empower a ruling class (of nobles, masters, priests, capitalists, etc.), which, in its most generic form, we call a state. So, 'once its needs are fully satisfied nothing could induce primitive society to produce more, that is, to alienate its time by working for no good reason when that time is available for idleness, play, warfare, or festivities' (Clastres, 1989: 197). Nothing could induce them to waste their time and energy, except coercion and violence, which the Spanish unleashed with great ferocity. Such coercion and violence is exemplified by King Leopold's Congo, where rubber earnings increased almost a hundredfold between 1890 and 1904. Steamboats and railways were needed to get the rubber out of the Congo, and their construction required porterage on a vast and deadly scale.

> It took eight years – from 1890 to 1898 – to build that railroad, against some of the most difficult terrain, climate, disease, and labor problems that ever beset such an enterprise. Meanwhile, Stanley and ... Leopold ... were eager to begin tapping the wealth of the Congo. That meant transporting steamboats in pieces on the heads of porters from Matadi to Stanley Pool. ... By the time the first train arrived in Leopoldville in 1898, porters had carried forty-three steamers, weighing in all 865 tons, to the upper river. (Headrick, 1981: 197)

As we previously noted, much of the cargo moving upriver was the weaponry needed to operate the regime of terror that compelled the natives to undertake work even more gruelling than porterage: rubber harvesting. Congolese women, children, and elders were taken hostage until such time as the men had harvested a sufficient quota of natural rubber to secure their release, and in the meantime the hostages were often abused, starved, and murdered. Hundreds of thousands of natives were subjected to this regime of terror, and tens of thousands perished as a result. Taking hostages was so routine that the *Manuel du Voyageur et du Résident au Congo* included detailed instructions. 'Every state or company post in the rubber areas had a stockade for hostages.' 'If a village refused to submit to the rubber regime, state or company troops or their allies sometimes shot everyone in sight, so that nearby villages would get the message' (Hochschild, 2006: 161 and 165, respectively). Natives who fled into the forest were hunted down and killed. In order to claim the bounty, the regime required proof: severed hands, which were often smoked to preserve them during a prolonged hunting expedition. 'As news of the white man's soldiers and their baskets of severed hands spread through the Congo, a myth gained credence. ... The cans of corned beef seen in white men's houses, it was said, did not contain meat from the animals shown on the label; they contained chopped-up hands' (Hochschild, 2006: 166). This myth is perfectly attuned to the cannibalistic nature of capitalism, which, according to Marx, renders human flesh and brains (i.e. labour power, brain power, and the 'general intellect') into a gelatinous substance drip-fed to the bourgeoisie (Sutherland, 2011). For commodities are congealed masses of amorphous human labour whose social substance appears in the fetishistic form of objects that have commerce amongst themselves. Commodities relate to one another as exchange-values, not use-values.

The opening up and exploitation of inhospitable regions has invariably entailed regimes of terror imposed by a state apparatus. The construction of the Kolyma Highway, or 'Road of Bones', in the Russian Far East (1932–52), and the Thailand–Burma Railway, or 'Death Railway' (1942–3), are infamous examples. So too is the 141-mile White Sea–Baltic Canal in Russia (1931–3). This folly required 170,000 Gulag labourers, 25,000 of whom died in the process. Everything was done by hand, even the fabrication of rudimentary tools, such as wooden spades and wheelbarrows. 'As work progressed, new camp sites had to be built along the course of the canal. At every one of these new sites, the prisoners and exiles arrived – and found nothing. Before starting work they had to build their own wooden barracks and organize their food supply' (Applebaum, 2004: 80). They were lethal-labour camps: not because the Bolsheviks wanted the inmates dead, but because their living or dying was a matter of indifference. Having been 'reduced to "nonpeople" or creatures from the Stone Age' (Brent, 2008: 14–15), the death camps were immune to criticism from 'the "medieval" fossils caterwauling in Europe, as Stalin put it' (Brent, 2008: 12).

Given the horror that accompanies every state like a diabolical shadow, Clastres (1989) argues that far from lacking a state, so-called 'primitive' societies proactively stopped one from emerging. They did so by warding off either an endogenous seizure of power or an exogenous subjugation. For what good is a state to a subsistence community? And conversely: what good is a subsistence community to a state? A state and its ruling classes can only be sustained once the community produces a surplus for them to appropriate and accumulate. Every state is essentially parasitic and vampiric; every ruling class superfluous. Clastres (1989) argues that the Amerindians successfully thwarted the emergence of a state until they were conquered by the Spanish. They were driven out of their subsistence communities and into the mines and plantations, and forced to produce a surplus of wealth for the Europeans to accumulate and enjoy at their leisure.

There is, then, a profound difference between communities that limit themselves to subsistence and communities that generate surpluses. While the latter readily succumb to despotism and the capitalist delirium of 'accumulation for accumulation's sake', as Marx put it, the former ensure that any inadvertent surplus is squandered rather than accumulated. This is why Georges Bataille (1988b: 46) argued that the Aztecs 'were just as concerned with sacrificing as we are about working'. Sacrifice is the principal way for a society to thwart accumulation and prevent the formation of a state. Sacrifice puts to death swiftly what would otherwise be put to death slowly. As 'willing slaves of capital' (Lordon, 2014) we have become accustomed to calling such a slow death 'work' or 'labour'. To place sacrifice at the heart of the community, then, is to orchestrate a society of consumption and expenditure, rather than a society of accumulation and growth.

In Aztec mythology the gods sacrificed themselves to bring life to the world, which thereby placed a sacred duty on the Aztecs to sacrifice themselves and others in return. Such is the gift of death.

> [T]he gods assembled ... and spoke among themselves, saying: 'Who will take it upon himself to bring light to the world?' ... Nanauatzin ... threw himself into the fire [and became the Sun] ... Tecuciztecatl also cast himself into the flames [and became the Moon] ... Then the gods had to die; the wind, Quetzalcoatl, killed them all: The wind tore out their hearts and used them to animate the newborn stars. (Recounted in Bataille, 1988b: 46–9)

The fundamental obligation placed on the recipient of a gift is to give something back in return. So, the gift of life must be returned whence it came – to the sacrificial Gods. Accordingly, the Aztecs sacrificed thousands of people a year. These sacrifices fed 'the hungry Gods' (Bataille, 1988b: 54), for without it the Sun would dry up and life on Earth would wither away. It is in this sense that midwives reputedly told newborn baby boys that 'your duty is to give the sun the blood of your enemies to drink and to supply the earth with the bodies of your enemies to eat [and] you are offered and promised to the earth and the sun' (Bataille, 1988b: 53).

Once bloodshed is seen as a sacred obligation one can begin to understand why victims were treated relatively humanely. As gifts to the gods, those to be sacrificed were precious. 'The victim is a surplus taken from the mass of *useful* wealth', Bataille (1988b: 58) contends. 'It suffices for the sacrificer to give up the wealth that the victim could have been for him' (Bataille, 1988b: 60). So, although the Aztecs killed hundreds of thousands of people, they did not systematically dehumanize them or render them worthless. They were simply returned whence they came. Or rather, the Sun's energy (*tonalli*) that they embodied was given back to the gods.

Christian Duverger (1989) offers an account of the quintessential form of human sacrifice. Prior to being sacrificed the victim would endure all kinds of things that were designed to excite the energy that they embodied: from dancing and intercourse to sleep deprivation and drugging. The sacrifice itself would be performed in public, at a sacred location, and by priests. It was not a spectacle, but a ritual. The victim, arched over a sacrificial stone, would have his or her chest cut open with a flint knife, and the heart excised whilst still beating in order to maximize the blood loss. This nourished the 'Sun, Lord of the Earth'. Death in battle, and self-sacrifice, had the same effect as ritual sacrifice, but without the opportunity to maximize the bloodshed. A violent death was preferable because a 'natural' death (from old age, disease, accident, or suchlike) meant that much of the energy would drain into the underworld rather than back to the gods. The sacrificial ritual often ended with mutilation, decapitation, dismemberment, and cannibalism.

Aztec ritual sacrifice stands in stark contrast to the profane cannibalism and vampirism of capitalism. Capital is a monstrous, artificial, and undead life form that feeds off the slow release of the worker's energy, the draining of which is often strung out over a lifetime. Little wonder, then, that in those societies given over to capitalism's insatiable thirst for living labour, so-called 'premature' and 'preventable' deaths should have become such a scandal, and that the desire for immortality should have taken hold (Bauman, 1992). Contemporary capitalism is literally banking on death and investing in life (Blackburn, 2002; Tyner, 2016). Naturally, some obtuse souls have sought to escape capitalism's voracious appetite for the living and its ebullient 'health fascism' by choosing swift deaths instead (Baudrillard, 1993). The irony, of course, is that the desire to enforce and exploit immortality came in the wake of Europe's headlong rush into total war. The scandal of mortality is merely the inverted echo of the continent's willingness to sacrifice everything. It is to this suicidal death-drive that we now turn.

4

The European Way of War

From Abattoir Christianity to Godforsaken Total War

> When I search for Man in the technique and the style of Europe, I see only ... an avalanche of murders.
>
> Franz Fanon, 2008: 79–80

Medieval Europe's quintessential form of warfare was the crusade. Solicited by Pope Urban II, the first (1095–9) sought to regain Jerusalem from Islam. Around 100,000 crusaders, mostly Franks, who considered themselves to be 'Soldiers of Christ' (*milites Christi*), waged 'holy war' against the recently vilified Muslims of the Near East, although its initial victims were Jews in places such as Cologne, Mainz, and Worms (Phillips, 2009). This first crusade included major battles in and around Nicaea, Dorylaeum, Antioch, Edessa, Mosul, and Arqa, as the crusaders advanced from Constantinople to Jerusalem via Asia Minor and the Levant (Syria, Lebanon, and Palestine). It ended in July 1099, with the sacking of Jerusalem: 'one of the most ... horrifying events of the medieval age' (Asbridge, 2005: 316). The Soldiers of Christ massacred the city's vanquished Muslim population, and then worshiped at the Holy Sepulchre. Their victory emphatically confirmed 'God's support for ... sanctified violence' (Asbridge, 2005: 336–7).

Unlike a St Augustinian 'just war' (*bellum iustum*), whose lesser-evil violence is tolerated by God because it is well intentioned, authorized, and restrained, a 'holy war' (*bellum sacrum*) is a form of sanctified violence 'that God actively supported, even demanded, and which could be of spiritual benefit to its participants' (Asbridge, 2005: 25). Whereas a just war leaves the souls of those who kill untarnished, a holy war actually does them some good. Pope Urban II took the esoteric notions of sanctified violence and holy war, and made them appealing to lay folk by grafting them onto the familiar practice of pilgrimage. Crucially, this coupling let Frankish knights 'pursue two of their favourite pastimes – warfare and pilgrimage' (Asbridge, 2005: 37). As Zygmunt Bauman (1988: 77) wryly said of our own consumer society, whose key injunctions are wholly permissive (*Please yourself! Choose yourself! Be yourself! Enjoy!*), 'With duties like these, who needs rights?'

Pilgrimages were the ur-form of the tourist experience, exemplified by the Grand Tour and wanderlust (Hudson, 1993; Solnit, 2002), but they were edifying rather than educational, and penitential rather than pleasurable. They were 'devotional journeys to sites of religious significance ... specifically designed to be gruelling ... and thus capable of purging the soul' (Asbridge, 2005: 37). Urban II 'interwove the theme of holy war with that of pilgrimage to produce a distinct, new class of sanctified violence: a crusade (Asbridge, 2005: 37). Moreover, looting made crusading lucrative, thereby enriching the crusaders in this world as well as the next.

Given the success of the First Crusade, prosecuting holy war in the East and quashing heretics at home became European passions from the twelfth century onwards (Moore, 1990; Tyerman, 2005). Killing infidels and heretics was not only just, it was necessary, and it was not only good for the Church, it was good for the soul. It was also good for the ruling nobility, since heretics were as likely to be political dissidents as spiritual deviants. For example, the 'Cathar heresy, a pacifist brand of Christianity embracing tolerance and poverty, rose to prominence in ... the twelfth century', says Stephen O'Shea (2001: 7). 'Catharism thrived in regions farthest along the road from the Dark Ages: the merchant cities of Italy, the trading centres of Champagne and the Rhineland, and ... Languedoc' (O'Shea, 2001: 8). The Cathars subscribed to the Gnostic notion that an evil demiurge had created the world, rendering it irredeemably evil. For the Cathars, the Roman Catholic Church was in league with the evil demiurge. It was the 'Church of Satan'. Ordinary Cathar believers (*credentes*) delayed receiving baptism – 'heretication' – until death was near, thereby enabling them 'to lead a fairly agreeable life, not too strict from the moral point of view, until their end approached. But once they were hereticated' and became pure (*parfait*), 'they had to embark ... on a state of ... suicidal fasting' (Le Roy Ladurie, 1990: ix).

The brutal Albigensian Crusade (1209–29), which was launched by Pope Innocent III, and prosecuted by French armies, laid waste to Languedoc, forcing the region to renounce Catharism and submit to French rule. As with other crusades, 'this was a war not fought simply for religion ... but for territorial conquest' (McGlynn, 2015: 12). Indeed, 'Cathars were not the only ones to oppose Rome' and regard 'both the northern army and the Papal agents as foreign invaders' (Martin, 2005: 12). Holy war enabled a 'dual state' to pursue its sacred and profane interests simultaneously, although tensions often arose between the Pope and the crowned heads, the clergy and the nobility, Rome and elsewhere. '*Kill them all. For the Lord knoweth them that are His*' is the apocryphal aphorism attributed to the Crusade's papal legate, Arnaud Amaury (quoting 2 Timothy 2:19), on the eve of the massacre of the entire population of Béziers on 22 July 1209, which indiscriminately killed Cathar heretics and ortho-dox Catholics alike (my italics). O'Shea (2001: 86) aptly calls this 'abattoir Christianity'. Innocent's successor, Pope Gregory IX, established the Papal Inquisition in 1231, appointing the first 'Inquisitors of Depravity' to root out heretics – including the vestiges of Catharism – although it would take the Inquisition of Jacques Fournier (1318–24), based in Carcassonne (Languedoc) and focused on Pamiers (Ariège), to wipe it out in France (Le Roy Ladurie, 1990). In 1252, Gregory's successor, Pope Innocent IV, authorized judicial tor-ture during inquisitions – to be performed by the secular authorities rather than Inquisitors. Such a vicarious arrangement finds a contemporary echo in the prac-tice of 'extraordinary rendition' and 'coercive interrogation'.

Scrutinized by torture, the body of the patient (from the Latin, *patior*, to suffer) disclosed its truth to the Inquisitors (DuBois, 1990; Silverman, 2001). Recourse to torture was an almost inevitable outcome of the abolition of the Ordeals by the Fourth Lateran Council (1215), which 'destroyed an entire sys-tem of proof' (Langbein, 2006: 6). Ordeals solicited the judgement of God, who revealed guilt or innocence by miraculously sparing the innocent and leaving the guilty to their fate. With the end of the Ordeals, 'humans were going to replace God in deciding guilt or innocence' (Langbein, 2006: 6), and they would do so by way of judicial duels, compurgations, and Inquisitions. Once the latter took root in an already persecuting society, torture was refined to perfect its efficacy. In the service of truth, torture was neither sadistic nor savage. It was exquisite. This state of affairs lasted until the middle of the eighteenth century, when 'the leading states of Europe abolished judicial torture within the space of a generation' (Langbein, 2006: 10): Prussia in 1740; Saxony in 1770; Austria, Bohemia, and Poland in 1776; and France in 1780. 'By the next generation, abolition was complete throughout Europe' (Langbein, 2006: 10). A new, more enlightened 'law of proof' came into existence that made recourse to judicial torture obsolete – although torture lived on in some extrajudicial settings, and many of its techniques, although no longer truth seeking, were nevertheless recast as instruments of terror.

At this point in our non-linear historical geography of mass killing I would like to introduce two breaks. The first is neatly summed up by Darnton (2003: 79): 'An ideological interlude in the history of war took place between 1648, when the Peace of Westphalia marked the end of religion as a crucial element in international relations, and 1792, when the outbreak of the revolutionary wars signaled the beginning of wars between nations'. Wars amongst religious sects made way for wars amongst competing nations, set within a secular framework (especially mod-ern diplomacy). The peace treaties of 1648 brought to an end both the Holy Roman Empire's Thirty Years War (1618–48), during which 'the Swedes razed and destroyed 1,976 castles, 1,629 towns and 18,310 villages', and 'the population of Bohemia dropped from 4,000,000 to 800,000' (SIPRI, 1975: 17), and the Eighty

Years War (1568–1648) between the Dutch Republic and Spain, while the Revolutionary and Napoleonic Wars (1792–1815) put an end to the vestiges of the Holy Roman Empire and initiated an age of 'total war' between the imperial war-machines of nation–states that culminated with two 'world' wars (1914–18, and 1939–45). Although the cult of Christianity survived, Christendom was defunct. 'With it died one of its most distinctive features, the crusade' (Tyerman, 2007: 919). Europe certainly retained a taste for warfare, but it no longer did so in the name of God; it did so in the name of nations. However, 'the relentless ambition of imperialism and colonialism, coupled with the cultural phenomena of Romanticism and Orientalism, overlapped and combined to produce a dramatic revival in imagery and ideas descended from crusading' (Phillips, 2009: xx). Like holy wars of old, the violence that European imperialists exercised in their colonies was rationalized, declared goodly, and made rewarding.

The second break in our non-linear historical geography of mass killing is neatly summed up by Tzvetan Todorov with regard to Europe's encounter with the New World. 'What the Spaniards discover is the contrast between the metropolitan country and the colony, for radically different moral laws regulate conduct in each' (Todorov, 1992: 144). In the Old World of Europe, killing invariably required justification. In the New World of the Americas, killing required no justification because the lives of those killed were a matter of indifference. Europeans could kill indigenous people with impunity. It could even be rationalized as noble and edifying, especially if placed in the aristocratic tradition of hunting or the moral instruction and domestication of animals, slaves, women, and children through violence.

On the basis of Europe's 'discovery' of a New World in which everything was permitted, Todorov argues that two types of society crystallized: 'sacrifice-societies and massacre-societies, of which the Aztecs and the sixteenth-century Spaniards would be the respective representatives' (Todorov, 1992: 143). Through its superior means of violence, the profanity of massacre prevailed over the sacredness of sacrifice.

> Sacrifice ... is a religious murder: it is performed in the name of the official ideology and will be perpetrated in public places, in sight of all and to everyone's knowledge. The victim's identity is determined by strict rules. ... Massacre, on the other hand, ... should be performed in some remote place where the law is only vaguely acknowledged. ... The more remote and alien the victims, the better: they are exterminated without remorse, more or less identified with animals. The individual identity of the massacre victim is by definition irrelevant. ... [O]ne cuts off the Indian's nose, tongue, and penis without this having any ritual meaning for the amputator. (Todorov, 1992: 144)

The Spanish 'settlers' of Mesoamerica were neither farmers nor craftsmen, but soldiers and mercenaries: conquistadors (conquerors). Between 1494 and

1515, following Christopher Columbus's fortuitous encounter with the New World in 1492 (the same year that Spain, under pressure from Rome, expelled its entire 200,000-strong Jewish population), waves of Spanish conquistadors devastated indigenous communities on Caribbean islands, such as Cuba and Hispaniola, before moving onto the mainland, where they vanquished the Aztec, Incan, and Mayan Empires. A few hundred conquistadors led by Hernán Cortés defeated tens of thousands of Amerindian warriors. The latter's Stone and Bronze Age weaponry (wooden swords with obsidian shards, stone and bronze axes, slings and arrows) and flimsy battle dress (fabric armour, wooden shields and helmets, often adorned with leather and feathers) were no match for lance-bearing cavalry and sword-wielding infantry, all encased in virtually impregnable plate armour and chain mail. Although the Spaniards' arquebuses and crossbows were largely redundant (since their *raisons d'être* were to penetrate steel armour), their frightful noise had a terrorizing effect on the Amerindians that would echo down the centuries. 'Weapons are tools not just of destruction but also of perception', argues Paul Virilio (1989: 8), which he illustrates with the example of the '*Stuka* or Junker 87, the German dive-bomber of World War Two that swept down on its target with a piercing screech designed to terrorize and paralyze the enemy'. Roman 'whistling' sling bullets had a similar terrorizing effect.

The European massacre societies that unfurled across the globe were more accomplished killers than the sacrifice societies they annihilated. 'In the year 1800 Europeans occupied or controlled thirty-five percent of the land surface of the world; ... by 1914 over eighty-four percent' (Headrick, 1981: 3). Technological innovations were key: gunboats and railways; breechloaders and machine guns; quinine prophylaxis and canned food. 'Confrontations between Europeans and Africans after 1870 rank among the most lopsided in history' (Headrick, 1981: 115). For instance, at Omdurman in 1898, General 'Kitchener confronted the main Dervish army of 40,000. ... After five hours of fighting, 20 Britons, 20 of their Egyptian allies and 11,000 Dervishes lay dead' (Headrick, 1981: 117–18). European weapons were especially effective when used defensively. 'Against an open assault of masses of warriors, the imperialist forces resurrected the square of Napoleonic times, a human fortress surrounded by an impenetrable hail of bullets' (Headrick, 1981: 121). In October 1893, for example, '50 British South African Police ... encountered the 5,000 Ndebele warriors of King Lobengula. ... Within an hour and a half 3,000 Ndebele lay dead' (Headrick, 1981: 121–2).

When Europeans repatriated their fondness for colonial massacres at the start of the First World War, they began to forge a synthetic form of killing that Todorov (1992: 253, italics in original) calls '*massacrifice*'.

> As in sacrifice societies, a state religion is professed; as in massacre societies, behavior is based on the Karamazovian principle of 'everything is permitted.' As in a sacrifice, killing is performed first of all on home ground;

> as in a massacre, the very existence of such killing is dissimulated and denied. As in a sacrifice, the victims are chosen individually; as in a massacre, they are exterminated without any notion of ritual. (Todorov, 1992: 253)

A foretaste of 'massacrifice' came in the entrenched battlefields of the First World War. 'The soldier in the trenches ... was indeed as invulnerable to enemy attack as his counterpart had been in the square at Omdurman or in the wagon laager in Ndebeleland. But conversely, the soldier going over the top of a Flanders trench was as vulnerable as any Dervish or Ndebele warrior' (Headrick, 1981: 123–4). Indeed, industrialized warfare had promised nothing but horror from the start of the nineteenth century. The Battle of Borodino, fought between Napoleon's invading *Grande Armée* and Tsar Alexander's forces on 7 September 1812, in the countryside to the west of Moscow, engaged around a quarter of a million troops, 70,000 of whom were killed or mortally wounded. At the time, this was the highest death toll for any day's fighting in recorded history, and it remains one of the most lethal classical formation battles in the history of warfare, alongside the Battles of Wagram (1809), Leipzig (1813), Waterloo (1815), Gettysburg (1863), Königgrätz (1866), and the first day of the Battle of the Somme (1916), and is surpassed only by the interminable besiegement of cities such as Moscow (1941–2), Stalingrad (1942–3), and Berlin (1945), each of which consumed over a million lives (Beevor, 1998, 2002; Nagorski, 2008).

The full horror of massacrifice was first experienced by prisoners of war (POWs). The French Revolution swept away three key practices that had regulated the treatment of POWs: exchange, impressment, and parole. First, in September 1792, the French Legislative Assembly abolished the well-established practice of exchanging prisoners for money, and decreed that they could only be exchanged man for man – although the imbalance of prisoners amongst the warring nations produced unequal exchanges, typically in France's favour. Nevertheless, the suspicion that many French officers harboured counter-revolutionary sympathies risked turning even their 'polite correspondence with enemy commanders over prisoner-exchanges' into *prima facie* 'evidence of treasonous intent' (Andress, 2005: 218). Second, since people had been lent inalienable national identities, such as 'French' or 'Russian' (a peculiar modern contrivance that still skewers people today), they could no longer be indiscriminately impressed into any military service whatsoever. Accordingly, in May 1793, the French National Convention decreed that foreign soldiers could not be solicited to swap sides. (Nevertheless, Napoleon still conscripted manpower from conquered territories to fight in French wars.) Finally, in June 1793, the Convention prohibited parole for officers, since the pre-revolutionary code of honour had proscribed their resumption of active military service. Such an aristocratic privilege was anathema to the Revolutionaries.

Since these and similar decrees inflated the number of prisoners, belligerents faced a growing problem. During the Napoleonic Wars over 100,000 French POWs were held in Britain alone (around 5,000 at any one time). Britain constructed the world's first purpose-built prisoner-of-war camp at Norman Cross in Cambridgeshire, in 1797. By the end of the First World War, however, there were an astonishing 6–7 million POWs (Yarnell, 2011). And when Germany invaded Russia in June 1941, it expected tens of millions of Soviet POWs – both soldiers and civilians, which exemplifies how warfare had become 'total'. As Kristin Ross says of the French campaign to 'pacify' Algeria, its colonial possession, in the 1950s and 1960s, for an Algerian 'to be "at home," an inhabitant, is to be at the center of the conflict: ... to be at home is possibly the most politicized state, ... in solidarity with ... the nationalist struggle' (Ross, 1995: 110).

The Revolutionary and Napoleonic Wars were the first 'total wars', in the double sense of engaging an entire population in warfare, and then endeavouring to wage war with the enemy completely – for the aim was 'no longer to *defeat an enemy* but to *annihilate a foe*' (Bernstein, 2013: 160, italics in original). The first sense is usually traced back to the National Convention's emergency decree of mass mobilization (*levée en masse*), issued on 23 August 1793, which 'requisitioned all adult males and all the country's resources in the first modern attempt to wage "total war"' (Rapport, 2013: 28). The mobilization aimed to defend the Revolution against counter-revolutionary forces at home and abroad (Cobb, 1987; Roberts, 1990). 'From this moment until such time as its enemies shall have been driven from the soil of the Republic, all Frenchmen are in permanent requisition for the services of the armies', the decree began. 'The young men shall fight; the married men shall forge arms and transport provisions; the women shall make tents and clothes and shall serve in the hospitals; the children shall turn old lint into linen; the old men shall betake themselves to the public squares in order to arouse the courage of the warriors.' By the end of 1794, over a million Frenchmen had been enlisted into the Revolutionary Army (*Armée révolutionnaire française*), an egalitarian feat unmatched by its royalist enemies in the rest of Europe who feared arming the people: 'the governing elites agonized over whether a "revolution from above," as one Prussian official called it, could take place without provoking a French-style revolution from below' (Bell, 2008: 252). Indeed, Adam Zamoyski (2014: 22) argues that none of the European states 'was remotely prepared to meet the challenge of the Revolution' because they were primarily geared up to control political strife within the elite (the aristocracy and nobility), rather than political agitation arising from the vast bulk of the population (peasants, workers, merchants, etc.). The masses had counted for nothing. Now, in France, they counted for all. The 'spectre of communism' was indeed spooking the medieval fossils of Old Europe. And ever since, Tyrants have feared this 'phantom terror', as Zamoyski (2014) calls it. Nevertheless, one monarch did attempt a limited mass mobilization. Following defeat at the legendary Battle of Austerlitz (1805), Francis the *Doppelkaiser*, who was simultaneously the last Holy Roman Emperor (Francis II) and the first Emperor of Austria (Francis I), tentatively established an Austrian 'home army' (*Landwehr*) between 1808 and 1813, but it was stymied from the off by a sceptical military elite: recruitment was disappointing, and 'those who did come into service, provided with poor weapons and worse leadership, fared from badly to disastrously on the battlefield' (Bell, 2008: 252).

The second sense of 'total war' marks the transition within Europe from a form of warfare characterized by orchestrated battles between like-minded and well-matched armies, the art of which had been refined in the eighteenth century to minimize the inconvenience that they caused, to a form of warfare in the nine-teenth century characterized by the increasingly merciless pitting of all against all, the art of which was subsequently refined in the twentieth century to become wars of annihilation and extermination. If the former could still feign a sense of redemptive chivalry, as if it were essentially a duel between gentlemen, the latter was killing pure and simple, and its heroes and heroines were those who could stomach it. Scorched earth methods, such as burning crops and settlements, slaughtering livestock, poisoning wells, and destroying infrastructure, which date back to Antiquity, came to the fore in conflicts such as the Napoleonic Wars, the American Civil War (1861–5), and the Boer War (1899–1902). For example, in the First World War, Lord Tiverton advocated using Britain's newly formed Royal Air Force (RAF) to drop planeloads of Colorado Beetles onto Germany's farm-land to destroy the potato crop and starve Germany into submission (Tanaka, 2009). Bombing crops and strafing livestock became a routine way for imperial powers to quell anti-colonial insurgencies in the 1920s and 1930s, especially in North Africa and the Middle East. 'The British *Manual of Air Tactics* of 1937 advocated them as a means of punishment' (SIPRI, 1975: 82). Indeed, the RAF considered bombing the German countryside with incendiaries during the Second World War, but the vegetation was judged to be insufficiently flammable. Meanwhile, amid the Second Italo-Ethiopian War (1935–6), the Italians terror-ized Ethiopians from the air: 'Except for Addis Ababa most of the centres of Ethiopia were subjected to substantial bombing, often with incendiaries' (SIPRI, 1975: 27). And in a final illustration that brought 'air frightfulness' much closer to home, during the Spanish Civil War (1936–9) the Germans bombed Durango and Guernica with incendiaries as 'experiments in terror bombing designed to break the morale of the civilian population' (Preston, 2012: 434). Few would countenance terror bombing civilians to destroy their civility. Yet terror bombing them to destroy their morale would soon become a military imperative. 'When bombing cannot hit anything else, it can strike at morale' (Strachan, 2006: 13).

Moving ever worstward, armed forces in a 'total' war tend to make recourse to rape, torture, terror, and desecration to defile and destroy the ease with which one can be at home with oneself and amongst others. 'In modern con-flicts rape reminds us that waging war is more than simply engaging in mechanical slaughter', writes Joanna Bourke (2007: 357). Sexual abuse, sexual violence, sexual torture, and sexual murder frequently accompany invasions, occupations, and liberations – as both weapons and spoils of war; as both ret-ribution and recreation – and they played an important role in 'the order of terror' of the SS concentration camps: to punish, intimidate, and dehumanize (Sofsky, 1997; Wachsmann, 2015). The ebb and flow of warfare leaves in its wake sexual horror, much of which is orchestrated. In the Second World War 'more rapes occurred in this war, particularly in its final stages, than during any other war in history' (Lowe, 2013: 51), and they were committed by Axis and Allied forces alike: 'at least 2 million German women are thought to have been raped' (Beevor, 2002: 410).

Sexual horror is also at work in the libidinal economy that saturates and invests warfare from beginning to end (Lyotard, 1993). Whether sacred or profane, violence and war – and the *desire* for violence and war – are first and foremost *pleasures*, as Klaus Theweleit (1987, 1989) reveals in his seminal study of the anti-Semitic and misogynistic male fantasies of the interwar *Freikorps* ('free regiments' of mercenaries). *Freikorps* were ultra-right-wing paramilitary volunteer units, mostly made up of German First World War veterans. In the 1920s, they battled the real and imagined communist 'Red flood' flowing from the East. They also lent their weight to the rise of Hitler's National Socialist German Workers Party (NSDAP or Nazi Party), into which they were assimilated via the SA (*Sturmabteilung* – the Party's paramilitary 'storm detachment' or 'brownshirts', founded in 1921), and the SS (*Schutzstaffel* – the Party's paramilitary 'protection squad' for the leadership, founded in 1925), into which the SA itself was assimilated following the 'Night of the Long Knives' in 1934. Thereafter, the explosive growth of the SS spawned a powerful array of organizations that shadowed, rivalled, and often usurped their state counterparts: the Reich Main Security Office (*Reichssicherheitshauptamt* or RSHA, that dealt with political and ideological enemies); the SD security services and Gestapo (that rivalled the criminal police force); the vast *Waffen-SS* (the Party's military wing that rivalled the regular armed forces, the Wehrmacht); and the *SS-Totenkopfverbände* (Death's Head concentration-camp units that rivalled the regular prison system); as well as the *SS-Sonderkommandos* (not to be confused with concentration-camp *Sonderkommandos*, which were squads of inmates forced to do the arduous work of mass killing, such as corpse disposal); and the *Einsatzgruppen* killing squads – all of which were responsible for planning and implementing the Holocaust or Shoah, from ghettoization and 'destruction through labour' to mass shooting and mass gassing. The *Freikorps* served as a 'vanishing mediator' between the proto-fascism of the 1920s and the rise of Nazism in the 1930s.

Nazi concentration camps were created for the mass incarceration of the Party's political opponents (communists, social democrats, trade unionists, etc.). The detention of political rivals was intended to cement the Party's grip on power following Hitler's appointment as Chancellor on 30 January 1933. In March, Adolf Wagner, the Bavarian Minister of the Interior, suggested that 'when state prisons were full arrested enemies should be exposed to the elements in "abandoned ruins"', and by the summer of 1933, the Nazis had established over 170 impromptu 'prisons' focused on 'Red Berlin' that included 'run-down or vacant hotels, castles, sports grounds, and youth hostels' (Wachsmann, 2015: 36). Such improvised spaces of incarceration – many of which 'were nothing more than warehouses acquired for the purpose of having detention centres separate from the German police' (Jaskot, 2000: 13) – held many thousands of people in extra-judicial 'protective custody' – 'kidnapping with a bureaucratic veneer' (Wachsmann, 2010: 19). Nazi guards 'used violence to communicate a simple message: the prisoners were worthless and at their mercy. Screaming men surrounded bewildered newcomers and showered them in abuse' and they 'kicked, beat, and whipped their victims' (Wachsmann, 2015: 39). However, this early regime of terror was not yet systematically lethal. Most taken into custody were terrorized for a while and then released. 'Murder remained the exception, as the early camps were more about intimidation than killing' (Wachsmann, 2010: 19). It would not be long, however, before 'a new species of absolute power was unleashed that shattered all previous conceptions of despotism or dictatorial brutality – the businesslike annihilation of human beings. In the span of twelve years, the concentration camp metamorphosed from a locus of terror into a universe of horror' (Sofsky, 1997: 5).

As Hitler and the Nazi Party consolidated their power in 1933–4, the number of improvised camps dwindled, and the SS took control of them all, thereby instituting an extrajudicial regime of detention and terror that separated itself from the regular criminal justice and prison systems administered by the Ministry of the Interior. For a while, however, it looked as though the SS camps, like the *Freikorps*, would be vanishing mediators.

> The emerging SS system was a small-scale operation with doubtful prospects. By summer 1935, there were just five concentration camps, holding no more than 4,000 … [T]hey were dwarfed by hundreds of regular prisons, which held well over 100,000 inmates … [I]t seemed as if extra-legal detention in camps might no longer be necessary. (Wachsmann, 2010: 21–2)

Himmler, however, regarded the release of political prisoners from protective custody as a grave error, and, with Hitler's support, set about rebuilding the SS concentration-camp system. By the end of 1937, there were just four camps: two established ones, at Dachau and Lichtenburg; and two new ones, at Buchenwald and Sachsenhausen. The latter were 'planned as small cities of terror, with rows of barracks and roads, command posts and guard towers, sewers and electricity, workshops and SS quarters. The new model, Himmler enthused in February 1937, was a "concentration camp for the modern age, which can be extended at any time"' (Wachsmann, 2010: 22). Within a year, Dachau was being rebuilt to this 'modern' specification. By 1938, then, a handful of SS camps, with barely 8,000 inmates, formed the kernel of the vast concentration-camp system that would soon emerge in the wake of the invasions of Poland and the Soviet Union in 1939 and 1941, respectively. They were extrajudicial, staffed by SS Death's Head units, with inmates required to wear standard uniforms with identifying emblems: colour-coded triangles, such as red for political prisoners, purple for Jehovah's Witnesses, pink for homosexuals, and black for the 'asocial' and 'workshy', all of which could be inverted and superimposed on a yellow triangle, thereby forming a star to differentiate the Jews (such as yellow on yellow for ordinary Jews, red on yellow for Jewish political prisoners, and pink on yellow for Jewish homosexuals); and other distinguishing marks to denote things like national affiliation and previous criminal convictions (e.g. 'SU' for Soviet subhuman).

The SS's sartorial system for concentration-camp prisoners was reminiscent of the requirement in many parts of medieval Europe for Jews, Muslims, and heretics to distinguish themselves from Christians by wearing conspicuous clothing (such as yellow stars, yellow crosses, and turbans), a practice that dates back to the Fourth Council of the Lateran (1215). While the latter, like other sumptuary laws, was not necessarily incompatible with the Papal position of *sicut Judaeis* (which sought to protect Jews from harassment, forced conversion, and desecration of their sacred places), the SS's system of discrimination was persecutory from the off. It 'regulated the distribution of misery, the dissemination of wretchedness' (Sofsky, 1997: 19). The stratification of the prison population determined 'who was granted temporary protection, who was exposed to ruinous, ravaging labor, what rations a prisoner received'. And while not yet systematically murderous, the Nazis nevertheless operated a regime of terror in tune with the biopolitical and necropolitical death function (Foucault, 1998, 2004; Mbembe, 2003).

When war began in 1939, 'the SS held 21,400 inmates in six concentration camps' (Wachsmann, 2010: 23), many of whom had been rounded up as recidivists, 'asocials', and 'workshy' – the unemployed, 'beggars and tramps, pimps and prostitutes, those on benefits and alcoholics, hooligans and traffic offenders' (Dams and Stolle, 2014: 110). They had been detained partly to enforce labour discipline amongst the German population, and partly to create a labour force within the camps for the Nazis' building programme. Buchenwald and Sachsenhausen were close to brick works, and Flossenbürg and Mauthausen to quarries. There had also been mass arrests of homosexuals, Jehovah's Witnesses, and – after the nationwide pogrom launched on 9–10 November 1938, the so-called 'Night of Broken Glass' (*Kristallnacht*) – Jews, which briefly raised the inmate population to 50,000, as part of the concerted effort 'to terrorize Jews into emigration' (Wachsmann, 2010: 26). Around 100 Jews died during *Kristallnacht*, and thousands were brutalized in the camps. 'The abuse of Jewish prisoners was unprecedented: deprivation, torture, suicide and murder reached new heights' (Wachsmann, 2010: 25). *Kristallnacht* was devastating. 'To destroy a community's institutions is ... almost as satisfying as destroying its people. As a general "cleansing" of Germany of Jewish synagogues, *Kristallnacht* was a proto-genocidal assault' (Goldhagen, 1997: 140–1).

When the centre of gravity of the concentration-camp system moved eastwards following the invasions of Poland and the Soviet Union, expanding enormously and reconfiguring itself to eliminate millions of Soviet POWs (through lethal labour) and then to exterminate millions of Jews (through shooting and gassing), the 'order of terror' and its sadistic 'welcome' would be taken to the limit, most infamously at the Auschwitz–Birkenau and Treblinka death camps, especially during the selection process for each new trainload of 'evacuees' pre-selected for destruction as the Jewish ghettoes were systematically liquidated: 'as the empire ... had no "outside" left where the dumping ground for the Jewish litter could be disposed of', writes Bauman (1989: 105). 'Only one direction of deportation remained; upward, in smoke.'

Meanwhile, the regular prison system was recast as a brutal regime of legal terror. As early as 1933, the Prussian State Secretary for Justice, Roland Freisler, called for prison to become a 'house of horror' (quoted in Wachsmann, 2004: 76). Unlike Germany's Weimar Republic (1918–33), which had focused on reform and rehabilitation, the Nazi regime focused on the 'protection' of the 'national community' from 'community aliens' and 'folk pests' (*Volksschädlinge*). This resulted in an explosion of the prison population and a dramatic increase in capital punishment. 'In 1943 and 1944, some 9,600 death sentences were passed in the German Reich. In these two years alone, more people were sentenced to death than in the entire 80-year period between 1861 and 1941' (Wachsmann, 2004: 218). The 1939 *Decree Against Public Enemies* ('Folk Pest Law') was the most frequently cited legal pretext for the death penalty between 1941 and 1945. The measures fell disproportionately on foreigners, especially Czechs, Hungarians, and Poles, which 'betrayed the growing paranoia about foreign workers, as the war turned against Germany and the number of these workers on German soil increased; by August 1944, there were almost six million, as well as two million POWs, labouring in Germany' (Wachsmann, 2004: 220).

The courts and prisons were a crucial apparatus of legal terror that complemented the extrajudicial terror of the secret police and concentration camps. 'Ultimately, they pursued one and the same goal: the fight against "community aliens" in the Third Reich. ... Most importantly, they provided each other with inmates for their respective sites of imprisonment' (Wachsmann, 2004: 380). The police could have taken all suspects to concentration camps without any court process, but most were transferred to the legal authorities. 'Penal institutions were the main sites of imprisonment in Nazi Germany before the war, eclipsing SS concentration camps, at times by an inmate ratio as high as 25:1', and for the bulk of the war they held 'more inmates than the SS concentration camps (excluding the death camps). Only in the last years of the war ... was this balance finally reversed' (Wachsmann, 2004: 374 and 376, respectively). Nevertheless, many of those held by the legal authorities were transferred into SS custody. 'In the case of certain political prisoners, criminal offenders and "racial aliens" coming to the end of their sentences, many legal officials believed that the inmates still needed to be locked up to protect the "national community," even though this was no longer legally possible' (Wachsmann, 2004: 381). Some of those acquitted by the courts, and even some whose cases were dismissed, were still handed over to the SS.

The SS's regime of terror was fronted by a double figure: guards barking orders accompanied by dogs barking ferociously. Terror bared its teeth upon arrival. 'The teeth of power – trained dogs as instruments of organized coercion and bloodletting – reveal themselves in the historical records of some of the worst instances of modern state violence' (Wall, 2014: 4). They were especially vicious in the camps, where fascism's insatiable appetite for destruction was unleashed. It was a voracious appetite that devoured itself as well as others. The Nazis were 'masters of death' (Rhodes, 2002), forging a 'suicidal state' rather than a 'totalitarian state'. They created '*a war machine that no longer had war as its object*', since it 'would rather annihilate its own servants than stop the destruction' (Deleuze and Guattari, 1988: 231, italics in original).

> Nazi statements ... always contain the 'stupid and repugnant' cry, *Long live death!*, even at the economic level, ... where investment veers from the means of production toward the means of pure destruction. ... 'Telegram 71 is the normal outcome: *If the war is lost, may the nation perish.* Here, Hitler decides to join forces with his enemies in order to complete the destruction of his own people.' (Deleuze and Guattari, 1988: 231, quoting Paul Virilio, *L'insécurité du territoire*)

As Marshall Berman (1999: 139) said of capitalist modernity, fascism feeds 'on its own self-destruction'. The all-consuming suicidal drive of total war stands in marked contrast to the more or less continuous yet moderate warfare that characterized Europe before the French Revolution.

> Western rulers saw war as their principal purpose and fought continually – during the 1700s, no more than six or seven years passed without at least one major European power at war. But since the end of the terrible religious conflicts of the Reformation, war had also become relatively easy to control and to restrain. Armies were relatively small, major battles relatively infrequent ... and civilians relatively well treated. ... This state of virtually permanent but restrained warfare ... allowed the aristocratic values of honor and service to find full expression without serious threats to social stability and prosperity. (Bell, 2008: 5)

In a sense, then, eighteenth-century Europe enjoyed the best of all possible wars, since their conduct had been optimized for the aristocratic theatre of chivalry with minimal disruption to everyday life. Enlightenment thinkers challenged the notion that war was endemic to human existence: 'the prevailing state of restrained warfare did not represent a natural equilibrium but rather a stage on the way to war's eventual complete disappearance' (Bell, 2008: 6). They argued that war should become something rare – perhaps even inconceivable. Many came to believe that the advent of the balloon, railway, and submarine would make war impossible – either because these transport revolutions would bring people ever closer together in friendship, 'realizing the

Universal Brotherhood of Universal Man' (Carey, 1992: 208), or else because they would unleash an unbearable form of warfare that no nation could endure. The Napoleonic Wars jolted Europe out of its daydreaming. For they heralded a new form of conflict – total war – along with the suicidal death-drive that such a totalization of warfare entails.

> [W]hen France took up arms in 1792, it was not to fight anything like the limited wars familiar to the powers of the Old Regime. ... Before 1790, only a handful of battles had involved more than 100,000 combatants; in 1809, the battle of Wagram, the largest yet seen in the gunpowder age, involved 300,000. Four years later, the battle of Leipzig drew 500,000. ... During the Napoleonic period, France alone counted close to a million war deaths. ... The toll across Europe may have reached as high as 5 million. (Bell, 2008: 7)

Total war emerged as an absolute limit that belligerents approached asymptotically. 'What marked the conflicts that began in 1792 was not simply their radically new scope and intensity but also the political dynamic that drove the participants relentlessly *toward* a condition of total engagement and the abandonment of restraints' (Bell, 2008: 8). What fuelled this was the conviction that the nation and the Revolution were at stake, thereby unleashing a reciprocal and escalatory logic of 'absolute enmity' and exterminatory warfare (Schmitt, 2007). The desire for total war, like the desire for Terror, emerges from perceived weakness rather than strength (Chase, 2001; Getty and Naumov, 2010; Wahnich, 2012). On 22 May 1790, the revolutionary government of France renounced 'wars of conflict' and declared that its armed forces would be limited to self-defence. Two years later, France invaded Austrian-ruled Belgium, ostensibly in self-defence, thereby initiating the Revolutionary and Napoleonic Wars that would consume Europe in an orgy of violence for the next 23 years: 'it sometimes seemed as if time itself had become impossibly compressed – "this quarter-century equalled many centuries," to quote [François-René de] Chateaubriand' (Bell, 2008: 17). War was no longer an aristocratic theatre of chivalry that left almost everything undisturbed, not least the aristocratic order itself, but rather an increasingly disinhibited struggle of revolution against counter-revolution that left unprecedented destruction in its wake. 'The phenomenon of total war reached a hideous peak in 1793–94, in the French region of the Vendée' (Bell, 2008: 18).

It would be a mistake to presume that 'the origins of modern total war are surely to be found on the early modern imperial frontiers', argues David Bell (2008: 18); that 'it was here, long before the Revolution, that Europeans first dispensed with notions of chivalric restraint and waged brutal wars of extermination against supposed "savages" ... in Asia, Africa, and the Americas'. First and foremost, Bell reminds us that the 'Europeans hardly needed colonial empires to learn the art of mass murder' (Bell, 2008: 18). 'The horrendous slaughters of the Reformation-era wars of religion began well before most European empires had developed much beyond trading posts, and the worst examples occurred in the German states, which had no colonies.' Moreover, the European empires of the eighteenth century were spread too thinly and their grip on far-flung peoples and places was too fragile to unleash exterminatory violence willy-nilly. Since they depended upon the cooperation of colonized populations, the violence inflicted on them tended to be functional rather than total. The aim was invariably occupation and exploitation; and only rarely extermination – typically as part of a broader land-clearance process, alongside deforestation and enclosure.

The final element of total war is how it broke out of the solid confines of the battlefield, flowed freely across the face of the earth, and in so doing precipitated a gaseous resistance.

> The warfare of the *Ancien Régime*, which resembled a carefully choreographed and complicit movement of solid masses, was destroyed by ... the liquid, wave-like offensive of the revolutionary armies. ... From the defeat of the massed solids of the armies of the *Ancien Régime* by the liquid mass of the revolutionary army emerges the People's War (*Volkskrieg*) of episodic and pointillistic attacks, momentary condensations of an intangible political vapour or cloud that is the actualization of a new capacity to resist. (Caygill, 2013: 24)

In an attempt 'to awaken, shock, wound the viewer', Francisco Goya depicted the 'ghoulish cruelties' (Sontag, 2003: 40) of this new kind of warfare in 82 etchings (1810–20), which were posthumously published as *The Disasters of War* in 1863. 'Goya shows the flotsam left by the flood of the passing revolutionary army: destroyed buildings, crops and heaps of mutilated bodies' (Caygill, 2013: 24). This harrowing series, from which 'the trappings of the spectacular have been eliminated', and whose 'cumulative effect is devastating' (Sontag, 2003: 40), was inspired by the atrocities committed by Napoleon's *Grande Armée* as it invaded Spain in 1808 to quell the insurrection against French occupation. This Peninsular War (1807–14) was one of the first wars of national liberation and entailed protracted guerrilla warfare. It also fed into the War of the Sixth Coalition (1813–14), which resulted in the defeat of the *Grande Armée*, the exile of Napoleon, and the restoration of Louis XVIII, the 'Bourbon pretender', to the throne of France.

The Revolutionary and Napoleonic Wars unleashed a flood of violence that could only be effectively countered by a vaporous resistance. 'A general uprising ... should be nebulous and elusive; the resistance should never materialize as a concrete body, otherwise the enemy can direct sufficient force at its core, crush it, and take many prisoners. ... On the other hand ... the fog must thicken and form a dark menacing cloud out of which a bolt of lightning may strike at any time' (Clausewitz, 1993: 581). Such vapoury became the hallmark of resistance, liberation, and revolutionary movements the world over, such as the International Anarchist Congress of 1881, which adopted the strategy of 'propaganda by deed' – political assassinations and quotidian bombings.

The trialectical struggle between solidity, liquidity, and gaseity gave rise to the asymmetrical conflicts to which we have become accustomed, such as the tragi-comic 'War on Terror' and a series of spin-offs that include the ongoing Iraqi and Syrian Civil Wars. The world's great military masses are frozen rigid in relation to one another, and yet they continue to exhaust themselves fighting vapours. What is striking is not only the 'strength of the weak', but also the fact that the asymmetry between the flood of total war and the fog of guerrilla resistance has been over-coded by a technological asymmetry mistaken for a moral opposition: the world's most advanced armaments are pitted against improvised weapons cobbled together by military *bricoleurs* (e.g. indiscriminate Scud ballistic missiles as opposed to discerning Tomahawk cruise missiles, or goodly drones as opposed to frightful hell cannons). Weapons manufactured by the military–industrial–humanitarian complex are blessed with exacting standards, the aura of advanced engineering, and the grandeur of high technology. Indeed, since the 1980s the US Department of Defense has led the way in implementing Total Quality Management (US DoD, 1990), the fallout from which has irradiated almost every organization in the empire of neoliberalism. Meanwhile, weapons improvised from recycled and repurposed materials that are ready to hand are cursed with an absence of standards, an embarrassing reliance on amateur mechanics, and a shameful recourse to lowly and debased technologies. Despite the recent fetishization of all things 'slow', 'local', and 'artisanal' amongst discerning middle-class consumers (such as real ale and urban allotments), this transvaluation has yet to embrace the artisans of improvised warfare. On those rare occasions when 'slow violence' has been brought to light, it is invariably to draw attention to 'violence that is neither spectacular nor instantaneous, but rather incremental and accretive'; to reveal slow-motion 'calamities that patiently dispense their devastation while remaining outside our flickering attention spans ... of a spectacle-driven corporate media' (Nixon, 2011: 2 and 6, respectively). For example, the swift violence of disasters such as Bhopal (1984), Deepwater Horizon (2010), and Fukushima (2011) is mirrored by the slow violence unleashed by the routine operation of the chemical, oil, and nuclear industries. In fact, I wager that the slower the calamity, the more murderous it will have been – from the adventure of capitalism to human-induced climatic change. According to Slavoj Žižek (2009), this structural and systemic violence forms a 'degree-zero' background against which other forms of violence periodically erupt and clamour for attention: wars, massacres, famines, floods, murders, crises, crashes, etc. The true horror is not what flares up but what endures: 'What is scandalous isn't the pit explosion, it's working in coalmines. "Social problems" aren't "a matter of concern" when there's a strike, they are intolerable twenty-four hours out of twenty-four, three hundred and sixty-five days a year' (Perec, 1999: 209).

With an eye towards the horror that is coming, consider how one of the world's most powerful liquid war-machines extinguished a guerrilla insurgency. During the Second Anglo-Boer War (1899–1902), the British devised a cunning plan to break the military deadlock by weaponizing a mass-produced agricultural product strewn across rural South Africa: barbed wire. In March 1901, Lord Kitchener 'decided to break the stalemate by a double sweeping operation: to flush out the guerrillas in a series of systematic "drives," organized like a sporting shoot, with success defined in a weekly "bag" of killed, captured and wounded; and to sweep the country bare of everything that could give sustenance to the guerrillas: not only horses, but cattle, sheep, women, and children' (Pakenham, 1991a: 493). In order to accomplish the first of these operations, a vast barbed-wire net was cast over the Transvaal and Orange Free State, so that the elusive Boer guerrillas could be hunted down. By May 1902, the British had erected 8,000 pre-fabricated tin-and-concrete gun emplacements ('blockhouses'), spaced out by lines of sight, connected by 3,700 miles of barbed wire, and guarded by 50,000 British troops and 16,000 African scouts. It was 'a gigantic grid-mesh of blockhouse lines: barbed wire, alternating with blockhouses, each miniature fort within rifle range of each other' (Pakenham, 1991a: 499). Columns of hundreds of troops would move through each cell, 'flushing out' the Boer guerrillas, and 'driving' them into the barbed wire, where they could be 'bagged' (shot or captured). It was an extraordinarily novel strategy, combining the age-old aristocratic passion for hunting with horses and dogs, and the relatively newfangled technologies of railway lines, barbed wire, and machine guns. To illustrate the perverse 'exhilaration of the new-style war, hunting down the Boers like "game"', Thomas Pakenham (1991a: 541) quotes Colonel Rawlinson's account of a night raid by 2,500 troops and scouts: 'we had a good long gallop of nearly 7 miles … rewarded by collecting 53 prisoners'.

The first hunt happened on 5–6 February 1902, in a cell covering 50 square miles, three sides of which were enclosed by wire and machine guns. Nine hundred soldiers advanced from the open edge: 'roughly one man for every ten yards, lined out across the fifty-four miles of the open end. … Meanwhile, other columns were sent to reinforce the blockhouses on the three other sides, and seven armoured trains, equipped with guns and searchlights, steamed up and down the railway tracks' (Pakenham, 1991a: 545). This first hunt was only partially successful, however, 'bagging' fewer than 300 guerrillas, with many more evading the trap by cutting the barbed wire under the noses of the blockhouse gunners. Nevertheless, such operations became more effective with time, netting up to 2,000 a month, and eventually extinguishing Boer resistance to British occupation.

At this point it is worth noting that Nazi police units undertook similar 'man-hunts', not only to extinguish partisans, but also to ensure that occupied areas were completely 'free' and 'clean' of Jews (*Judenfrei*). The 'Jew hunt' (*Judenjagd*), which commenced in earnest in the autumn of 1942, was 'a tenacious, remorseless, ongoing campaign in which the "hunters" tracked down and killed their "prey" in direct and personal confrontation … an existential condition of constant readiness and intention to kill every last Jew who could be found' (Browning, 2001: 132). While some Jew hunts were large operations in forests and the countryside, others focused on towns and villages. 'The most common … was the small patrol into the forest to liquidate an individual bunker' (Browning, 2001: 126). The police units 'built up a network of informers and "forest runners," or trackers, who searched for and revealed Jewish hiding places', says Christopher Browning (2001: 126). 'Time and again the same scenario was played out, with only minor variations. The policemen followed their Polish guides directly to the bunker hideouts and tossed grenades in the openings. The Jews who survived … were forced to lie face down for the neck shot.'

The second of Lord Kitchener's sweeping operations comprised two counterinsurgency strategies pioneered by the Spanish during the Cuban War of Independence (1895–8). The Spanish had compelled, on pain of death, the entire civilian population in Cuba to leave the countryside and 'reconcentrate' in cities. The depopulated countryside was then subjected to a systematic scorched earth policy designed to starve the Cuban guerrillas of food, shelter, and support. In the wake of reconcentration, however, epidemics and starvation in the overcrowded cities killed around 200,000 people. In the Boer War, the British also applied these scorched earth and reconcentration policies, but rather than concentrate people in cities, they concentrated them in clusters of tents modelled on military encampments. These 'concentration camps', as critics dubbed them, were presented to the world as 'camps of refuge', but the 100,000 or so women and children taken to them were internees rather than refugees. A barbed-wire perimeter was soon added to each camp, ostensibly to prevent Boer guerrillas from making clandestine raids for food, but the barbed-wire perimeter also imprisoned the internees. Barbed wire was soon deployed internally within the camps to enforce 'order' and 'hygiene' amongst people that the British regarded as inherently unruly and unclean. These barbed-wire settlements were presented as a benign environment to civilize the Boers. However, the overcrowded and under-resourced 'concentration camps' met the same fate as the 'reconcentrated' cities of Cuba: at least 30,000 died, mostly from typhoid and measles. Similarly, Britain's suppression of the Mau Mau rebellion in Kenya in the 1950s entailed the detention of hundreds of thousands of Kikuyu women and children in around 800 'emergency villages' hastily erected in the countryside. They 'were surrounded by spiked trenches, barbed wire, and watchtowers, and were heavily patrolled by armed guards' (Elkins, 2005: 59). They were also ravaged by malnutrition, starvation, and disease, which the colonial administration regarded with indifference.

Suffice to say that while these Spanish and British policies of concentration unintentionally resulted in civilian deaths on a massive scale, the Nazi policy of ghettoization was not only intended to kill Jews through malnutrition and disease, it also entailed precisely calculated starvation diets. The British pioneered minimal human-subsistence diets in India during the famines of 1876–9, and 1886–1902, which killed somewhere between 12 million and 30 million people: the so-called 1877 'Temple Wage' in Madras, for example, 'provided less subsistence for hard labor than the diet inside the infamous Buchenwald concentration camp', and to qualify for this lethal diet 'required starving applicants to travel to dormitory camps outside their locality for coolie labor on railroad and canal projects. The deliberately cruel "distance test" refused work to able-bodied adults and older children within a ten-mile radius of their homes' (Davis, 2002: 38). As millions of Indians starved to death, British 'famine relief' amounted to lethal labour, starvation diets, and death marches to concentration camps. This was not an isolated case, as demonstrated by Britain's disastrous response to the Irish Famine of 1845–9 (O'Regan, 2013).

Nazi ghettoization took many spatial forms, some of which were remarkably diffuse – such as the 'Yellow Star' houses in Budapest (Cole, 2003) – and they all mutated over time. Segregation, concentration, enclosure, and liquidation were on-going processes rather than settled states (Cole, 2011; Cole and Giordano, 2014; Giaccaria and Minca, 2016; Michman, 2014). Ghettoization was also a well-established practice in Europe, dating back to the fourteenth-century quarantining of lepers and plague victims, typically on boats and islands near port cities such as Dubrovnik, Marseilles, and Venice, as well as in pest houses and plague hospitals (McNeill, 1979; Moore, 1990; Slack, 2012). This paved the way for the seventeenth century's 'Great Confinement', when the dangerous and delinquent were taken into the protective custody of workhouses, asylums, prisons, etc. (Foucault, 1979). 'Paupers, petty criminals, layabouts, streetwalkers, vagabonds, and above all beggars formed the bulk of this monstrous army of the unreasonable, but symbolically their leaders were the insane and the idiotic' (Porter, 2002: 92). The Great Confinement was rendered in brick and stone. Moving ever worstward, much of the twentieth century's mass murder was housed in improvised settlements enclosed by barbed wire.

As disease decimated the Jewish ghettoes, Hans Frank, the Nazi Governor-General of occupied Poland, issued the so-called 'shooting order' in October 1941. The order decreed that any Jew found outside the ghettoes should be sentenced to death, because 'only the most draconian punishment could deter starving Jews from leaving the ghettos to smuggle food and thereby spreading the typhus epidemic' (Browning, 2001: 122). However, since the personnel 'available to escort captured Jews was too limited, the distances to be covered were too great, [and] the judicial procedures of the special courts too cumbersome and time-consuming' (Browning, 2001: 122), the 'shooting order' soon lost its judicial veneer, enabling the police to shoot errant Jews on sight. Moreover, Frank's authorization of summary executions paved the way for the 'Jew hunts' once the ghettoes were liquidated.

The entitlement to kill Jews found outside the ghettoes was not entirely dissimilar to the treatment of those convicted of crimes such as arson, parricide, or fraud according to the Roman Code of the Twelve Tables (c.450 BC): they 'could be killed with impunity' (Kyle, 2001: 41). Similarly, since ancient Germanic law was established on the basis of 'peace' (*Fried*), those who were excluded from the community for wrongdoing were 'without peace' (*friedlos*), and, like the *sacri* (or *homo sacer*) of Ancient Rome, 'anyone was permitted to kill [them] without committing homicide' (Agamben, 1998: 63). Likewise, '[t]he medieval ban also presents analogous traits', notes Giorgio Agamben (1998: 63), since 'the bandit could be killed ("'To ban' someone is to say that anyone may harm him") or was even considered to be already dead ("Whoever is banned from his city on pain of death must be considered as dead").' And foreshadowing the racial ideology of the Nazis, which defined Jews (and many others) as 'subhuman' (*Untermensch*), 'Germanic and Anglo-Saxon sources underline the bandit's liminal status by defining him as a wolf-man' (Agamben, 1998: 63). The common strand that runs through these various instantiations of *homo sacer* is not only abandonment by the law, but also by humanity. Such abandonment was paradoxically aided and abetted by the Enlightenment, as we shall now see.

5

Enlightened Killing

From the Delicacy of the Wet Guillotine to the Damp Squib of Electrocution

We feel like laughing when we consider the solemn commandment 'Thou shalt not kill' followed by a blessing on armies.

Georges Bataille, 1986: 63

Few readers of Michel Foucault's *Discipline and Punish* will forget the juxtaposition of a gruesome public execution and a dreary set of rules for an enlightened workhouse. On 2 March 1757, Robert-François Damiens, 'a weak-minded servant who had wounded Louis XV with a penknife' (Andress, 2005: 103), became the last Frenchman to be drawn and quartered. The account Foucault crafts from contemporary sources is excruciating: 'the flesh will be torn from his breasts, arms, thighs and calves with red-hot pincers, his right hand ... burnt with sulphur, and, on those places where the flesh will be torn away, poured molten lead, boiling oil, burning resin, wax and sulphur melted together'. The drawing and quartering became unexpectedly tortuous 'because the horses used were not accustomed to drawing; consequently, instead of four, six were needed; and when that did not suffice, they were forced ... to sever the sinews and hack at the joints' (Foucault, 1979: 3). So it goes, as Kurt Vonnegut (2000) was fond of saying.

In stark contrast to this botched spectacle of sovereign violence in the twilight of the *ancien régime*, which divided the public as to whether it was edifying or horrifying, the routine drawn up in the 1830s by Léon Faucher for a 'House of Young Prisoners' seems refreshingly humdrum:

'Art. 17. The prisoners' day will begin at six in the morning in winter and at five in summer. They will work for nine hours a day throughout the year. Two hours a day will be devoted to instruction. Work and the day will end at nine o'clock in winter and at eight in summer.

Art. 18. *Rising.* At the first drum-roll, the prisoners must rise and dress in silence, as the supervisor opens the cell doors. At the second drum-roll, they must be dressed and make their beds. At the third, they must line up and proceed to the chapel for morning prayer.' (Foucault, 1979: 6)

The banality goes on and on: Article 19. *Prayer*; Article 20. *Work*; Article 21. *Meal*; Article 22. *School*; culminating with Article 28. *Bedtime*: 'At half-past seven in summer, half-past eight in winter, the prisoners must be back in their cells after the washing of hands and the inspection of clothes in the courtyard; at the first drum-roll, they must undress, and at the second get into bed' (Foucault, 1979: 7). So it goes, day after day.

Unlike the episodic demonstration of sovereign power, which touched people tangentially and infrequently (taxation, requisition, mobilization, etc.), and only rarely to the quick (exile, excommunication, execution, etc.), the exercise of disciplinary power aspired to be continuous, routinized, and penetrative – it sought to comport the body and mould the person, treating them as raw materials to be ceaselessly worked over and sculpted (Foucault, 2004). While sovereign power primarily required a stage on which to perform its theatre of cruelty (such as a scaffold), and an audience to lend it legitimacy and atmosphere (crowds of civically minded witnesses and bystanders), disciplinary power required an institutional apparatus for the serial production of generic social types: prisons for moulding prisoners; factories for moulding workers; barracks for moulding soldiers; schools for moulding children; hospitals for moulding invalids; churches for moulding credents; etc. Sovereign power ventriloquizes the patient to address the entire community. The systematic destruction of Damiens' body was an exquisite, eloquent, and edifying discourse, despite the embarrassing stuttering and stammering (the ineffectual pincers, the incapable horses, the inept hacking, etc.). By contrast, disciplinary power is essentially mute and tends to work in isolation, housing its moulds and other body-and-soul-sculpting apparatuses in spaces of enclosure behind closed doors, barred windows, and high walls. This anti-social tendency also has the advantage of dispensing with the crowd that played such an ambivalent role for sovereign power. For while sovereign power needed the crowd to witness justice being done, it could always turn riotous. This danger was increasingly acute in large cities such as London, Paris, and Rome, which lent themselves to mob formation under the cover of collective anonymity (Badiou, 2012; Bloom, 2012; Ross, 2008; Shoemaker, 2004; Žižek, 2012).

I am loath to call this re-articulation and redistribution of the political economy of violence 'progress', still less 'humane', but I am willing to call it 'enlightened'. Punishment ceased to be a live theatre of cruelty for the enjoyment and edification of the masses, and became a dreary routine, typically performed within spaces of enclosure – except for those rare occasions when it is vicariously resurrected by the media as a form of grim entertainment. The first seismic precursors can be traced back to the 1750s, and the emergence of a peculiar new sensibility with respect to witnessing executions – a visceral feeling of 'horror', ostensibly born of natural 'compassion' in the presence of suffering. Suddenly, it became fashionable for public executions, and especially exemplary executions, to engender 'horror' amongst those newly squeamish, faint-hearted, and compassionate souls who witnessed them. The 'ideal of *sensibilité*, which had originally been conceived of as the unique gift of the privileged few, was increasingly being understood as … a natural human reflex that made it impossible for one human being to witness the suffering of another without suffering themselves' (Friedland, 2012: 165). As the erstwhile aristocratic pleasure of 'compassion' was duly democratized, spreading through all classes of French society like a virus, the 'affective atmosphere' surrounding corporal and capital punishment turned decidedly sour. For example, in 1772, Siméon-Prosper Hardy, a Parisian diarist who had enjoyed executions for decades, suddenly and inexplicably found the execution of suicides 'distasteful'. He was evidently not alone. 'Hardy mentions a variety of different pretexts by which those who had committed suicide were spared postmortem executions', notes Paul Friedland (2012: 188), and there was 'a general caution – one might almost say an *embarrassment* – in the last decades of the ancien régime when it came to … capital punishment' (italics in original). A century later in America, Minnesota's so-called 1889 *Midnight Assassination Law*, which 'accelerated a nationwide trend toward in-private, after-dark executions' (Bessler, 2003: xvi), was symptomatic of a similar embarrassment with the *spectacle* of capital punishment: 'the "evident purpose" of Minnesota's law was "to surround the execution of criminals with as much secrecy as possible, in order to avoid exciting an unwholesome effect on the public mind," with the effect being that executions "must take place before dawn, while the masses are at rest, and within an inclosure, so as to debar the morbidly curious"' (Bessler, 1996: 580, quoting a 1907 Minnesota Supreme Court decision that upheld this law). The *Midnight Assassination Law* was contentious because it prohibited reporters from attending executions and restricted newspapers to merely announcing that an execution had taken place. Capital punishment was no longer edifying. There was nothing to witness, understand, or enjoy.

The reaction to the execution of Damiens – '*the* execution of the eighteenth century' (Friedland, 2012: 176) – was symptomatic of the new squeamish sensibility. Yet 'commentators were expressing their horror, not so much at the execution itself, but at those spectators, and those female spectators in particular, who could watch Damiens die without a trace of natural compassion' (Friedland, 2012: 165). It would not be long before the new sensibility of 'horror' would also affect more humdrum forms of capital and corporal punishment, such as hanging and beheading, and even branding and mutilation. Hereinafter, the trope of the cold-hearted woman unmoved by horror reappears in practically every subsequent scene of modern cruelty, from revolutionary Terror to the death camps. Needless to say, the newfound squeamishness did little to dampen the public's appetite for spectacular punishments. 'At the execution of the Comte de Lally, ... beheaded for treason in 1766, Hardy reports that "all the windows on the Grève were rented at insane prices, the roofs of many houses were uncovered in order to build scaffolds, and one could see men even on the chimneystacks"' (Friedland, 2012: 186). By the time of the French Revolution in 1789, 'the wealthier classes had largely forsaken the penal spectacle, abandoning the now "horrible" spectacle of public executions to the masses who continued to watch, as yet unaware that it was a perversion of natural human sensibilities to do so' (Friedland, 2012: 165) – and perhaps they never would, judging by the propensity for passers-by to stare agog at motorway pile-ups. (Car crashes are arguably the closest thing to public executions that many of us now witness, and works such as Andy Warhol's *Death and Disaster* series created in the 1960s, and J. G. Ballard's 1973 novel, *Crash*, dramatize the absolute proximity of pleasure and pain, death and eroticism.)

Despite the new sensibility of 'horror' when faced with suffering, most continued to watch executions with pleasure (often with opera glasses), while some started to watch in horror (which delivers its own kind of pleasure), but few seem to have watched in trepidation. 'This vulgarization of the penal spectacle would provoke a crisis in its own right, as the very individuals who were now the only ones taking delight in the penal spectacle were precisely the ones to whom exemplary deterrence was meant to be teaching a lesson' (Friedland, 2012: 165–6). The *raisons d'être* of spectacular punishment – edification and deterrence – were becoming anachronistic, and some enlightened reformers began to advocate what sounded like a contradiction in terms: *unspectacular* capital punishment, especially the 'simple' deprivation of life. Enlightened killing is not only dreary, however, but also cold. Unlike sovereign violence, spectacular violence, and divine violence, which are always soaked in blood-red hues, enlightened killing dons the pallid complexion of the bureaucrat, merchant, and capitalist: blue-grey (Lyotard, 1998). Rather than make a show of violence, enlightened killers trade in violence. They make it their business. Enlightened killing is speculative rather than spectacular; profitable rather than demonstrative; and experimental rather than expressive. Violence is no longer made to speak; it is set to work. Denis Diderot's essay on 'Anatomy' in the *Encyclopédie* perfectly illustrates this cold and calculated use of capital punishment as an investment vehicle:

> I should like to see established ... the custom of turning criminals over to [anatomists] for dissection, and I would desire these latter to have the courage to perform this task. Whatever one's opinion of the death of a malefactor, it would be as useful to society in the lecture hall as on the scaffold – and this form of punishment would be no less fearful than any other. ... Who, rather than undergo execution, ... would not allow their thigh to be amputated at the joint; or their spleen to be removed; or some

portion of their brain to be extracted; … or some other operation to be attempted on some other internal organ? For the rational, the advantage of these experiments will be reason enough. (Quoted in Arasse, 1991: 3)

The enlightened anatomist proclaims that in the name of reason everything is permitted. Little wonder, then, that the medical profession, like so many others (academia, accountancy, law, science, engineering, etc.), should have become complicit in all manner of state-sponsored horrors, such as genocide, the Holocaust, and the weaponization of life itself (Ericksen, 2012; Fleischman, Funnell and Walker, 2013; Weindling, 2015). Telford Taylor, in his opening statement for the prosecution at the Nuremberg Doctors' Trial in 1946, coined a new word for 'the science of producing death', *thanatology*, and enumerated some of the thanatological experiments conducted on concentration-camp prisoners by SS doctors, including: high-altitude, sea-water, and freezing experiments; malaria, typhus, and sterilization experiments; and poison, gas, and incendiary experiments (Annas and Grodin, 1992). The humane medical scientist is practically obliged to make use of what would otherwise go to waste. For it would surely be better to *make suffer* for some higher purpose than to *let suffer* for no reason at all. What matters, then, is not the extent to which the patient suffers, but whether such suffering is squandered or capitalized. Enlightened killing and judicial torture are kindred spirits. Neither sadistic nor savage, they are exquisite (from the Latin, *exquirere*, to seek out). They are truth seekers. Both investigate the patient: one to disclose its workings; the other to disclose its depravity. Fortuitously, such a painstaking investigation also has the merit of punishing the guilt-ridden patient as it proceeds.

The ambivalence of enlightened killing is beautifully exemplified by Dr Joseph-Ignace Guillotin, who proposed a 'humane' killing machine. He wanted to alleviate suffering – not only for the condemned patient, but also for those who had to perform and witness executions. On the one hand, echoing Diderot, Guillotin had argued in 1775–6 that medical science would benefit from convicts undergoing 'all such experiments as have been … attempted with animals' (quoted in Arasse, 1991: 4). On the other hand, he was dismayed by the myriad forms of execution employed in eighteenth-century France, which resulted in a wide variation in suffering. For example, highwaymen were generally broken on the wheel, witches burnt at the stake, and thieves hung. By contrast, on those rare occasions when nobles were executed, they were usually beheaded. The aristocratic privilege of receiving the 'dignity of the block' was reminiscent of a privilege afforded to Roman citizens. 'A citizen of status condemned to death, if his appeal to the assembly failed and he declined to go into exile, faced summary execution by the sword (*gladio*)' (Kyle, 2001: 41). However, whilst beheading by sword was an aristocratic privilege, most commoners were decapitated using an unwieldy 'heading axe' that bludgeoned its way through the neck – often requiring several attempts so to do. 'It was, after all, a weapon of punishment, not mercy' (Abbott, 2005: 15). Executioners in the *ancien régime* were often called headsmen.

In the wake of the 1789 Revolution, Guillotin petitioned the government to abolish the myriad forms of execution, all of which had been refined to extort more or less suffering in spectacular fashion (drowning, boiling, burying, breaking, hanging, etc.), and to introduce a single, enlightened form of execution that would minimize suffering: simple decapitation. His call echoed those of other penal reformers, such as Jean-Paul Marat in 1777: 'Even for the most serious crimes … the machinery of execution shall be fearful, but the death shall be an easy one' (quoted in Arasse, 1991: 12–13); and Maximilien Robespierre in 1783: 'The wheel, the gallows … disgrace the family of those who perish by these means, but the blade that severs the head of the criminal debases his family not at all. … Would it not be possible to … extend this means of punishing crime to all classes of citizen? We thus eliminate an unjust discrimination' (quoted in Arasse, 1991: 12). In 1791, the National Assembly decreed that all executions would be egalitarian, humane, and individualistic. This was a bold move, since Europeans were accustomed to the innumerable ways 'in which authority enacted itself on the suffering bodies of those who offended it' (Andress, 2005: 102). For example, by the 1780s, England's 'list of capital offenses had grown to 350 and was used throughout most of the British colonies' (McAllister, 2003: 18), even though its glaringly obvious inconsistencies and idiocies were already bringing capital punishment into disrepute:

> Juries, judges and prosecutors were no longer prepared to send people to the gallows for a theft of a few pence. With the connivance of the whole courtroom, women indicted of a double felony [a capital crime] were routinely found guilty of a single felony and sentenced to transportation instead of death. Even when a death sentence could not be avoided, female offenders were rarely hanged; a petition for pardon would be drawn up by the sentencing judge and the sentence commuted to transportation to 'Parts Beyond the Seas,' the vague name given to the rest of the world by the Elizabethan Transport Act. (Rees, 2001: 47)

The 1790s, then, were ripe for the introduction of a simple killing machine that 'might bear the legend: Humanity, Equality, Rationality' (Arasse, 1991: 13). 'What, in 1789, had seemed like a very odd suggestion and had been the butt of countless jokes, was now beginning to seem like a logical, humane, and rational method of executing people' (Friedland, 2012: 243). And with the introduction of that 'Great Machine' of swift, inflexible, egalitarian, and enlightened justice – nicknamed 'Saint Guillotine', 'Holy Guillotine', 'Sword of Liberty', and 'National Razor' – the citizens of France would hereinafter be expected to attend executions out of a sense of civic duty, just as their descendants would be expected to visit the Paris Morgue, which opened to the public in 1864, to help identify the anonymous corpses that increasingly washed up in the rapidly expanding city of strangers – although recall that the Morgue quickly became a key venue for the 'collective tourist gaze' until the public were barred in 1907 (Schwartz, 1999; Urry, 1990).

In 1791, however, two forms of execution had been in contention for the new egalitarian, humane, and individualistic approach to capital punishment: hanging and beheading. Neither found immediate favour. Although some, like Raymond de Verninac Saint-Maur, had argued in the immediate aftermath of the Revolution that instead of elevating 'the masses to the dignity of the block, we should reduce the nobility to the modesty of the gibbet' (quoted in Arasse, 1991: 16), hanging was nevertheless deemed unsuitable because it was gruesome, associated with repression in the *ancien régime*, and had been a spontaneous means of delivering 'revolutionary justice' by fashioning impromptu gallows out of lamp posts – those ghastly symbols of state control that had facilitated the extension of both police surveillance and the working day into the night (Schivelbusch, 1988). Beheading was also unsuitable because it was impractical to give everyone sentenced to death the privilege of decapitation by sword. Each beheading required a new sword, and only two were available in Paris at the time. New ones were expensive, and occasionally broke in use. Moreover, beheading required precision, patience, and a compliant patient, who had to remain perfectly still whilst kneeling. As France's foremost executioner, Charles-Henri Sanson, cautioned: 'If prisoners cannot hold themselves up ... the execution becomes a struggle and a massacre. ... It is therefore indispensible that ... some means should be found to avoid delays, and assure certainty, by *fixing* the patient so that the success of the operation shall not be doubtful' (quoted in Abbott, 2005: 126).

Accordingly, in March 1792, the Assembly decreed that a mechanical device be created for beheading swiftly, accurately, and as painlessly and unspectacularly as possible. 'The spectacle of suffering was to be replaced by a kind of surgical precision, excising the condemned from the social body as neatly as possible' (Friedland, 2012: 219). Although Dr Guillotin was not awarded the contract for creating such an enlightened device (that pleasure went to Dr Antoine Louis, the permanent secretary of the Academy of Surgery, and erstwhile surgeon to Louis XVI, although it was actually built, in less than a week, to Louis's specification, by Tobias Schmidt, a German piano-maker), the eponymous 'guillotine' became legendary thanks to the Terror of 1792–4, which used this humane 'Sword of Liberty' for the fast and furious transformation of enemies of the people into headless corpses. Fortuitously, 'the introduction of such a machine was timely, for within a matter of months the Revolution would demand the heads of not just a score or two of common criminals but of thousands of hated aristocrats' (Abbott, 2005: 129). Rather than aristocrats, however, most victims of the guillotine were drawn from the same classes as the revolutionaries themselves, since the Terror primarily consumed those citizens suspected of being counter-revolutionaries. A lack of revolutionary zeal, plain indifference, or even incompetence and ineffectiveness were sufficient for someone to become suspect and deserving of swift and inflexible revolutionary justice – decapitation. 'At the height of the Terror Sanson decapitated 300 men and women in three days, 1,300 in six weeks, and between 6 April 1793 and 29 July 1795, no fewer than 2,831 heads fell into the waiting baskets' (Abbott, 2005: 133). This number pales, however, when compared to Nazi Germany's use of the guillotine: 16,500 from 1933 to 1945. 'Shortly after coming to power, Hitler ... ordered twenty additional machines to be built and began recruiting executioners' (Gerould, 1992: 240).

From 1933 to 1938, the courts of Nazi Germany delivered fewer than 100 death sentences each year. The number grew rapidly in the war years, however, and in a climactic 10-month period spanning 1944 and 1945, 'over 10,000 heads fell' (Gerould, 1992: 240). Johann Baptist Reichart, an eighth-generation German executioner, 'guillotined 2,876 victims (almost all of them political), setting the world record for the number of heads severed ... [T]he Allies used the services of Reichart after the defeat of Germany and had him prepare the gallows for the Nuremberg war criminals' (Gerould, 1992: 242). Many of those sentenced to death by Nazi Germany's civilian courts were so-called 'racial aliens', mostly Poles, often for trivial crimes, such as unlawful animal slaughter or illicit sexual relations with German women. Others were so-called 'national pests' (whose supposed ingrained criminality necessitated elimination from the 'national community'), and political enemies of the Nazi regime (especially foreigners). 'The torrent of judicial death sentences turned some penal institutions into killing factories', argues Wachsmann (2004: 315). 'As the numbers of prisoners on death row grew ... the Reich Ministry of Justice introduced measures to speed up the killings.' The number of prisons administering capital punishment doubled (from 11 in 1937, to 21 in 1945), and executions were no longer limited to dawn, the guillotine, or official executioners. Shooting and hanging were adopted, and army and police units were roped into killing prisoners. After a visit to Auschwitz in June 1944, the Ministry 'even toyed with the idea of building "gas cells" to kill prisoners' (Wachsmann, 2004: 316).

The swiftness of the guillotine lent itself to acceleration. 'In the early days of mass executions, staggering records were set. On October 31, 1793, twenty-one Girondins were killed in thirty-eight minutes' (Gerould, 1992: 65). Even so, some, like Joseph Fouché, 'an ex-monk, revolutionary terrorist, and later Napoleon's chief of police and father of the modern police state', bitterly complained that 'the guillotine works too slowly' (quoted in Gerould, 1992: 65). One amateur mechanic, fortuitously called Guillot, experimented with a nine-bladed guillotine in July 1794, but to no avail. Less ambitious multi-bladed guillotines for dispatching several people at once were dreamt up, but none ever materialized. Even during the so-called 'batch' executions of the Terror, the enemies of liberty would continue to be executed in their anti-social individuality: one by one.

The quantitative 'success' of the guillotine belies a qualitative ambivalence that dogged the great machine from the off. After a series of experimental decapitations of animal carcasses from a local abattoir and fresh cadavers from the Bicêtre Hospital, the public debut of the world's first proto-industrial killing machine on 25 April 1792, in Place de l'hôtel de ville, had a mixed reception. It was ridiculed in the press for its 'gentle', 'delicate', and 'effeminate' action, and stoked public resentment with its lightning-quick operation, which killed 'faster than the speed of sight', thereby depriving the crowd of the spectacle of violence. 'The guillotine … obscured the view of spectators … through speed rather than through obstruction', says Paul Friedland (2012: 248). It was 'a non-spectacular public spectacle, one that allowed spectators to watch without being able to see'. The guillotine was neither a horrid pleasure nor an edifying spectacle. It was just frightful. Did the guillotine dispense egalitarian justice and deliver humane executions? Or did it dispense mechanical slaughter and deliver frightful terror? Indeed, Derrida (2014: 192) raises a profound question with respect to 'this humanitarianism of the guillotine'. Echoing his meditation on the proximity of 'the beast' and 'the sovereign' (Derrida, 2011), he asks: 'What must be that which is called man so that at a moment of his history he comes to consider the guillotine as an advance in human progress, an advance in man's appropriation of his essence?' (Derrida, 2014: 192). Naturally, the guillotine was just the first attempt to enlighten the act of killing. Others included the 'electric chair', invented in New York in 1890, and the 'gas chamber', the first of which was installed in the Nevada State Prison in Carson City in 1924, although as early as 1791, citizen Girardet had proposed to the French National Assembly a glass 'asphyxiation booth' set on a scaffold, and filled from below with charcoal smoke and sulphur fumes, for public executions. 'One will see through the panes of glass, notwithstanding the thickness of the smoke, *death by suffocation*; horrors will be concealed; and justice will be done promptly. The cadaver will be removed from the booth, it will remain for a quarter hour in the public gaze, and then carried to the *field of sleep*' (quoted in Friedland, 2012: 240, italics in original). Girardet's suggestion, like citizen Thomas's proposal for a 'strangulation machine', fell on deaf ears. The Assembly was wedded to a beheading machine.

Since we will return to guillotines and gas chambers, I will round off this chapter by considering the advent of the electric chair. 'By the 1880s most [American] states had outlawed public hangings, and an anti-gallows movement had taken firm hold' (Simon, 2005: 221). The last *public* hanging in the US took place in Kentucky in 1936, while some states (such as Massachusetts, New Jersey, New York, and Pennsylvania) had outlawed public executions a century earlier, in the 1830s (Bessler, 1996). At that time, only suspension and short-drop forms of hanging were available to executioners. These all killed by slow and painful strangulation (taking up to 20 minutes or so), and were effectively forms of judicial lynching (Berg, 2011; Bessler, 2003; Pfeifer, 2004; Wood, 2009). The patient is hung from something like a tree, gallows, or lamp post, and is either hauled up directly or with the aid of a support (such as a stool, ladder, or cart) that is abruptly pulled away. Humane forms of hanging intended to break the patient's neck, causing instant paralysis and unconsciousness, were only introduced from the late 1860s (using a standard drop of 4–6 feet) and 1870s (using a measured drop tailored to the patient's weight and height). Even so, death by strangulation (too little force) and decapitation (too much force) were not uncommon. The latter invariably resulted in a media storm, such as happened after the botched hangings of Thomas 'Black Jack' Ketchum in New Mexico in 1901, and Barzan Ibrahim al-Tikriti in Iraq in 2007.

New York State had repealed judicial hanging back in 1860, prior to the neck-breaking innovations, and in 1885, with the number of prisoners on 'death row' steadily increasing but no legal way to cull them, the state established a Commission to find a solution that would meet 'the requirements of humanity' – neither cruel nor unusual (quoted in Simon, 2005: 222). The Commission concluded that the guillotine, garrotte, and shooting were all too bloody; that lethal injection was vehemently opposed by the medical profession because the public already regarded needles and doctors with fear and suspicion; and that a gas chamber had little support, not least because of its association with explosions. (One of the most memorable gas explosions occurred in London in 1865, 'when eleven workmen were killed by the accidental lighting of 1,000,000 cubic feet of gas at the London Gaslight Company' (Ackroyd, 2011: 94). Gas pipes had been installed beneath city streets from as early as 1805, and the rest of the century would resound to subterranean blasts from this frightful infrastructure. Some of these blasts were deliberate, such as when Irish nationalists blew up a gas main in Clerkenwell, London, in the 1860s.) Having discounted guillotining, garrotting, shooting, injecting, and gassing, the Commission was left with electrocution as its preferred method of execution, despite the concerted opposition of the electrical profession, which was already struggling to persuade the public to electrify their homes with an accident-prone technology that was just as lethal as gas.

New York followed the advice of the Commission, and its *Electrical Execution Act* (1888) came into force in 1889. Meanwhile, the state established an 'Electrical Death Commission' to implement the Act, and Thomas Edison's laboratory was used for animal experiments to develop a suitable apparatus. The first 'electric chair' execution took place in Auburn Prison on 6 August 1890. It took 2 minutes to complete, during which time witnesses smelt burning flesh and saw smoke rising from the man's head. The *New York World* reported how he 'died in agony, by slow torture'. The *Chicago Evening Post* said that 'the wretch was actually tortured to death with a refinement of cruelty that was unequalled in the dark ages'. Other newspapers likened it 'to burning at the stake and to the tortures of the Inquisition' (Simon, 2005: 238–9). Electrocution is far from humane. Once paralysed, the patient 'may feel himself being burned to death while he is conscious of his inability to breath' (Abbott, 2005: 95). Indeed, 'too little current caused agony, too much literally grilled the flesh and fried the brain' (Abbott, 2005: 85). It was certainly no improvement on judicial lynching. So it goes. *Worstward Ho!*

Far from meeting the requirements of humanity, the electric chair was intended to be frightful. For it came straight out of a negative marketing campaign, as part of the so-called 'War of the Electric Currents' that took place between Thomas Edison and George Westinghouse in the 1880s and 1890s. They were competing to electrify American cities using two different transmission systems: direct current (DC) and alternating current (AC), respectively. Edison's early domination of the market with DC was increasingly threatened by Westinghouse's newfangled AC technology. So, Edison spread disinformation about fatal AC accidents and staged AC electrocutions of cats, dogs, horses, and cattle at fairs and shows. Despite his own opposition to capital punishment, Edison's desire to disparage AC led him to influence the Commission's adoption of electrocution for state executions, and to power those electric chairs with AC. Edison reputedly paid the chair's inventor to promote the false notion that AC was deadlier than DC, and that it was wholly unsuited to the home. He even tried to popularize the term 'Westinghoused' for being electrocuted to discredit his rival. For his part, Westinghouse tried to prevent Auburn Prison from acquiring a Westinghouse AC generator to power its electric chair, but to no avail.

Ironically, the advent of the electric chair did nothing to stop AC from winning the 'War of the Electric Currents'. In 1903, having long since been forced out of the domestic electricity business, Edison's blossoming film company captured the public electro-execution of an old circus elephant called Topsy, at Coney Island's Luna Park. Topsy had been 'convicted' of murdering a (reputedly drunken and abusive) handler. It is not known if this quasi-legal stunt was mere coincidence or Edison's final, futile strike at an old enemy: AC. What is certain, however, is that the faux 'execution' was a profitable spectacle for these enterprising Brooklyn showmen: 'Fifteen hundred people showed up one cold Sunday in January to watch as three-ton Topsy was zapped with 6,600 volts of electricity for ten seconds' (McAllister, 2003: 30). Edison's 70-foot film (*c*.1¼ minutes), entitled *Electrocuting an Elephant*, played in Kinetoscope parlours, cinemas, and fairgrounds the world over, and can still be viewed today. The film may even have been directed by the legendary film pioneer, Edwin S. Porter, who produced one of the most famous films of the silent era in exactly the same year: *The Great Train Robbery* (1903). By happy coincidence, the topsy-turvy violence of the railway age lies immediately ahead.

The Animal Slaughter Industry

Perfect Cities of Blood – Paris and Chicago

A stone's throw from the stock exchange the air is filled with the aroma of roasting coffee; a few hundred feet from Times Square with the stench of the slaughterhouses.

Regional Plan Association of New York and Its Environs,
1929 Master Plan, quoted in Joe Flood, 2010: 142

Enlightened killing did not only revolutionize capital punishment, it also revolutionized the broader mass killing of animals and humans. This chapter will be devoted to the enlightened killing of animals, particularly in Paris and Chicago, and then I will turn to the enlightened killing of people in subsequent chapters. My argument takes off from a parallelism that Daniel Pick articulates in his wonderful book, *War Machine: The Rationalisation of Slaughter in the Modern Age* (1993), at the heart of which is the industrialization of killing that makes machinic slaughter the common denominator of both modern abattoirs and modern warfare. The revolution started in the 1860s, amid the squalor of the artisanal meat trade that permeated the whole of Paris (although it is worth mentioning in passing that a few animals were occasionally guillotined in the 1790s, invariably for political crimes, rather than for eating, and usually alongside their aristocratic masters and mistresses – this perpetuated a tradition widely practised by the Inquisition: witches were frequently burnt at the stake alongside their diabolical familiars, typically birds and cats). The slaughter and butchery of animals, and the selling of meat, took place in small establishments scattered throughout the city, using techniques inherited from the *ancien régime*. This meant that animals destined for the meat trade needed to move throughout the city, along with the various waste products of their living and dying (feed, dung, blood, urine, etc.). Dung was not too much of a problem, since it could be collected, along with 'night soil', and used as an agricultural fertilizer. The rest of the waste wound up in the Seine, which served as an open sewer for the city and a source of terrible pollution for those downstream. Since Paris had expanded so rapidly, doubling in size to 2 million people between the 1830s and 1860s alone, this waste became a major health hazard, and the stench of death and decay hung over the city.

Under the direction of Napoleon III, Baron George Eugène Haussmann, Prefect of the Seine region and architect of Second Empire Paris, envisaged an ideal abattoir for the whole city: 'a perfectly engineered, centralised, hygienic meat location, catering to the needs of millions' (Pick, 1993: 180). Haussmann oversaw the construction of a new abattoir complex at La Villette, on the north-eastern edge of the city, which opened in 1867. 'It became *the* abattoir, a prototype for the rest of the century' (Giedion, quoted in Pick, 1993: 180, note 36). The concentration of slaughter and butchery on the periphery of the city was a great success, and it chimed perfectly with the embourgeoisement of the city as whole, in so far as the city centre could be more easily turned over to leisure and pleasure: 'the guiding imperative behind the slaughterhouse's creation was the extraction of animal slaughter from quotidian experience. ... By the late nineteenth century, no Parisian *flâneurs* would wander into steers or hogs when they strolled through the city's broad boulevards' (Lee, 2008: 239). It would be a mistake, however, to see this expulsion of the meat industry and its livestock from the city centre as the origin of the alienation of urban consumers from rural producers. The formation of the Revolutionary Armies in 1793, for instance, was precisely to ensure that the Republic's urban strongholds were not starved into submission by a counter-revolutionary peasantry predisposed to hoarding (Andress, 2005). Entrusting 'the task of requisitioning grain to those most interested in the supply of the main towns was an original ... idea. Equally original was the idea of attaching an armed force, chosen for its political orthodoxy, to the urban "apostles" sent to preach the revolutionary gospel to the rural populace. ... They represented the Terror on the move, the village Terror' (Cobb, 1987: 1–2).

However, behind the ultra-modern iron-and-glass façade, La Villette retained the artisanal workspaces (a set of private stalls rather than a series of connecting spaces for distinct stages of butchery), abattoir practices (with little division of labour), and guild values that were unchanged from the *ancien régime*. 'La Villette was a closed culture with its own traditions and codes of honor, hierarchies, and generations of clan alliances. ... La Villette stubbornly cleaved to the history and traditions of French artisanal slaughter (*abattage*)' (Claflin, 2008: 27). For all of its apparent modernity, then, La Villette was inimical to two of its key aspects: acceleration and intensification.

Haussmann had set the precedent of seeking to construct an ideal slaughter-house, but he had only managed to concentrate the activity by harnessing the old and new mass transportation technologies of canals and railways. The industrialization and rationalization of slaughter itself would take place elsewhere – in North America, and especially in Chicago – and this revolution would leave La Villette looking like a pale imitation. 'Within thirty years of its opening, a growing circle of opponents considered the renowned model of a modern European abattoir to be one of the most primitive slaughterhouses on the continent' (Claflin, 2008: 38). The qualitative difference between La Villette, the 'City of Blood' (*La Cité du Sang*), and Chicago, 'Hog Butcher for the World', is neatly summed up by Kyri Claflin: 'In Paris, butchers were artisans; in Chicago, there were only unskilled laborers. French *abattage* proceeded at a man's pace, in contrast to slaughter in Chicago, which was dictated by the mechanical processes of the assembly line' (Claflin, 2008: 37). Similarly, Paula Lee (2008) notes that a British journalist coined the phrase 'slaughter factories', rather than 'slaughter houses', to convey the fact that in America, unlike Europe, animals were treated as nothing more than a raw material to be processed according to the imperative of profit maximization. Their killing and disassembly was an industrial rather than a craft activity. What made this industrial process so frightful for many sensitive commentators was not only the scale and speed of the mass killing, but also the impassivity that it produced amongst the killers and bystanders alike. For example, Rudyard Kipling – drawing on a trope familiar from the advent of the guillotine – was appalled by the indifference of a young woman as she watched a Chicago 'slaughter factory' operate. Once industrialized and rationalized, mass killing risked becoming utterly banal – a matter of fact that neither elicits nor merits any concern, least of all moral concern, except for the optimization of its technical operation: the maximization of its functioning and the minimization of its malfunctioning. 'What is truly startling in this mass transition from life to death is the complete neutrality of the act. One does not experience, one does not feel; one merely observes' (Sigfried Giedion, 1948, quoted in Pick, 1993: 185).

By the 1830s, Cincinnati in Ohio had become the largest centre for pork-packing in North America, and the meatpackers of this 'Porkopolis' pioneered new forms of mechanization to cope with the volume of work involved in slaughtering, processing, packing, and distributing huge quantities of pork products (barrelled pork, cured pork, lard, soap, candles, and glue). These new forms of mechanization included a rotating overhead wheel from which dead pigs hung whilst 'workers at the eight points of its compass cleaned and gutted the animals in eight separate steps before sending them off to a storage room for cooling' (Cronon, 1992: 228). To this detailed division of labour, which broke the whole process down into a series of discrete tasks, 'Cincinnati packers later supplemented the wheel with an overhead rail which carried pigs through each step of the butchering process, and with multistoried packing plants in which animals and carcasses moved by the force of gravity from station to station'

(Cronon, 1992: 228). The combination of a detailed division of labour and a moving production line would enable managers to demystify the craft of meat-packing, deskill the meatpacker, and optimize the time and motion of the work both as a whole and in its constituent parts. 'The whole system came to be called the disassembly line and was among the most important forerunners of the mass production techniques that swept [through] American industry in the century to come' (Cronon, 1992: 229). The most famous of these was Henry Ford's 'assembly line' for the mass production of cars in Detroit, which came to define the rise and fall of an entire 'regime of accumulation' ('Fordism' and 'Post-Fordism'), although Ford and his eponymous 'Model T' were actually latecomers compared to meatpacking, textiles, and shipbuilding – specifically Venetian shipbuilding.

Venice's Arsenale (*Arsenale Nuovo*), a huge shipbuilding and armaments complex established in the fourteenth century, was mass producing galleys using assembly line techniques by the sixteenth century. It was 'the largest productive complex and the greatest concentration of skilled labour in the world prior to the industrial age' (da Mosto, 2004: 53). Up to 16,000 workers produced a ship in a day or so, whereas other European shipbuilders would typically take weeks or even months so to do. 'In 1570, when the Turks attacked Cyprus, the Arsenale had furnished a hundred galleys ready for combat within just two months, in part building them, in part adapting the commercial fleet. A century earlier ... for the benefit of King Henry III of France, an entire galley was assembled during a banquet' (da Mosto, 2004: 53–4). The mass production of ships made the Republic of Venice a major naval power for centuries. It dominated European trade with the Middle and Far East (the 'Orient'), and accrued vast wealth in the process: not through conquest, plunder, and enslavement, but through commerce – especially its control of the lucrative spice trade. 'For the people of the Middle Ages, spices were emissaries from a fabled world. ... The aroma of spices was believed to be a breath wafted from Paradise over the human world' (Schivelbusch, 1992: 6). Pepper was the most valuable commodity at the time, and even more coveted than gold. Venice controlled the spice trade. It was Europe's portal to Paradise. Consequently, the gulf between the *salty* Holy Roman world and the *spicy* Venetian world could hardly be starker: 'Salt and pepper represented two fundamentally different phases of human civilization' (Schivelbusch, 1992: 3). Between the twelfth and sixteenth centuries, the flooding of Europe with pepper and other paradisiacal spices 'signaled the end of the Middle Ages and the dawn of the modern age' (Schivelbusch, 1992: 10). The Latin Crusades and Venetian Arsenale were the vanishing mediators that bridged the one and the other by opening Europe up to the Orient: the Crusaders for plunder and the Venetians for trade.

Along with the Dutch, the Italians made the socially necessary but sordid business of trade, commerce, and money-lending respectable, as well as profitable. Venice, which was 'more exposed ... to Oriental influences' than other Italian commercial centres, such as Florence and Pisa, 'became Europe's great lending laboratory' (Ferguson, 2008: 33). The subsequent ascent of rational calculation was fraught with deeply heretical implications, just one of which was the mercantile attempt to smuggle the demonic zero (0) into Latin Europe under the noses of the Inquisition (Rotman, 1993). Zero may be better for bookkeeping and accounting than tallying and Roman numerals, but it is much more diabolical than the number 666 or 665. Zero opens a void in both thought and existence. It perforates God's plenum with nothingness so that it leaks in all directions, and its unholy repetition induces a sorcerous multiplication that would make the worst usurers, counterfeiters, and 'quantitative easers' blush: 1, 10, 100, 1,000, … 1,000,000, etc. Zero is the demonic naught (*no thing*) into which every thing and every thought plunges. Nothingness is the accursed share that not only mocks the infinite ($1/0 = \infty$), it also mocks the finite by mirroring every thought and thing with an uncanny, inverted double (± 1, ± 2, ± 3, etc.). God's world is not only found to be lacking and imperfect, it is infinitely lacking, full of imperfection, saturated with negativity, and revolves around the void. And then, to add insult to injury, the Renaissance reorganized representation around this diabolical sinkhole: the perspectival vanishing point into which both reality and vision plunge (Foucault, 1974; Rotman, 1993). So, when merchants trafficked zero into Christendom, they did much more damage to the faithful than the Black Death (1346–53), which was carried into Europe by merchant galleys arriving in Genoa, Pisa, and Venice, or even the so-called 'Copernican Revolution' of the sixteenth century, which merely promulgated a heliocentric cosmology. Little wonder, then, that those merchants and bookkeepers who smuggled the void into Christendom provoked profound theological anxiety (as did the 'discovery' of a diabolical 'New World'), a kind of Middle-Aged 'moral panic', and many were persecuted as heretics by the Inquisition. For all of its subsequent mutations, capitalism has remained stained by diabolism and nihilism ever since, and no amount of money laundering will ever make it clean. The extraordinary splendour of Venice's built environment reflects the ascent of the commercial void, the eclipse of the sacred by moneyed profanity, and the 'urbanization of mercantile capital' over half a millennium. Once the cutting edge of modernity shifted to industrial capital in the wake of the Industrial Revolution, however, the world of mercantile capital was left to rot (Taylor, 1999). It is now the turn of the world of industrial capital to fall apart and decompose: from the post-industrial ruins of America's so-called 'Rust Belt' to the legions of Chinese 'ghost cities' at home and abroad (Beauregard, 1993; Shepard, 2015; Vergara, 1999).

What Venice did for shipbuilding, and Detroit for automobile production, Cincinnati did for animal disassembly. The place where the mechanized animal slaughter industry reached its perfection was not Cincinnati, however, but Chicago, from the 1860s to 1880s. 'The abattoir was to become a complex factory involving a precise separation of tasks and mechanical operations – stabling, killing, cleaning, refrigerating, transporting, inspecting, preparing foodstuffs, and so forth' (Pick, 1993: 180). Meanwhile, both Cincinnati and Chicago further dramatized the ambivalence of modernity. For while in one part of each city hundreds of thousands of animals were being disassembled in slaughter factories, in another part members of an entirely different class of animal (often exotic) were being pampered in purpose-built enclosures: sometimes for educational purposes, but mostly for entertainment. The first zoos in Chicago and Cincinnati opened in 1868 and 1875, respectively. The Cincinnati Zoo 'sheltered its animals in decorative buildings that were spaced generously along softly rolling grounds' (Horowitz, 1996: 126). The modern living conditions that many zoos provided for their animals were far superior to the squalid housing endured by ordinary folk. For example, the state-of-the-art Gorilla House and Penguin Pool installed at London Zoo in 1933–4 stood in stark contrast to the working-class slums of London (Gruffudd, 2000).

In the first half of the nineteenth century, Chicago, unlike Cincinnati, was not a major focus of the American meat industry. 'At the start of the 1850s, Chicago packed 20,000 hogs, compared with Cincinnati's 334,000' (Cronon, 1992: 229). Yet while Cincinnati had peaked by mid-century, not least because of the limits of the river transportation system upon which it relied, Chicago was just beginning its ascendancy, thanks to the seemingly limitless potential of railway transportation. The coming of the railways in the 1850s was crucial for Chicago's rise as a stockyard and meatpacking location. Rail was a cheap and efficient way to transport livestock, animal feed, dressed meat, and even the ice needed for refrigeration to sustain the industry on a continental scale over winter and summer months alike. 'For cattle, this meant traveling east by rail in heretofore unheard-of numbers while still alive, since beef packing was not at first a major activity at the Chicago stockyards', writes William Cronon (1992: 211). 'For pigs, it meant passing through the "disassembly line" … that divided animals into their most minute constituent parts so that the greatest possible profit from their sale could be gained.' By 1862, Chicago had surpassed Cincinnati in pork-packing, and by the 1870s it processed a million pigs a year.

American consumers were accustomed to preserved pork products (salted, smoked, and canned), and so were willing to accept them from distant locations, just as they were accustomed to canned salmon from places such as the Columbia River. Indeed, canned and other preserved foodstuffs fuelled European imperialism and colonialism, and were as important as coal and oil. American consumers preferred fresh beef, however. This was an initially insurmountable obstacle to the emergence of a Chicago-based, long-distance beef-packing industry, because decay – and therefore waste – set in from the moment that a cow was killed. Refrigeration with ice would eventually solve this problem in the 1870s, for both packing and distribution (refrigerated factories and railcars). 'As late as 1871, less than 4 percent of the cattle that arrived in Chicago were packed there, those few being shipped mainly to England and imperial outposts like India' (Cronon, 1992: 232). By 1884, refrigeration enabled the volume of packed cattle to surpass the number of live cattle that it shipped to the east coast. Railways and refrigeration 'brought the entire nation – and Great Britain as well – into Chicago's hinterland' (Cronon, 1992: 238).

The railways were also indirectly responsible for the abundance of Longhorn cattle on the Great Plains. They came in the wake of the annihilation of millions of bison after the Civil War. 'Within four years of the appearance of the railroads and a market in tannable hides, well over four million bison died on the southern plains alone. In Kansas, the slaughter reached its peak between 1870 and 1873, and then collapsed' (Cronon, 1992: 217). Hunters then moved on to decimate the bison populations of Texas, Dakota, Montana, and the Canadian prairies. The destruction was truly catastrophic for Native Americans. 'The Indian wars of the 1870s took place in the shadow of hunger and starvation' (Cronon, 1992: 218). 'By 1890, the ten million or more bison that had still grazed the Great Plains at the end of the Civil War were gone. In their place were nearly as many cattle' (Cronon, 1992: 247). Having helped wipe out the bison, replacing them with cattle, the railways also enabled Chicago to gather up this 'great tide of animal flesh' and facilitate 'the emergence of the midwestern feedlot system, in which farmers raised corn and hay together to fatten western cattle and midwestern hogs before their final journey to the Chicago slaughterhouses' (Cronon, 1992: 247). 'Chicago was the end of the line. It was the place, more than any other, where animals went to die. In the grim brick buildings that sprung up beside the great stockyard, death itself took a new form' (Cronon, 1992: 225).

Chicago's 'great stockyard' – the Union Stock Yards – opened on Christmas Day, 1865. It replaced the patchwork of stockyards and slaughterhouses that had been hemmed in by the sprawl of a rapidly expanding city. The Yards occupied a large and open area adjacent to the river and the railroads, 4 miles from the city centre. It opened with 500 animal pens on a 60-acre site that required 30 miles of drainage pipes, 3 miles of water troughs, and 10 miles of feed troughs. 'In 1866, the stockyards' first full year of operation, the "livestock hotel" catered to 1,564,293 animals' (Pacyga, 2008: 154). Three years later, the Yards had grown to '2,300 pens on a hundred acres, capable of handling 21,000 head of cattle, 75,000 hogs, 22,000 sheep, and 200 horses, all at the same time' (Cronon, 1992: 210). By 1900, an astonishing '14,622,315 animals filled its vast pens and chutes' (Pacyga, 2008: 154). This was animal slaughter on a gargantuan scale, made possible by the railways, which even supported the harvesting of vast quantities of ice for refrigeration from further and further afield, such as the lakes of Wisconsin in the 1880s and 1890s. 'Harvesting the winter', as Cronon (1992: 235) aptly calls it, was a huge industry in its own right, until it was rendered obsolete by artificial refrigeration fuelled by diesel. Even before the end of the nineteenth century, however, the Chicago stockyards and meatpacking industries were in relative decline, with the major firms opening factories in places such as Kansas City and Omaha. Diesel trucks accelerated the process of decentralization. 'By the 1930s, the output of the stockyards was in steady decline; by 1960, all the major packers had shut down their Chicago factories. Ten years later, the stockyards finally closed altogether. ... Grass began to grow again amid the ruins' (Cronon, 1992: 259).

As Chicago's meatpacking industry took off in the 1860s, the Chicago River served as an open sewer for its waste. This infamous 'River of Blood' soon became known as 'Bubble Creek'. There was, however, commercial pressure to reduce the volume of waste. With meatpacking only marginally profitable, and often loss-making, there was a relentless imperative for cost-saving innovations, such as substituting skilled labour with unskilled labour (especially East European immigrants and even women), resistance to unionization, substituting machinery for labour (such as steam-powered lifts and circular saws), and speeding up production and distribution to accelerate the turnover of capital. This was accomplished by organizing the slaughtering, butchering, and packing in terms of a finely graded and largely unskilled division of labour that was subservient to the stages and rhythms of a moving disassembly line. The full array of activities was often housed in a single multistorey building: stunning, exsanguination, skinning (cattle), scalding and dehairing (pigs), evisceration, and splitting. Live animals were driven up onto the roof. The killing floors were directly underneath. Then the carcasses were systematically disassembled on the floors below. At the end of the disassembly line, on ground level, there was almost nothing left to discard into Bubble Creek. Moreover, each stage in the line could be refined for optimal performance, and sped up to maximize profits. Through mechanization and rationalization, these 'slaughter factories' gained an insatiable appetite for animals. 'Once the slaughter had begun, the flow of carcasses seemed endless' (Pacyga, 2008: 154).

One of the most significant cost-saving exercises was the continuous drive to eliminate waste by using every conceivable part of the animal, from hooves to bristles. Gradually, the vast amount of waste that was once dumped into Bubble Creek was diverted into an ever-expanding array of byproducts: pet foods, fertilizers, brushes, cosmetics, margarine, lard, glue, candles, soap, cutlery handles, etc. By the 1890s, the disassembly line was so efficient that it enabled virtually wasteless production. Cincinnati's motto coined in the 1830s had been literalized in Chicago – they used *'Everything but the squeal'*. One processed foodstuff was so problematic for public health that it spawned legislation to uphold food standards: the so-called 'Bologna sausage', which 'became the great waste disposal product because it could hide such a multitude of sins: ... even sawdust and dirt' (Cronon, 1992: 252–3).

Although both La Villette and the Yards were conceived in the 1860s to be ideal slaughterhouses, the gap between them was enormous: 'Remarkable for its planning and its scale, La Villette retained elements of a handicraft tradition at odds with the routinised mass slaughter to come. Aspects of the killing arrangements remained cumbersome, since each ox was held in a separate booth', argues Pick (1993: 180). 'With the development of the Union Stockyards of Chicago in the 1860s, however, mechanised animal butchery moved towards its apotheosis. Chicago became the greatest cattle market in the world and quickly reached the point of slaughtering and processing some 200,000 hogs a day.' By the 1900s, the difference between La Villette and the Yards was even starker.

Chicago's '"Packingtown" employed thirty thousand men on assembly lines to perform relatively unskilled tasks, used mechanization wherever and whenever possible, ... to meet the demands of thirty to forty million American consumers and a growing export market', notes Claflin (2008: 34). 'By contrast ... there were about 350 artisan butchers ... working at La Villette, and another fifty or so at two smaller Paris abattoirs.'

In its heyday, the Chicago Yards would elicit an ambivalent response from commentators. While some regarded it as a wonder of the modern age, and duly added it to the list of world-class tourist sites (Pacyga, 2015), others regarded it as Hell on Earth, most famously depicted in Upton Sinclair's 1906 novel, *The Jungle*, as 'the Great Butcher' and the 'spirit of Capitalism made flesh' (Sinclair, 2012: 300). Such hellishness is a distant echo of Dante's recourse to the Venetian Arsenale for the poetic justice that awaits 'peculators' (swindlers, embezzlers, fraudsters, profiteers, usurers, etc.) in the fifth trench of the eighth circle of Hell in his epic poem, *Divine Comedy* (*c*.1308–20): immersion in a trench full of boiling pitch, overseen by demons armed with grappling hooks. The horror of entrenched battlefields and barbed-wire settlements once again springs to mind; along with the cannibalistic rendering down of human flesh and brains by capital, which oozes from its vats as a gelatinous mass of commodities that 'nobody is likely to call manna from heaven', as Raoul Vaneigem (1979: unpaginated) once sarcastically said of the avalanche of gadgets raining down on the consumer society.

What made the Yards so disconcerting was the fact that the railroads had not only taken millions of animals to industrial slaughter, they had also taken hundreds of thousands of men to meet the same fate in the Civil War. 'The 1860s was to inaugurate a new systematic mechanisation of death in both military and industrial killing machinery', says Pick (1993: 185). 'A new "humane" order of killing ... went hand in hand with a new vastness of death, a hitherto inconceivably rationalised and industrialised processing of meat. Not by chance was the metaphor of the slaughterhouse to become so inextricably intertwined with the language of modern war.' Indeed, in an 1866 letter to Engels, Marx aptly dubbed modern warfare 'the human slaughter industry' (quoted in Pick, 1993: 185).

What we begin to glimpse in the co-evolution of modern abattoirs and modern warfare is that capitalism in its entirety is a slaughter industry. Consider Baron Haussmann, the self-styled 'demolition artist' (*artiste démolisseur*) of Second Empire Paris (Benjamin, 2002: 12), or Robert Moses, the axe-wielding 'Butcher of New York'. In relation to brutal redevelopment schemes such as the mid-twentieth-century construction of the Cross Bronx Expressway, a 'seven-mile-long trench of a highway that cut through the very heart of a dozen different neighborhoods', which required the eviction of 'at least sixty thousand mainly Jewish and Italian Bronxites' (Flood, 2010: 164–5), and left the Bronx in 'spectacular ruins', Moses famously quipped that: 'When you operate in an overbuilt metropolis, you have to hack your way through with a meat ax' (quoted in Berman, 1983: 293–4). In keeping with the 'creative destruction' of urban redevelopment, Moses was fond of quoting Joseph Stalin's maxim that you cannot make an omelette without breaking eggs. 'Moses was destroying our world, yet he seemed to be working in the name of values that we ourselves embraced', laments Berman (1983: 295); values such as 'progress', 'renewal', and 'reform'; values that could be encapsulated in the passion for 'the tradition of the New'. 'Here in the Bronx, thanks to Robert Moses, the modernity of the urban boulevard was being condemned as obsolete, and blown to pieces, by the modernity of the interstate highway' (Berman, 1983: 295–6). Before Moses cut through the Bronx with his meat axe, the strikingly 'modern' 1930s Art Deco apartment buildings, reminiscent of a Parisian boulevard, 'could be admired for free, like the rows of glamorous ocean liners in port downtown'. After the meat axe had done its work, these buildings resembled 'shell-shocked battleships in drydock' (Berman, 1983: 295).

The fortuitous mention of 'shell-shock' is an opportune moment to turn our attention away from the industrial slaughter of animals to consider the industrial slaughter of humans more fully, which will no doubt lead us back to wet and dry guillotines, barbed-wire settlements, and purpose-built death factories with their gas chambers and crematoria fed by far-flung railway networks. For we are still living through the aftershocks and airquakes of optimism and Enlightenment, which continue to shatter our world. Some, like La Villette and the Yards, open up vast sinkholes that swallow entire regions in an orgy of creative destruction, while others open up almost imperceptible abysses into which reality plunges, such as early cinema (c.1895–1906), whose 'dynamite of the tenth of a second' (Benjamin, 1985: 236) pulverized the present – the 'Here and Now', upon which everything hinges – through editing and montage. As Georges Duhamel (1931) astutely noted in *America the Menace*, Chicago slaughterhouses and New York cinemas both 'struck him as manifesting the same annihilative enterprise' (Damisch, 2001: 71). Hereinafter, the modern world is always primed to explode – in both the real and the imaginary.

7

The Human Slaughter Industry

War-machines, Speed-space, and Shell Shock

Maybe humankind's a pinnacle, but only a disastrous one.

Georges Bataille, 1988a: 7

As the Second Anglo-Boer War began (1899), delegates from 26 countries gathered at the Hague to discuss how war might be avoided through arbitration and, in the event of war, how it might be constrained. Given its military supremacy and worldwide empire, the British Government instructed its delegation to avoid 'restricting innovations in weaponry' because that would 'favour the interests of savage nations' (quoted in Preston, 2015: 16). Unrivalled superiority would be the most effective deterrent, the world's greatest superpower insisted. Needless to say, the 'reason of the strongest' prevailed, yet the Convention nevertheless proscribed 'asphyxiating and deleterious gases', but only in projectiles; and the second Hague Convention (1907) further proscribed 'poison or poisoned weapons', and weapons causing 'unnecessary suffering'. The gas warfare that started in April 1915 arguably did not, strictly speaking, break these Conventions because it was conducted from canisters, and many of the agents were neither gases (they were aerosols) nor poisons (they were irritants or blister agents). I mention this because gas warfare, like the guillotine, has accrued a frightful reputation, whereas incendiaries have been regarded as more humdrum – except, perhaps, in connection with thermobaric weapons, nuclear radiation, and burning at the stake. Perhaps the truly frightful thing was not particular kinds of weapons but the way in which the modern war-machine weaponized industrial processes and products, such as petroleum jelly and pesticides. Indeed, 'gases could be manufactured in bulk using the methods and machinery normally employed in making dyestuffs' (Harris and Paxman, 2002: 8), and Germany weaponized gas not only because it had the requisite chemical industry, but also because the British naval blockade starved it of the nitrates needed for manufacturing explosives.

While Germany had an advanced chemical industry the British lagged behind. Nevertheless, Britain could still muster 33 laboratories to test '150,000 ... compounds ... to develop the most poisonous war gas' (Harris and Paxman, 2002: 21), and, in 1916, it established the War Department Experimental Ground at Porton Down – complete with a faux trench system – to develop chemical weapons. A farm and breeding facility were added in 1917, thereby ensuring a sustainable supply of animals for experimentation: 'Cats, dogs, monkeys, baboons, goats, sheep, guinea pigs, rabbits, rats and mice' (Harris and Paxman, 2002: 40).

The First World War also saw significant attempts to incorporate biological agents into the war-machine. For instance, the Germans attacked Allied horses and cattle with glanders and anthrax. Again, this was not unprecedented. Infecting water supplies with diseased carcasses has a long pedigree. In 1346, the Mongols catapulted plague-ridden bodies into Caffa, as did the Russians in Reval in 1710, and, in 1763, the besieged British at Fort Pitt (now Pittsburgh) passed smallpox-infected blankets to Native American emissaries during Pontiac's Rebellion. However, the scientific and industrial explication (unfolding) of biological weapons truly took off in the 1930s, spearheaded by the Imperial Japanese Army, whose Pingfan Institute engaged '3,000 scientists, technicians and soldiers' in the weaponization of everything from anthrax, botulism, and cholera to plague, smallpox, and typhoid. During the Second World War, the Institute and its 18 satellites could produce eight imperial tons of bacteria a month, while American's main 'germ warfare factory', at Vigo in Indiana, would ... have been capable of producing twelve times' as much (Harris and Paxman, 2002: 77).

The Institute was constructed in a remote part of Japanese-occupied Manchuria. It comprised 150 buildings set within a square-mile compound and a large exclusion zone, with a proving ground in another remote part of Manchuria. The development of the Uji 'plague bomb' gives a flavour of the macabre fusion of biomedical expertise and advanced engineering. In 1940, dropping drums full of plague-carrying fleas from aircraft proved more effective than 'spraying "bare" bacteria from aircraft' (Williams and Wallace, 1990: 121), but it was still accident prone and inefficient. It took until 1944, however, for the Institute to perfect the 25-kg porcelain-encased Uji bomb, each of which contained around 30,000 plague-carrying fleas.

Shortly after the First World War became entrenched, the Germans tested tear-gas shells at Neuve Chapelle in France, on 27 October 1914, and at Bolimov in Poland, on 31 January 2015, but neither the French nor the Russians realized that they had been attacked: the gas froze solid in sub-zero temperatures. The Germans then tested chlorine gas at Hasselt in Belgium on 2 April 1915, but the cloud was so diffuse that it barely incapacitated anyone. The infamous chlorine gas attack at Ypres in Belgium, on 22 April 1915, was so successful partly because the surprised Allied soldiers ran in the same direction as the drifting gas cloud, thereby extending their exposure. The Germans had released 150 imperial tons of chlorine from 6,000 canisters, which formed a dense cloud 4 miles wide and 0.5 mile deep. However, 'the German high command, not anticipating significant success, had laid no plans to exploit the advantage' (Richter, 1994: 10). Moreover, despite their 'heinous' and 'diabolical' reputation, chlorine gas, sulphur (mustard) gas, and similar chemical weapons were ineffective compared to machine guns, incendiaries, and shells: 'gas warfare was anything but reliable or effective except in the most unusual circumstances, and a defensive capability developed very rapidly' (Richter, 1994: 1). For example, within days of the Ypres attack, Britain's *Daily Mail* newspaper appealed for homemade respirator pads. Within weeks, pads had been distributed to almost all British soldiers in France – although they were quickly withdrawn as defective. Shortly thereafter, factories were mass producing more robust gasmasks. Both sides quickly became accustomed to gas warfare, protected by gasmasks, alerts, and drills. Indeed, the 'ratio of deaths to casualties was dramatically lower for gas casualties (3–4 per cent) than for other injuries (over 25 per cent)' (Richter, 1994: 218). Many regarded tear gas (a non-lethal irritant), mustard gas (a rarely fatal blister agent), chlorine gas (a more potent irritant and asphyxiant), and even phosgene gas (a powerful asphyxiant responsible for four fifths of chemical fatalities) as amongst the war's least atrocious weapons. 'In the majority of cases of minor gassing, the invariable result was temporary incapacitation' (Richter, 1994: 218).

Another experimental chemical weapon, the flamethrower, also had some success. In July 1915, for instance, some British soldiers were driven from their trenches by German flamethrowers (SIPRI, 1975). However, incendiaries were even less effective than gas. They accounted for just 0.5 per cent and 5 per cent, respectively, of battlefield casualties in 1918. Other First World War innovations in killing were equally ineffective, including 'airships' and 'military tractors', both of which, like barbed wire and pesticides, had been *détourned* from their civilian milieux and weaponized. The armour-plated, caterpillar-tracked, diesel-powered, and gun-toting military tractors (dubbed 'tanks' because they resembled cisterns) were even gendered: 'female' tanks sported a machine gun, while 'male' tanks enjoyed a small cannon.

The weird notion of weaponizing an 'iron horse' nearly met the same fate as other crackpot proposals for newfangled weapons in the Machine Age. Since the British Army dismissed the idea as a folly, the Navy was left to take it up. Winston Churchill, First Lord of the Admiralty, formed a 'Landships Committee' in February 1915. The Admiralty conceived of the 'military tractor' as a 'land battleship', and its prototype, nicknamed 'Little Willie', was built by an agricultural machinery manufacturer, with the production version, 'Big Willie', appearing on its paperwork under the misnomer 'water carrier' ('tank'). After the Army took over the project and brought it to fruition, all that remained of the poetic discourse of 'land battleships' was the nickname 'tank'.

Churchill envisaged these 'military tractors' ploughing up the barbed-wire entanglements that had overrun the entrenched battlefield like metallic briar patches, thereby rendering it penetrable by infantry and cavalry (another anachronistic occupant of the industrialized battle 'field', which would soon be forced to dismount its horses and mount motorized vehicles instead). However, when the entire fleet of 48 combat-ready 'tanks' was mobilized for the first time at the Battle of Combles–Flers–Courcelette in France in September 1916 (part of the final Somme Offensive), only 36 managed to cross the British front line, and just 18 survived the day. Nevertheless, the fearsome sight of these monstrous machines had such a demoralizing effect on German troops that many fled or surrendered. General Douglas Haig was sufficiently impressed to request another 1,000, but 'tanks' remained bedevilled by mishaps for the rest of the war. Tanks would only thrive in the Second World War, once they had been perfected as dependable killing machines. And one might add that weaponized construction vehicles – such as the Caterpillar D9 armoured bulldozer used by the Israel Defense Forces (IDF) in Gaza – have become fearsome tools of residential destruction and 'splintered occupation' (Weizman, 2007, 2011a, 2012). They leave in their wake historical geographies of violence written in rubble, which chime with other landscapes of 'creative destruction' and 'scab architecture' (Hell and Schönle, 2010; Woods, 1993).

Like tanks, gas attacks were neither capable nor dependable in the First World War. The peregrinations of gas clouds depended on the vagaries of the topography, the microclimate, and the weather. They frequently dispersed without ever sufficiently concentrating to have the desired effect, and they often engulfed the attacker's own troops. The British discovered this on 25 September 1915, during the Battle of Loos in France, when their inaugural chlorine gas attack, delivered from a 7-mile section of trenches, sunk back into those trenches. 'Perhaps the most fatal flaw of gas warfare was, after all the expense and the trouble, the very real risk of doing as much damage to one's own troops as to the enemy's' (Richter, 1994: 223).

Germany's last gas attack on the Western Front was on 8 August 1916, after which it redeployed its gas regiments to the Eastern Front, where the prevailing winds favoured German gas attacks against an ill-equipped Red Army. The Russians 'suffered almost half a million [gas] casualties' (Harris and Paxman, 2002: 11). The British, however, persisted with gas attacks, largely due to a gas fanatic: Charles Foulkes. His 'Special Brigade' of 6,000 men conducted '768 gas operations involving 88,000 gas cylinders' that 'discharged 5,700 tons of various gases' (Richter, 1994: 228), but to little avail. Nevertheless, gas clouds have retained an aura of frightfulness. In fact, the term 'frightfulness' (*Schrecklichkeit*) became a media buzzword during the war, peppering accounts of dastardly deeds such as gassing soldiers, bombing civilians, and torpedoing merchant ships.

Asphyxiating gases and incendiary weapons have been instruments of war since Antiquity, such as flaming arrows, burning oil, and Greek fire. The Chinese have been particularly adept. Consider the Siege of Yü-Pi in AD 546, which involved extensive tunnelling beneath the cliff-side citadel. The defenders used bellows to send 'smoke and noxious gasses into the tunnels, quickly choking and burning the enemy' (Sawyer, 2004: 349). Indeed, sieges have always lent themselves to incendiary and gas attacks. For instance, the Spartans laid siege to Plataea in Greece in 428 BC, during the Peloponnesian War (431–404 BC), using sulphur and pitch fumes. Even the Bible 'relates how Samson affixed firebrands to the tails of foxes and released them amongst the cornfields of the Philistines' (SIPRI, 1975: 15). Scorched earth practices have an ancient pedigree. In the Napoleonic Wars the British considered using 'stink ships' – vessels filled with coal, tar, and sulphur, and ignited when close to the enemy – and, in the Crimean War (1853–6), shells filled with cacodyl cyanide. In the American Civil War, chlorine and chloroform gas shells were suggested as a way to flush out Confederate soldiers from their trenches and fortifications, and patriotic inventors tried in vain to create flamethrowers (Hasegawa, 2015). In short, the use of chemical weapons in the First World War was far from unprecedented. Indeed, in the same year that gas warfare erupted on the Western Front, 1915, the Turks were systematically exterminating Armenians in the Ottoman Empire: 'the epicenter of death was the region of Deir el-Zor, ... where Armenians died not only of massacre, starvation, and disease but were stuffed into caves and asphyxiated by brush fires – primitive gas chambers' (Balakian, 2005: 176). The extermination began in April, when the Turks, having lost ground on the Caucus Front, 'blamed the local Armenian population for co-operating with the Russian invaders' (Gilbert, 1995: 142). By May, the Turks were being accused of 'deliberately exterminating' the Armenians, and of committing 'crimes ... against humanity and civilisation' (quoted in Preston, 2015: 173–4). This was one of the first occurrences of such a phrase. 'In a broad belt more than five hundred miles behind the Russian front, from the former Ottoman capital of Bursa to the crusader city of Aleppo, the killings continued', writes Martin Gilbert (1995: 166–7). 'By September as many as a million Armenians were dead [and] 200,000 were forcibly converted to Islam.' On the eve of Germany's invasion of Poland in 1939, Adolf Hitler posed a chilling rhetorical question: 'Who today, after all, speaks of the annihilation of the Armenians?' (quoted in Balakian, 2005: 377). Who indeed?

The decisive shift, then, was not the deployment of morally 'frightful' weapons, but rather the advent of 'war as a machine' (Pick, 1993: 165). The epoch of 'the human slaughter industry' had arrived, as Marx dubbed it in 1866, and its 'violent motor' could be traced back to the French Revolution. The industrial war-machine cut 'a vast and ghastly sanguinary spiral across the nineteenth century, stretching perhaps from 1789 to 1914, or even to Auschwitz', argues Pick (1993: 161). It unfurled a ferocious dialectic 'of blood and madness, of reason and violence' that implicitly posed an urgent question that would resound throughout Modernity: could the war-machine be kept under control or would it inevitably run amok? 'Every technology produces, provokes, programs a specific accident', cautions Paul Virilio (Virilio and Lotringer, 1997: 38). 'The invention of the boat was the invention of shipwrecks. The invention of the steam engine and the locomotive was the invention of derailments. ... The invention of the airplane was the invention of the plane crash.' Likewise, the invention of the industrial war-machine was the invention of the human slaughter industry, and the simultaneous invention of all manner of anticipated and unanticipated 'accidents' of more or less apocalyptic proportions: from the incalculable risks of weaponizing life itself (biogenetic weapons) to the prospect of nuclear Armageddon (mutually assured destruction or the meltdown of nuclear reactors, from Chernobyl to Fukushima).

The formation of the war-machine depended not only on industrialized weaponry but also on railways, telephony, and timetables that enabled warfare to be scaled up to continental and global proportions. As we have noted, some optimists thought time–space compression wrought by the railways would put an end to war. In France, for example, 'a theory developed that the railroads would increase familiarity among people and that the new forms of human universality made possible would render war impossible', notes Michel Foucault (1989: 262). What this failed to appreciate, however, 'was that, on the contrary, the railways rendered war far easier to wage'.

The railways made travel a disembodied and effortless experience; a kind of 'stationary trip' that would find its perfection in the revolutionary teleportation device that hit the streets in 1895: the Lumière Brothers' *Cinématographe*, whose celebrated debut in Paris included the arrival of a train. The railway shot passengers through space in a trajectory that did not so much take place as take time. It traversed a 'speed-space' that connected the points of departure and arrival whilst dissolving what lay in between. Train travel elapsed and became something to endure – through sleeping, daydreaming, or immersion in other worlds (newspapers, magazines, novels, soundscapes, etc.). The time-lapse character of train travel gave rise to a revolutionary new form of representation, the 'timetable', and a new urge: acceleration. As a speed-space wedded to acceleration, 'the railroad annihilated space and time' (Schivelbusch, 1986: 36), bringing once distant places connected by rails (and later wires) closer together, whilst flinging everywhere else further away. Accordingly, 'travelers gradually got accustomed to what at first seemed frightening: the demolition of traditional time-space relationships and the dissolution of reality' (Schivelbusch, 1986: 160). These were hastened by the telegraph, whose cabling was strung out beside the tracks: initially for distanciated signalling, and then for distanciated communication.

The first commercial use of an electric telegraph was on the London and Blackwell Railway in 1840. It was used to signal when engines should start and stop, an innovation that revolutionized the collision-prone, single-track railroads in the American West. Before telegraphic switching, 'the Boston and Worcester Railroad, for one example, kept horses every five miles along the line, and they raced up and down the track so that their riders could warn engineers of impending collisions' (Carey, 1992: 214). Samuel Morse sent his first 'instant message' by telegraph in 1844, having predicted in 1838 that telegraphy would yield something akin to a global village – a transformation of the whole of America into 'one neighborhood' (quoted in Carey, 1992: 207). Although the public, commercial, and government reactions were lacklustre, the press appreciated the telegraph's potential for reportage. 'The Magnetic Telegraph annihilates distance', announced the *Albany Argus* in 1845 (Simon, 2005: 37), following the opening of a line from Washington to Baltimore. As more lines were installed, 'the exuberant proclamation that the telegraph had the power to "annihilate space and time"' became a cliché (Simon, 2005: 40).

One should not underestimate the shock and fatigue of rail travel and industrialized warfare on the mental and material fabric of people and machines: 'railroad disasters ranked among the most spectacular events of the nineteenth century', argues Wolfgang Schivelbusch (1986: 125). Nor should one underestimate the challenge of coordinating a manifold speed-space, even with timetables and telegraphy, especially when it increased in density and extent so rapidly. In railway pioneering Britain, for instance, there were just 100 miles of track in 1830, but 19,000 miles by 1900. Building on the cycling craze that swept through Britain in the 1830s, railways further democratized travel, giving the mass of the population access to speed for both work and leisure. By 1870, there were over 300 million railway trips, most of which were third class. The *Railway Regulation Act* of 1844 even legislated that third-class passengers were to be given protection from the weather, as well as seating, and affordable access to speed. Each line had to have at least one daily train in each direction, calling at all stations, with an average speed of at least 12 m.p.h., and at a cost of no more than a penny a mile. The mass mobilization of Britain was an accomplished fact by the 1850s.

As the British railways spread in the 1830s and 1840s, some stations became places where lines converged, enabling connections. 'A new contrivance was devised for this purpose, and it was called a "time table." These words were used by the London & Birmingham Railway in 1838, and then passed into general currency' (Simmons, 1995: 183). From 1839, George Bradshaw's *Railway Guide* was published every month for 120 years, and while it was the unrivalled timetable for the railway network, it baffled almost everyone. For right up to the 1870s, there was no standard time in Britain to assist the Herculean task of coordinating the patchwork of local times that had evolved over centuries (Glennie and Thrift, 2011). Britain in the 1830s was still temporalized by the vagaries of the sun and the moon, and soundscapes such as the dawn chorus, church bells, and signal guns – none of which gave much heed to the abstract monotony of clock-time (originally developed to regulate religious activities before passing into commercial and secular use), and still less to the choreography of trains. Like Borges' (2000) *Garden of Forking Paths*, Bradshaw's *Railway Guide* articulated a fiendish labyrinth of time rather than the usual labyrinth of space.

Originally, each British railway company ran according to the local time of the city where it was based, each differing by up to a quarter of an hour or so. This gave rise to the peculiar situation that 'in stations used by several different lines there were clocks showing different times' (Schivelbusch, 1986: 44). In the case of America, whose railway boom came several decades after Britain's, the array of railway times was even more baffling. For example, while Buffalo's station sported three clocks to keep track of the lines running through it, Pittsburgh's enjoyed six. That, however, was the least of the problems. 'Before standard time Michigan had twenty-seven time zones; Indiana, twenty-three; Wisconsin, thirty-nine; Illinois, twenty-seven. ... The railroads used fifty-eight local times keyed to the largest cities' (Carey, 1992: 224).

In the absence of a standard time for Britain each company maintained the time of its network. For example, a company that used London's time would dispatch a clock set to the time at the Royal Observatory in Greenwich on the first train departing from London that morning, and at each stop the station's timepieces would be synchronized with the clock. (Some Greenwich-set clocks were even ferried across the Irish Sea so that stations in Ireland and the colonial administration could be set to London time.) The clock would eventually return to London – often on the last train – so that the process could be repeated the next day. Soon, this cumbersome synchronization routine would be accomplished via telegraph wires, spreading London's time throughout Great Britain and into the far-flung empire (via submarine cables). After all, British ships ferried Greenwich time around the world on chronometers long before trains hauled it around on clocks. The distribution of time in Britain remained rail-bound until 1924, when radio – the 'wireless' – took over this onerous task, before passing over to telephonic 'speaking clocks' and suchlike from the 1930s.

In 1840, the Great Western Railway (GWR) was the first company based outside of London to synchronize its rail network with London's time. The adoption of 'London time' by other companies followed swiftly, and in its wake came pocket-watches blessed with two dials or minute hands: one for local time; the other for London time. By 1852, the entire British railway network was on London time or 'rail time' as it became known. However, the country at large retained its patchwork of local times. So, for example, while Swansea's station ran on London time, the city remained 10 minutes adrift, running on the local time that it had enjoyed since the Middle Ages.

Of course, many communities valiantly resisted being colonized by London time, just as they had resisted being colonized by street lighting. But London's time proved hard to repel, not least because it was backed by so many business interests that embraced the railways as a way to reduce the 'friction of distance' and its associated costs. So, the process of uprooting localities and letting them drift into a 'placeless' and 'timeless' state was well underway by the 1850s, long before the 'placelessness' misattributed to the twentieth century (Augé, 2009; Relph, 1976). Then, in 1858, a pyrrhic legal victory reaffirmed local time as official time. The final blow came in 1880, when Parliament legislated that the official time in Britain would be Greenwich Mean Time (GMT). In fewer than 50 years, London's time had surged through the railway network, spilt out from its stations, and flooded the entire nation with simultaneity. Other temporal rhythms persisted, and some even flourished, but they all paled before the cold, impersonal, and monotonous beat of clock-time, which hammered out the past, present, and future into a flat, empty, and homogeneous drone (Bergson, 1999; Lefebvre, 1991, 2004). Perhaps it was no mere coincidence that Martial Bourdin, a French anarchist, tried to blow up the Royal Observatory in 1894, in Britain's first international terrorist attack. GMT would go on to colonize the world, but it would have to wait until well into the twentieth century so to do. (Coordinated Universal Time took over from the 1960s.) Only one clock in Britain still maintains local time, although it is usually mistaken for an errant 'slow time' – but not in the positive sense that has accrued to other 'slow movements', such as 'slow food', 'slow fashion', 'slow science', and even 'slow travel'.

Meanwhile, a parallel process unfolded in America (Bartky, 2000). As late as 1870, there were 'still about eighty different railroad times' (Pick, 1993: 169). As well as parochial interests that hampered the adoption of a standardized railway time, there were two other key impediments. Standard railway time offended the devoutly religious since it violated 'divinely ordained nature', and it also became embroiled in 'populist protest against the banks, the telegraph, and the railroad' (Carey, 1992: 225). The eventual transition to a standard railway time, in 1883, 'was greeted by mass meetings, anger, and religious protest but to no avail' (Carey, 1992: 226). Nevertheless, although railway time 'was not made official US time until the emergency of World War I', by 1884 'the avalanche of switches to it by local communities was well under way'.

Moreover, the 'annihilation of space by time' was not only accomplished by the railway, but also by telecommunication. The advent of radio in the 1890s was arguably the first major 'wireless' telecommunication technology since Claude Chappe revolutionized military signalling with his 'optical telegraph' system in 1792, building on the age-old 'line-of-sight' (tele-vision) network of beacon hills. Chappe's system gave France a major communicative (speed-space) advantage in the Revolutionary and Napoleonic Wars. It covered France and beyond with over 500 stations connected by lines of sight that stretched 3,000 miles, thereby enabling military intelligence and orders to be exchanged via semaphore between Paris and places as far afield as Amsterdam, Brest, Mainz, Milan, Perpignan, and Venice in a few hours, rather than in a few days via dispatch riders. (The 3,700-mile barbed-wire net cast over South Africa by the British during the Boer War is reminiscent of Chappe's optical telegraph, although it transmitted bullets rather than signals along its lines of sight.) France used the optical telegraph until the 1850s, when it was superseded by the electrical telegraph. The optical telegraph was instrumental in cementing the authority of Paris over France, just as the electrical telegraph was instrumental in cementing the authority of Paris over the French Empire. As James Carey (1992: 212) said of the British Empire: 'Until the transatlantic cable, it was difficult to determine whether British colonial policy was being set in London or by the colonial governors in the field – out of contact and out of control.' Rapid worldwide telecommunication enabled the imperial core to be more active and less reactive to events unfolding in the periphery. Submarine cables began to be laid in the 1850s, and the first transatlantic cable, over 6,000 kilometres long, was completed in 1858, although it failed within a month. A secure connection was finally established in 1866. With the laying of a transpacific cable between New Zealand and Canada in 1902, the telegraph spanned the world, and the epoch of 'tele-presence' had dawned. This infrastructure was not only vital for the 'Age of Empire' (Hobsbawm, 1994), laying the basis for a 'world' war, it also proved sufficiently durable to sustain 'globalization' and the 'Empire of Capital' into the twenty-first century. Our 'global village' remains well and truly tethered to the Earth by submarine cables, despite the colonization of the planet by the 'World Wide Web', its encirclement by hundreds of telecommunication satellites, and its envelopment in noxious clouds of supersaturated data.

Railways, telegraphy, and timetables utterly transformed the mobilization for war, enabling it to be accomplished with lightning rapidity. When Napoleon's *Grande Armée* of almost 450,000 men and 160,000 horses invaded Russia in 1812, some troops took months to advance from France, across Germany and Poland, and into Russia, over increasingly inhospitable terrain that transformed the summer-time invasion into a drawn-out death march characterized by exhaustion, starvation, dehydration, and disease: 'The roadside was littered ... with the carcases of horses and the bodies of men who had died on the march', writes Zamoyski; 'the whole army had been reduced by a third by the time it reached Vitebsk, without fighting a single battle' (Zamoyski, 2005: 188 and 190, respectively). Merely 100,000 survived the final advance on Moscow, and barely half of those endured the winter retreat out of Russia. One of the first major conflicts of the railway age, the Franco–Prussian War (1870–1), stands in stark contrast to the slow decimation of the *Grande Armée*. The German railways transported 370,000 troops into France swiftly. This 'was not lost on other European powers, which soon commenced the construction of railway lines in coordination with military needs' (Kern, 1983: 269). The Russians, by contrast, used 'railroads to thwart an invasion of their homeland. They constructed lines on a broader gauge.'

The speed-space at the outset of the First World War was even more concentrated, making mobilization verge on the semi-automatic. For the first time 'the world went to war according to mobilisation timetables facilitated by standard time' (Pick, 1993: 169). Consider the French and German mobilizations in 1914. '"Improvisation when dealing with nearly three million men and the movements of 4,278 trains, as the French had to do, is out of the question." The German mobilization timetable was even more precise, for it led immediately to war on two fronts' (Kern, 1983: 270, quoting a contemporary observer). When such a speed-space depends on telegraphy, mobilization accelerates as never before. This is well illustrated by General Dobrorolski's mobilization of 2 million Russian troops from a telegraph office in Saint Petersburg.

> Dobrorolski recalled: 'Every operator was sitting by his instrument waiting for the copy of the telegram in order to send to all the ends of the Russian empire the momentous news of the calling up of the Russian people. ... When the moment has been chosen, one only has to press the button and the whole state begins to function automatically with the precision of a clock's mechanism.' (Kern, 1983: 272)

And so the First World War got under way, through a mechanical mobilization that was a harbinger of the industrial slaughter to come – except that it would not be a lightning war, but rather a slow torture even more disastrous than Napoleon's misadventure in Russia: 'Its more than four years' duration consumed human beings ... in an almost perpetual meat grinder of extraordinary proportions' (Levene, 2013a: 37). Consider one cog that got jammed up in this lumbering war-machine: the Battle of the Somme. On its first day, 1 July 1916, 'sixty thousand British soldiers were killed or gravely wounded – 30,000 of these in the first half-hour. At the end of four and a half months of battle ... the British and French front line had advanced by five miles' (Sontag, 2003: 22). With '419,654 killed, wounded and missing, the British had liberated a two-mile strip of blasted countryside and shattered French villages. French losses had reached 204,253 and ... the Germans about 500,000' (Winchester, 2010: 36). This 'was a time of enormous epidemics of neuroses, many of which can be traced back to shellshock' (Schivelbusch, 1986: 148). Gilbert (1995) estimates that over a quarter of a million men were left suffering from 'shellshock' or 'war neurosis', a condition first diagnosed in the American Civil War, and which echoes the inaugural 'shock' of the Machine Age: the traumata of the railway journey, such as 'railway spine' and 'accident shock', that came to prominence around 1865–85 (Schivelbusch, 1986).

The First World War was not, however, the first major conflict to combine railway mobilization with industrial firepower to yield entrenched battlefields and industrial traumata. That dubious accolade belongs to the American Civil War. This conflict saw 'a devastating increase in firepower, which in turn ushered in the entrenched battlefield. The Civil War soldier was obliged to dig in on the attack as well as on the defence – thus anticipating the First World War' (Pick, 1993: 177). Indeed, this was the first major war 'to see the use of military trenches, railways, vast and moving theatres of battle, mass mobilisation and civil destruction as war strategy rather than by-product' (Pick, 1993: 178, note 33). During the war, 'entrenchments reached their most elaborate forms in ... the Petersburg campaign of 1864–65', writes Gerald Linderman (1987: 146). 'Soldiers entered that phase of the war looking backward and rejoicing that open warfare had been left behind ... but few continued for long to consider it a change for the better.' The key difference between the entrenchments of the Civil War and those of the Great War was the addition of barbed wire in the latter. 'At Petersburg the opposing fortified lines of trenches, protected by ditches, *abattis* (felled trees), and *chevaux-de-frise* (sharpened stakes), were so complex that they began to seem permanent' (Linderman, 1987: 146). The barbed-wire entanglements of the First World War also seemed permanent, forming a 'river of steel' 475 miles long and 0.5 mile wide, flowing from Switzerland to the North Sea. One American manufacturer supplied 3 million miles of barbed wire: enough to encircle the Earth 120 times.

In the Civil War, industrial firepower and entrenchment resulted in a shift from infrequent battles characteristic of the old style of warfare to the continuous skirmishes of a war of attrition. The embattled 'soldier had no time to prepare himself for death, and its setting was no longer one of special drama' (Linderman, 1987: 147). Little wonder, then, that regular soldiers despised the arrival of a new protagonist: snipers, who killed without warning, usually from hidden or camouflaged positions, and often with telescopic vision. Some snipers even killed those attending to calls of nature. The disreputable nature of sniping would become most obvious during the besiegement of cities such as Sarajevo (1992–6) and Aleppo (2012–16), when used to terrorize civilians. Such an aversion to sniping is repeated in the current disdain for drone operatives engaged in targeted assassination (Chamayou, 2012; Massumi, 2011; Weizman, 2011b). Indeed, most technological advances have been accompanied by repugnance: musketeers, U-boatmen, and Zeppelin airmen were all said to kill in a dishonourable way: without warning, and without honour.

As well as railway mobilization, industrial firepower, and entrenchment, the Civil War is notable for the fact that civilian populations were targeted. It 'ushered in an age in which characteristically major warfare would be endured by populations as a whole rather than professional armies and those unfortunate enough to lie in their path' (Pick, 1993: 177). This 'warfare of terror' or 'warfare of frightfulness' (Linderman, 1987: 180) stood in stark contrast to the start of the war, when both sides sought to respect civilians and their property. Gradually, however, hunger and frustration drove soldiers to loot and destroy civilian property, drawing upon the scorched earth tactics employed against Native Americans in the preceding decades.

> The goal of the Indian wars was not the destruction of the enemy's forces, but the destruction of the enemies themselves. The wars were as much a part of land clearing as the deforestation of primeval woodlands and the burning of the prairies. At the beginning of one such Indian campaign, General Philip Henry Sheridan issued an order to his sub-commanders: 'Let it be a campaign of annihilation, obliteration, and complete destruction.' Sheridan and ... William T. Sherman would continue their scorched-earth policy during the Civil War. The only strategic component omitted ... was genocide. (Schivelbusch, 2003: 38)

Whilst anticipating the First World War, the Civil War nevertheless 'squats in the middle of the nineteenth century like a monstrous irony', writes Schivelbusch (2003: 37); 'the United States ... plunged into war with a bellicose fury that had not been seen since the Wars of Religion' (Schivelbusch, 2003: 37). Almost two thirds of a million people were killed; many towns and cities were deliberately destroyed ('Shermanized'); and the emancipation of slaves without compensating their owners was a form of wealth destruction amounting to 'some four billion dollars' (Schivelbusch, 2003: 38). The British had cannily extricated themselves from slavery by compensating slave owners on the one hand (the Treasury borrowed £15 million from Rothschild to fund the compensation scheme) and by transforming slaves into wage labourers on the other hand (thereby ensuring the continuity of the structural relations of exploitation), both of which required the 'sinister inscriptions' of accountancy to ensure a smooth transition from a regime of accumulation based on slavery to one based on wage labour: 'The abolition of slavery in the British West Indies in 1834 was followed by a four-year period of transition in which the "freed" slaves, now termed "apprentices," were obliged to work for their former masters while they were taught how to behave like responsible wage-workers' (Oldroyd, Fleischman, and Tyson, 2013: 145). Accountants monitored the work performance of the 'apprentices' to determine the ratio of incentives and punishments periodically meted out by the government. Meanwhile, the proslavery lobby argued that the system of wage labour was crueller than the system of slavery because the capitalist enjoyed all of the rights of a master (law-abiding exploitation) but without any of the responsibilities (socially necessary welfare): 'slaves had been "formerly protected" because they were "articles of value," whereas now no one had an interest in their preservation but themselves' (Oldroyd, Fleischman, and Tyson, 2013: 151). Slave owners argued they had an interest in cultivating their human property, particularly after 1807, when the British and American governments banned the replenishment of the stock of slaves in the Caribbean and US with fresh imports from Africa. Indeed, the notion that slaves were just a certain kind of property, and closer to animals than humans, was one that 'book-keepers helped to perpetuate through commonly classifying them with the mules and cattle in inventories and valuations of livestock' (Oldroyd, Fleischman, and Tyson, 2013: 149).

There is a final aspect of the American Civil War that I wish to mention: prisoners of war. The Civil War was the first conflict in which the number of prisoners became a major problem. 'Even the Napoleonic Wars were manageable: Britain, for instance, handled most of its French captives in a single prison at Dartmoor' (Netz, 2009: 148). However, 'the American Civil War signaled a new era. With its millions of soldiers, it had new levels of human concentration on the battlefield, and this necessarily led to new levels of concentration in the prisoner-of-war camps. This war had nearly *half a million* prisoners of war on each side' (Netz, 2009: 148–9, italics in original). In the First World War, with even swifter mobilization and greater concentration, there were over a million POWs on the Western Front and over 5 million on the Eastern Front. Barbed-wire camps became a cheap solution to this extraordinary number of POWs, and they sprang up everywhere. In the twentieth century millions would perish in barbed-wire settlements, the most notorious of which were the Nazi concentration camps and the Soviet Gulag: 'In the years of its full operation, 1929 to 1953, the Gulag had claimed some 12 million lives' (Netz, 2009: 194).

During the Second World War the Nazi regime sought the German colonization of the East, including Estonia, Latvia, Lithuania, Poland, Russia, and the Ukraine. This would have entailed the displacement, enslavement, and extermination of millions of people as part of the land-clearance process. Himmler's 'SS planners did not advocate cosmetic changes but butchery, with whole cities razed, vast regions Germanized, and tens of millions of civilians deported, enslaved, and killed' (Wachsmann, 2015: 276). Himmler charged Oswald Pohl with overseeing the construction of the new Germany in Central and Eastern Europe, and concentration-camp prisoners would provide the labour. Accordingly, the SS set about transforming the concentration-camp (KL) system to accommodate the vast number of forced labourers that would be required to realize the RSHA's 'Masterplan East' (*Generalplan Ost*) (Jaskot, 2000). By October 1941, the invasion of Russia had yielded over 3 million POWs, reaped from two of the largest encirclements in the history of warfare, the Battles of Kiev and Minsk, and other operations. There were so many POWs that tens of thousands were simply left to die in barbed-wire enclosures. 'There was no shelter of any kind and the inmates resorted to digging holes in the ground with their bare hands. ... No food, water, or the most basic sanitation was provided, which reduced the starving prisoners to eating the grass in the "cages." Cannibalism was a fact' (O'Neil, 2008: 69).

A note in Himmler's diary for 15 September 1941 reads: '100,000 Russians – take over into concentration camps' (quoted in Wachsmann, 2015: 278). Within days of this entry, Himmler doubled the number that he coveted to 200,000. At the time, the entire concentration-camp system held fewer than 80,000 prisoners, only 5,000 of whom were Jewish. 'By October 1941, special areas, separated from the rest of the compounds and identified by signs such as "Prisoner of War Labor Camp," had been hastily completed in Neuengamme, Buchenwald, Flossenbürg, Gross-Rosen, Sachsenhausen, and Dachau, as well as in Mauthausen' (Wachsmann, 2015: 278). By the end of the war in May 1945, 'as many as 3.3 million Soviet prisoners of war [had] died at the hands of the Nazis as a result of mass executions, brutal mistreatment, intentional starvation, and lack of clothing or shelter' (Berenbaum, 1993: 127).

The expansion of the KL system was supplemented by the creation of two new gigantic camps to accommodate the anticipated Soviet slave-labour force. The first, Majdanek, was established near Lublin, in the General Government area of occupied Poland. When construction began in October 1941, the planned capacity was 50,000. By December 1941, 150,000 were expected. The second was constructed as a sub-camp of the main Auschwitz camp. This new sub-camp,

Auschwitz II, was located at Birkenau, two miles from Auschwitz I. It was built to accommodate 50,000, with plans to expand its capacity to 200,000. 'There were no signs yet that Birkenau would one day stand at the center of the Holocaust' (Wachsmann, 2015: 279). There was also another sub-camp, at Monowitz (Auschwitz III), which provided up to 11,000 slave labourers for the IG Farben industrial complex, which was the focus of 'one of the single greatest wartime investment programmes undertaken by the Third Reich' (Klemann and Kudryashov, 2012: 348).

The Nazi plan of turning the KL system into a vast slave-labour force building the new Germany quickly fell apart. The thousands of Soviet POWs initially transferred from Wehrmacht custody into SS custody were too exhausted, malnourished, and diseased to work; and given the appalling conditions, nearly all were dead within weeks. This was not necessarily a problem from the SS perspective since their lives were worthless. These 'masses from the East' (which included Jews, Roma, and Slavs) were 'subhuman'. The SS architects and planners 'subscribed to Himmler's views of Soviets as resilient "human animals"'. Their living or dying was a matter of indifference. Indeed, Birkenau had a 'lethal atmosphere' from the off: 'Death and disease were built into the plans, which envisaged 125,000 POWs packed into 174 barracks' (Wachsmann, 2015: 285). A total of 7,000 would share a latrine; 7,800 a wash hut. However, the destruction of the first tranche of POWs turned out to be a problem for two key reasons. First, no sooner had the KL system been reoriented for Soviet POWs than Hitler decided they should be fed into the German war economy instead since it faced severe labour shortages. (The shortages were exacerbated by the fact that Albert Speer, Reich Minister of Armaments and War Production, had prohibited 'labour hunting' in Western Europe and the Czech territories.) Second, the endless supply of POWs failed to materialize. The Red Army had thwarted the German invasion, and, after the Battles of Moscow (1941–2) and Stalingrad (1942–3), the Wehrmacht were in almost continual retreat, waging a 'defensive war' in the face of impending defeat, the so-called 'Rzhev Slaughterhouse' (1942–3) notwithstanding. There was not even enough labour (or materials) to complete the camps, let alone to realize the Masterplan East. Majdanek rarely held over 15,000 prisoners; and by the spring of 1942, fewer than 1,000 Soviets remained in Birkenau, almost all of whom soon perished. Nevertheless, if Birkenau was stymied from becoming a Soviet slave-labour camp, it was soon repurposed once more: as one of six 'death factories', which the Nazis intended as a 'Final Solution' to their deranged 'Jewish Question' – the total extermination of European Jewry: 'Judeocide', as Arono Mayer (2012) called it; or the 'Great Massacre', as Pierre Vidal-Naquet (1996) put it.

From early 1942, the Camp SS switched from gearing up for Soviet POWs and forced labour to gearing up for Jews and their extermination: 'it resolved to build a large crematorium in Birkenau, capable of disposing of eight hundred bodies in twenty-four hours', and 'prepared for the mass influx of women, who were part of Himmler's deportation plans' (Wachsmann, 2015: 296–7). On 26 March

1942, the first trainload of 999 Jewish women from Slovakia arrived. Auschwitz–Birkenau functioned as a death factory until the gassing stopped in November 1944, followed by a final burst of residual killing, including death marches amid the chaos of the Soviet advance and German collapse (Blatman, 2010, 2011; Goldhagen, 1997). The Red Army liberated the camp in January 1945, although survivors continued to suffer, not least in post-war 'displaced persons camps' (Stone, 2015). Over 1,100,000 were murdered at Birkenau; at least 870,000 were Jews. Meanwhile, Monowitz operated the SS's other mechanism for mass extermination: annihilation through labour. 'By the time the camp was closed in January 1945, the SS had brought a total of 35,000 people to Monowitz, of whom around 25,000 either fell victim to the inhuman working conditions or were selected for death in the gas chambers of Birkenau' (Wagner, 2010: 134).

Despite the Allied bombing campaign on Germany and German-occupied Europe, including the IG Farben complex at Monowitz, neither the six death factories nor the rail lines that served them were targeted. Nevertheless, Auschwitz–Birkenau was inadvertently bombed on a couple of occasions when aircrews mistook it for the IG Farben complex. By May 1944, the Allied air force could 'strike Auschwitz at will. The rail lines from Hungary were also well within range' (Berenbaum, 1993: 144), and yet the rail lines and 'death camp remained untouched'. Disrupting the deportations and exterminations was never a priority for the Allies. Indeed, the US 'War Department had decided in January [1944] that army units would not be "employed for the purpose of rescuing victims of enemy oppression" unless a rescue opportunity arose in the course of routine military operations' (Berenbaum, 1993: 145). Furthermore, there was virtually no Resistance activity directed against the transportation of the Jews to the death camps, despite widespread knowledge from early on that 'evacuation' and 'resettlement' meant journeys to places of mass murder: 'an estimated three million Jewish deportees were ... transported in freight cars to the camps in the "East". ... Only thousands survived' (Gigliotti, 2010: 2). It is striking that neither the Allies nor the Resistance disrupted either the death factories or the transports that fed them, despite many other attacks on the railways. 'Eighty-five rail conveys of Jews left France for the concentration camps, transporting over 70,000 people to their deaths, including 10,000 children. Not one train was stopped or even significantly delayed. Amazingly, this is not only true for France; it is also true for the whole of Occupied Europe, with two exceptions' (Cobb, 2009: 200). Denmark was the only country that prevented the deportation of its Jewish population. Following a tip-off that they would be deported in October 1943, the Danish Resistance organized the escape of almost all 8,000 of them to neutral Sweden. There was also Jewish resistance across occupied Europe: escapes, sabotage, and infrequent armed resistance, the most famous of which included the uprisings in the Warsaw Ghetto (April–May 1943) and the Sobibor death camp (14 October 1943).

It was not simply that people were transported in freight and cattle cars, as if they were goods or livestock, which would at least have been in keeping with the broader experience of railway travel since its inception: dehumanization and reification (Schivelbusch, 1986). Freight ordinarily has value, and it is usually handled with care. Deportation trains, however, were instruments of extermination in their own right. Thousands did not survive its 'excremental assault' (Des Pres, 1980): 'The initial push into the carriage, the rush for sitting and standing space, the train's unconfirmed destination, the compression of bodies, and the violation of social boundaries were nothing compared to the overpowering assault of excrement, urine, and vomit, and the dearth of water and food' (Gigliotti, 2010: 4). For those who survived transportation – which often took several days in extreme weather, typically claiming 5–10 per cent through hyperthermia or dehydration (Browning, 2001; Gigliotti, 2010) – what the SS euphemistically called 'evacuation', 'deportation', and 'resettlement' was either a swift or a slow death. 'At Belzec, Sobibor, and Treblinka, all but a few were dead within hours. At Auschwitz and Majdanek, which were also slave-labor camps, one could hope for a reprieve. Still, the vast majority were killed shortly after arrival' (Berenbaum, 1993: 127). Selection 'was a means to determine when and how they would perish. Some would be registered for murderous forced labour', and duly 'branded and sheared' (Berenbaum, 1993: 127), while the rest were killed immediately. Slave labour was the fate that awaited those 'selected' for a temporary reprieve: mostly for the war economy, although some worked in the camps and death factories themselves, as part of *Sonderkommandos* ('special squads') responsible for things like corpse disposal and the reclamation of valuables. At Auschwitz–Birkenau, for instance, the *Sonderkommandos* were already 400 strong by 1943, and swelled to over 900 in 1944, as the volume of killing escalated. Those selected for the camp *Sonderkommandos* were treated less brutally than other inmates, and tended to survive longer, but few outlived the war.

Children were especially vulnerable during selection. 'Between 1942 and 1945, around 210,000 were deported to Auschwitz. … In all, fewer than 2,500 Jewish children survived the initial selection' (Wachsmann, 2015: 310), and many of those – especially twins – were selected by Dr Josef Mengele and other SS doctors for medical experimentation. Importantly, selection was not limited to new arrivals, but repeated regularly. 'The officer in charge of the "selection" was a physician. His "expert opinion" was required to determine who would live and who would die. … The inmate who survived the first selection lived in constant fear of future selections' (Berenbaum, 1993: 127). Compliance was enforced through an all-encompassing regime of terror, which included individual and collective terror 'punishments', and arbitrary violence meted out at whim. But there was also solidarity and mutual aid amongst prisoners. The camps – even the death camps – were not, then, places where every inmate was utterly demolished and stripped back to a residual 'bare life' (Agamben, 2005), a life that was only 'life exposed to death' (Noys, 2005: 17). The extent of demolition was differentiated amongst the various social strata and groups within the camps, with age, gender, 'race', nationality, and ethnicity particularly significant. The most demolished were the *Muselmänner* – the 'living dead' or 'walking skeletons'. The least demolished were the *Kapos* ('prisoner functionaries'), who typically acted as block or work-group overseers, which put them in a liminal position with respect to victims and perpetrators. Like the *Judenräte* ('Jewish Councils') and the Ghetto Police, the liminality of the *Kapos* lent itself to both resistance and complicity, and their indiscernibility. Moreover, demolition was not so much an existential or ontological state as an unfolding process. 'Selection', then, which took place in the ghettoes, camps, and elsewhere was 'a general organizational schema by which "superfluous" human beings were sorted out from workers and then liquidated' (Sofsky, 1997: 241).

The explication (unfolding) of the human slaughter industry has made mass killing much easier to accomplish, and as we move ever worstward in the following chapters we will see that it has continued to become easier still. Perhaps an extreme optimist – or an optimistic extremist – would like it to become truly effortless. Meanwhile, just living becomes harder and harder. It is not a 'bare life' that verges on the inanimate, but a process that requires a tremendous amount of effort and courage, as the 'living dead' of our own consumer society demonstrate day after day: the homeless and the roofless; those 'street people' who are interned amidst the ruins of affluence; those 'people of the abyss', as Jack London (1903) called them, who are persecuted by the law, patronized by philanthropy, and misplaced by society at every turn: from Skid Rows to idyllic hedgerows.

8

Weaponized Air

From Forced Euthanasia to Military Ballooning

> The fighter plane ... soars above good and evil, a celestial goddess with an insatiable thirst for sacrificial tribute.
>
> Azmi Bishara, quoted in Eyal Weizman, 2008: 325

One can always concoct a more or less twisted rationale to justify any act of violence, from torture and assassination to terror bombing and poison gassing. So long as the ends are sufficiently noble, or at least tolerable when compared to the worst, then any means will invariably do – if only as exceptions that prove (demonstrate, validate, inflate, and aerate) the rule. For example, Professor Fritz Haber, the scientific director of the German gas-warfare programme in the First World War, and Nobel Prize-winning chemist, claimed that poison gas was 'a higher form of killing' (quoted in Preston, 2015: 1). Similarly, during the Second World War, the British Prime Minister, Winston Churchill, instructed his advisors 'to think very seriously over the question of using poison gas. I would not use it unless it could be shown that (a) it was life or death for us, or (b) it would shorten the war by a year', he wrote. 'It is absurd to consider morality on the topic', he added. 'In the last war the bombing of open cities was regarded as forbidden. Now everybody does it as a matter of course' (quoted in Preston, 2015: 273). Some went even further, as one delegate bluntly put it at the first Hague peace conference in 1899: 'The humanising of war, you might as well talk about the humanising of Hell!' Nevertheless, there have been countless attempts to humanize war: everything from technological innovations that have blessed the world with 'better' weapons to international humanitarian laws that have draped rights, responsibilities, and prohibitions over all and sundry – although 'better' is clearly a matter of perspective and the law never bites by itself. So, blessed are those peacekeeping weapons whose frightfulness 'better' dissuades than more muted weaponry, while the law obviously needs enforcing, which brings us circling back to the 'reason of the strongest' who wield the sovereign power to determine not only the law itself, but also the manner of its application – including the possibility of its suspension in a 'state of exception' or its remaining 'in force' but without any actual enforcement (Agamben, 1998, 2005; Friedländer, 2007a, 2007b). For instance, the Nazi regime's Anti-Jewish *Reich Citizenship Law* and *Law for the Defence of German Blood and Honour*, both of which were unanimously passed by the Reichstag on 15 September 1935, clearly demonstrate how the law can bite as savagely as any beast (Burleigh and Wippermann, 1991). These so-called 'Nuremberg Laws' stripped all full and three-quarter 'Jews' of Reich citizenship, along with many of those who were classified as half 'Jews' (*Mischling* of the first degree). This left them subject to the law but without any right to be protected by the state. Similarly, *Kristallnacht* was a chilling example of the law's withdrawal (Gilbert, 2006; Steinweis, 2009). On the eve of *Kristallnacht*, Dr Joseph Goebbels recorded in his diary what Hitler said to him about the anti-Jewish violence following Ernst vom Rath's murder in Paris: 'He decides: demonstrations should be allowed to continue. The police should be withdrawn. For once the Jews should get the feel of popular anger.' To which Goebbels added: 'I immediately give the necessary order to the police and the Party' (quoted in Gilbert, 2006: 29). With law enforcement suspended, and the SA unleashed,

> more than a thousand synagogues were set on fire and destroyed. ... Tens of thousands of Jewish shops and homes were ransacked. Jews were attacked in every German town, from the capital, Berlin, to the smallest towns and villages. ... In twenty-four hours of violence, ninety-one Jews were killed ... [and] 30,000 Jewish men ... – a quarter of all Jewish men still in Germany – were arrested and sent to concentration camps. ... More than a thousand died in these camps. (Gilbert, 2006: 15)

Accordingly, one should never take supposedly law-abiding and humane violence at face value. It is salutary to remember that Hitler once forbade gassing Jews on the grounds that such a 'merciful' death was too good for them: 'the benefits of euthanasia were to be reserved for true Germans' (Arendt, 2005: 50–1). The state-sanctioned killing programme of forced euthanasia, which began in 1939, was reserved for 'life unworthy of life', as a pro-euthanasia text entitled *Authorization for the Annihilation of Life Unworthy of Being Lived* (1920) famously put it, rather than for 'subhuman' and 'pestilent' lives that just deserved extermination through starvation, lethal labour, and shooting. The Nazi's *Aktion T-4* forced-euthanasia programme (named after the Berlin address from where it was coordinated: Tiergartenstrasse 4), which ran from late 1939 to mid-1941, administered, under medical supervision, 'mercy deaths' by lethal injection and gassing to upwards of 70,000 mentally ill and physically disabled patients drawn from Germany's asylums, hospitals, and care homes (Friedlander, 1995). When one also takes into account unauthorized euthanasia that continued after the official programme was stopped, and the separate euthanasia programme for children, the death toll may have reached 200,000. And once again, the killers faced the vexed problem of corpse disposal: 'it was simply not practical to clutter up the transportation system by shipping corpses all over the landscape. It was for this reason, as much as public health reasons, that caused [the chief of Hitler's Chancellery, Philip] Bouhler to insist upon immediate cremation at the major centers', argues Hugh Gallagher (1997: 213). 'Permanent furnaces were constructed at some of the sites, but other hospitals relied upon an ingenious device, a portable furnace on wheels. Some of the centers were so mechanized as to have a conveyer belt system installed to carry the corpses from the gas chamber to the oven.' In keeping with the logic of euthanasia, ashes were 'placed in ceremonial urns and delivered to their families along with a letter of condolence. No effort was made to distinguish the ashes of one victim from another' (Gallagher, 1997: 214).

Those subjected to forced euthanasia were singled out not primarily because of any medical condition or for any particular concern about their welfare, but for eugenic reasons. Their death would purge the 'race' of its deleterious elements. Expressed in some of the euphemisms of the time, granting 'final medical assistance' to 'refractory therapy cases' amounted to a beneficent 'negative population policy' (Gallagher, 1997). Forced euthanasia, which could be either *involuntary* (imposed on the unwilling) or *non-voluntary* (imposed on those who lacked the capacity or the opportunity to consent, acquiesce, or resist), followed the same eugenic logic as forced sterilization (Burleigh and Wippermann, 1991). And while the original regulations for *Aktion T-4* may have 'envisaged a "conservative" program with careful review procedures', like so many other policies in the Third Reich, once it was set to work in Germany's hospitals and asylums 'the program became a matter of killing in wholesale lots' (Gallagher, 1997: 213). Indeed, 'most of its victims were neither terminally ill nor in unbearable pain, nor were they anxious to die' (Gallagher, 1997: 208). The blithesome application of *Aktion T-4* was partly because those involved took advantage of their new-found freedom to kill, using criteria that were extraordinarily vague ('incurably sick', 'useless lives', 'senile maladies', 'chronic diseases', 'insanity', and 'paralysis'), but also because no one was ultimately responsible for taking the decision to kill: a stepwise bureaucratic process led from the ward to the gas chamber, and each person merely played their part in an extensive division of labour.

The bulk of the euthanasia took place at six killing centres, overseen by organizations bearing innocuous-sounding names, such as: the charitable 'Foundation for the Care of Institutions in the Public Interest', which handled the financial aspects of *Aktion T-4*; the 'National Group for the Study of Sanatoria and Nursing Homes', which handled all of the non-financial planning and administration; and the 'Limited Company for the Transport of Invalids in the Public Interest', which moved tens of thousands of patients around the network of hospitals, asylums, and killing facilities (Gallagher, 1997). After the adult programme stopped in August 1941, following protests from relatives, politicians, and the church (the euthanasia of children continued, however), many of its staff, and much of its equipment, and expertise was redeployed to assist the SS in killing concentration-camp prisoners unfit for work. 'Himmler decided to outsource the first extermination program of his prisoners to the T-4 killers, rather than leaving it to the Camp SS' (Wachsmann, 2015: 245). The mass murder of concentration-camp prisoners that followed was neither merciful nor humane. Those killed included disabled veterans of the First World War, long-suffering Jews on the verge of starvation, and, from 1942, some German soldiers wounded on the Eastern Front. The programme (dubbed *Aktion 14f13*) started in April 1941, at Sachsenhausen, where peripatetic T-4 doctors selected those to be killed from lists prepared by the local Camp SS. In the following months, a dozen or so T-4 physicians visited most KL camps, including Auschwitz, Buchenwald, Dachau (which had the longest list: 2,000 prisoners), Flossenbürg, Gross-Rosen, Mauthausen, Neuengamme, and Ravensbrück (which was primarily for women).

One T-4 doctor likened the selection process to a 'conveyor belt' or 'assembly line'. The fate of each prisoner was typically decided in 5–10 minutes, usually after a cursory examination of the appropriate file and a brief 'inspection' of the prisoner in question. Once the final selection had been ratified by the T-4 head-office in Berlin, the prisoners were transported from their KL camp to one of the euthanasia centres: Bernburg and Sonnenstein in Saxony, and Hartheim near Linz. These centres used carbon monoxide gas chambers for the killing operation and crematoria for corpse disposal – after removing any gold fillings, the revenue from which 'more or less covered the cost of the killings. The murder machine was self-financing, as victims paid for their own extermination' (Wachsmann, 2015: 248). Moreover, in stark contrast to the brutality of the Camp SS, the T-4 doctors beguiled the prisoners with talk of 'light labour' and 'recuperation' in hospitals and sanatoria. By the middle of 1941, however, the prisoners were no longer fooled by such dissemblance. The self-financing and dissimulation of mass murder ('special treatment') using a combination of gas chambers (mocked up to resemble disinfecting showers, which were a common feature of camps and barracks the world over) and crematoria would be replicated on a vast scale in the six SS death factories. They comprised the three purpose-built *Aktion Reinhard* death camps at Belzec, Sobibor, and Treblinka, which 'were treated as a single unit with interchangeable personnel' (O'Neil, 2008: 71); the two existing KL camps at Auschwitz–Birkenau and Majdanek, which were expanded and refurbished for mass murder, whilst also continuing to function as slave-labour camps; and the camp at Chelmno, which used a mobile gas van that, 'like a perpetual motion machine, recycled exhaust fumes to kill its human cargo' (Friedlander, 1995: 286) rather than stationary gas chambers, and mass graves, pyres, and cremation pits rather than crematoria for corpse disposal. The heterogeneity of these camps should be stressed: 'In Majdanek it took several days to murder a thousand Jews; in Chelmno 1,000 could be murdered in a day; in the *Reinhardt* death camps, on average, 10,000 were murdered every day – at each camp!' (O'Neil, 2008: 71). Other KL camps had facilities for mass shootings: Janowska, Plaszow, Poniatowa, and Trawniki. 'The *Reinhardt* "death camps" were used specifically for solving the "Jewish Question." When they closed down, Auschwitz remained the principal site for mass elimination by gassing' (O'Neil, 2008: 236).

Initially, the *Aktion 14f13* selections for 'special treatment' were primarily on 'medical' grounds (those unfit for work), aggravated by other factors, such as 'race', criminality, homosexuality, and 'asocial' behaviour. 'Operation *14f13* practiced wanton killing of the sick and disabled in the camps and elsewhere', argues Gallagher (1997: 215). 'What the Germans at the time referred to as "wild euthanasia" led to additional widespread, unorganized, and indiscriminate killing.' Later, the selections would become primarily 'racial'. 'Sometime in autumn 1941, the leaders of Action 14f13 stepped up the murder of Jewish prisoners. … Several months before the Nazi regime embarked on the systematic extermination of European Jews, almost all Jews held inside concentration camps were regarded as candidates for the T-4 gas chambers' (Wachsmann, 2015: 254). The *Aktion 14f13* programme that outsourced 'special treatment' of KL prisoners to the T-4 euthanasia centres in Bernburg, Hartheim, and Sonnenstein lasted for nearly a year, during which time around 6,500 prisoners were killed in their gas chambers. 'The focus of the T-4 organization had shifted to a far bigger program of mass extermination – the Holocaust', notes Nikolaus Wachsmann (2015: 256). 'By spring 1942, many officials had already relocated to occupied eastern Europe, where they were in great demand for the new death camps at Belzec, Sobibor, and Treblinka; in comparison, the murder of KL prisoners in the "euthanasia" killing centres in Germany lost its significance.' Meanwhile, local Camp SS began T-4 style mass killings under their own volition: 'SS men in different camps explored different killing methods, as the spirit of lethal experimentation became all-pervasive' (Wachsmann, 2015: 257). The focus of the experiments were now Soviet POWs, under the codename *Aktion 14f14*, and the lessons learnt would subsequently be applied to the Jews. Given the regime of terror in the camps, and the slow destruction of people through starvation, lethal labour, and disease, the introduction of 'killing by asphyxiation may be said to have intensified the torment of the camp's Jews in degree, not in kind' (Mayer, 2012: 362). Finally, it is worth noting that despite the veneer of instrumentality, the T-4 doctors enjoyed their eugenic killing programmes. Henry Friedlander recounts a chilling example from one of the T-4 killing centres. All of the staff were gathered in 'the basement crematorium to participate in the burning of the ten thousandth victim. A naked corpse lay on a stretcher, covered with flowers. The supervisor Bünger made a speech, and a staff member dressed up as a cleric performed a ceremony. Every staff member received a bottle of beer' (Friedlander, 1995: 110).

Thus far, we have largely considered gas from the perspective of chemical weapons used on the entrenched battlefield and in enclosed spaces. However, weaponized gas needs to be understood within a much broader context of what one might call military aeration and weaponized air. Specifically, what I want to consider now is the rising up of airborne vehicles that enabled terrifying weaponry to rain down on the ground below. Balloons, airships, aeroplanes, rockets, and suchlike have all given rise to what Peter Sloterdijk (2009) has aptly called 'air tremors' or 'air quakes' (*Luftbeben*). But whereas Sloterdijk traces this explication of 'atmospheric terrorism' back to the trenches of the First World War, it actually began its deadly ascent at least a century earlier, just before the earth-shattering tremulations occasioned by the French Revolution (1789), and shortly after those unleashed by the Great Lisbon Earthquake (1755).

Amid the unprecedented 'weather panics of 1783' (Hamblyn, 2009: xviii), on 23 August, barely two months after the Montgolfier brothers had given the first-ever public demonstration of a 'hot air' balloon, which rose on a tether to an altitude of 1,000 feet, the American statesman, Benjamin Franklin – who was in Paris to negotiate the peace treaty that would formally end America's Revolutionary War with Britain – witnessed an amazing thing. He saw the first-ever public ascent of Jacques Charles's 'lighter than air' or 'inflammable air' (hydrogen) balloon called the *Globe*, which took off from the Champ de Mars. The untethered balloon eventually came down in the countryside 15 miles away. Within a month, a large crowd, including King Louis XVI and Marie Antoinette, watched as a new Montgolfier hot air balloon with an onboard furnace took the first-ever aeronauts into the sky – not a group of humans, but a trio of farmyard animals: a sheep, a rooster, and a duck; all of whom returned safely back to earth (Evans, 2002). (The first-ever astronaut, Laika, a stray mongrel from Moscow turned Soviet space-dog, was not so lucky. She died of overheating within hours of being launched into space onboard Sputnik 2 on 3 November 1957. The intention had been to euthanize Laika when the oxygen ran out.) A month after the animal-balloonist experiment, the first-ever human passenger ascended in a moored hot air balloon, and then, on 21 November 1783, the first-ever untethered 'free-flight' of a manned balloon included a military man as one of its two passengers. For the rest of the decade, 'all of Europe became caught up in "balloon fever"' (Evans, 2002: 24); just as it had been caught up in 'see-fever' a few decades earlier (Oettermann, 1997: 22) as a result of the quotidian 'discovery of the horizon', when it became a matter of immediate sensory experience rather than a mere mathematical abstraction. Ascending everything from church spires to mountain summits in order to experience unobstructed views of the horizon suddenly came into vogue, a fashion that was soon satisfied by a burgeoning 'see-fever' tourism industry (for which the novelty of ballooning was ideally suited), and the erection of all manner of viewing platforms and structures (thereby initiating the modern passion for skyscraping adventures in general, and the ur-form of skyscraping architecture in particular). 'In all periods, the city has trained its gaze on itself, at eye-level, along its streets and squares, or from the top of towers offering plunging views', argues Hubert Damisch (2001: 12). 'But only in the nineteenth century did architects multiply panoramic prospects by erecting all manner of belvederes and terraces, bridges, viaducts, elevated trains, and, before long, towers on a scale quite other from those of the medieval period', the most famous of which is undoubtedly Gustave Eiffel's tower in Paris, erected (temporarily) for the *Exposition Universelle* in 1889.

The invention of the manned hot air balloon in Paris in 1783, and the first permanent, truly immersive panorama exhibition in London in 1793, exemplified the desire for an all-encompassing, unmediated, and pan-optic view (Huhtamo, 2013; Oettermann, 1997); for an all-seeing view previously reserved for the gods that all too clearly heralded the fact that 'total war' was also on the horizon. Europe was indeed on the cusp of drifting into a new totality, which would prove to be a shattering experience for all concerned. This was the culmination of a long process of systematic 'de-shelling' that left humanity in a state of 'over-exposed' vulnerability in the face of machine-age 'horrorism' (Cavarero, 2011; Sloterdijk, 2011). And just as famous battles swiftly became a popular subject for panorama painters, the balloon swiftly became subject to military speculation. For example, in a letter written on 16 January 1784, Benjamin Franklin conjectured that balloons would convince sovereigns of 'the folly of war … since it will be impossible for the most potent of them to guard his dominions' (quoted in Evans, 2002: 24). For while he thought it feasible to secure a territory from a ground assault, since only its perimeter needed to be defended, it would be impossible to protect the entire area of the territory from an aerial assault of thousands of 'men descending from the clouds'. Already in 1784, then, air power promised to deliver unexpected terror 'from above' (Adey, Whitehead and Williams, 2013) that no nation down below could endure. If the realization of this promise would have to wait until well into the twentieth century, it was already an accomplished fact in the imaginary. 'Aeromobility [was] militarized from its inception' (Kaplan, 2013: 39).

By the turn of the twentieth century the terrifying potential of air power gripped popular culture. For example, H. G. Wells's celebrated 1908 novel, *The War in the Air*, envisaged a 'world war' in which aerial bombing would destroy every major city, precipitating social collapse. The description of New York under attack was prescient.

> Something had dropped from the aeroplane, something that looked small and flimsy. … The little man on the pavement jumped comically – no doubt with terror, as the bomb fell beside him. Then blinding flames squirted out in all directions from the point of impact, and the little man who had jumped became, for an instant, a flash of fire and vanished. … In this manner the massacre of New York began. She was the first of the great cities of the Scientific Age to suffer. … For that night he proposed only the wrecking of Broadway. He directed the air-fleet to move in column over the route of this thoroughfare, dropping bombs.

Indeed, upon first seeing Manhattan's skyline, Wells said: 'What a ruin it will make!' a sentiment echoed by Alfred Ludwig, the city's Chief Buildings Inspector, in 1911: 'The Titanic was unsinkable – yet she went down; our sky-scrapers are unburnable – yet we shall have a skyscraper disaster that will stagger humanity' (quoted in Goldsmith, 2015: 856 and 863, respectively). Between 1911 and 9/11, New York was 'damaged, destroyed, or otherwise devastated' in countless films, such as: '*King Kong* (1933) – destroyed by a giant monster rampage; *Fire* (1951) – destroyed by nuclear weapons; *When Worlds Collide* (1951) – destroyed by multiple natural disasters; *Invasion U.S.A.* (1952) – destroyed by a nuclear war; *Captive Women* (1952) – unknown destruction of the city; *The Beast from 20,000 Fathoms* (1953) – destroyed by a giant monster rampage', etc. (listed in Goldsmith, 2015: 856). New York has been in the throes of cinematic wrecking ever since the American Mutoscope and Biograph Company famously experimented with time-lapse photography in April 1901 to capture the demolition of the Star Theatre, which appears to dissolve into the ground. Indeed, still photography and animated photography are explosive media. They are media of demolition and dissolution, a predilec-tion that they share with the modern city itself (Barber, 2002).

Since ballooning in pre-revolutionary France was a pursuit – and often a folly – of the ruling elites, one of many novel spectacles designed to fill the existential void left by 'cognitive drift' and to distract 'the restless and pleasure loving imagination of the public' (Stafford, 1994: 23 and 225, respectively), it is hardly surprising that the Revolution curtailed 'balloon fever'. However, as civilian ballooning plummeted, military ballooning took off. In 1793, the French military formed a balloon service (*Les Aérostatiers*) that undertook reconnaissance missions (weather permitting). For example, at the Siege of Maubeuge in 1793, French aeronauts observed Austrian and Dutch troop movements. Overall, however, the service was a disappointment, and Napoleon disbanded it in 1802. Meanwhile, on the other side of the Atlantic, despite Benjamin Franklin's evident enthusiasm for ballooning, and his speculation about its role in warfare, suggestions for the military use of balloons during the Second Seminole War in Florida (1835–42), and also during the Mexican War (1846–8) to capture Vera Cruz Castle, fell on deaf ears (Evans, 2002). Nevertheless, when the American Civil War began in 1861, a number of aeronauts (primarily showmen) offered their services to the Union Army for reconnaissance of the Confederate forces. On 17 June 1861, Thaddeus Lowe tethered a balloon on Pennsylvania Avenue in Washington, opposite the White House, and, using a battery-powered telegraph key installed in the balloon and a wire that ran down one of the tether cables, he transmitted a message to the President, Abraham Lincoln. This was the first time 'an electronic transmission was sent from an aerial platform to earth' (Evans, 2002: 70). Lincoln was so impressed that he established a Union Army Balloon Corps under Lowe's command, despite stiff resistance from an incredulous army leadership, and all manner of obstacles, such as adverse weather and the difficulties of field deployment.

Before Lowe's Corps was even established, however, a rival, James Allen, had tried in vain to gather useful reconnaissance for the Union Army at the Battle of Harpers Ferry (June 1861), and Allen was earning a reputation for having unreliable equipment. Nevertheless, Lowe's Corps proved successful; so successful in fact that the Confederate Army established its own corps in 1862. Lowe's Corps was very inventive, particularly in terms of field equipment, such as: a 'telegraph train' (in the form of a horse-drawn wagon) to accompany the balloon; powerful oxyhydrogen-fuelled lights for illuminating the battlefield at night from the air; and the world's first 'aircraft carrier', which he created from an old barge, the *George Washington Parke Custis*. The 'balloon carrier' became operational on the Potomac River in November 1861, during the Battle of Port Royal. Lowe also toyed with the idea of aerial photography, but he only pursued this after the war. Likewise, the enemy invented new ways of deceiving the aerial observers, such as the construction of so-called 'Quaker guns' (piles of logs made to resemble gun batteries) and other forms of deception and camouflage. Aerial surveillance ushered in an epoch of needing to hide in plain sight, using the 'air-mindedness' of a 'camoufleur – to "think," "act" and "see" aeronautically' (Robinson, 2013: 147).

In the Civil War, balloons were only used for reconnaissance, and not for shooting, bombing, or troop deployment. Nevertheless, some balloons, such as the one used by John Wise, had percussion grenades and bombs for ballast. 'If Confederate forces were to overrun the position where the balloon was moored, Wise could rain down a barrage of explosives and then sever the tethering cables and float off' (Evans, 2002: 81). Manned balloons, then, had the capacity to bomb, and even as reconnaissance platforms they reputedly had a seriously demoralizing effect on those they observed, invariably eliciting jeers and insults, along with a hail of bullets and a barrage of missiles, but rarely with any success. The balloons were nearly always out of range, such that Union ground troops typically had to bear the brunt of the retaliation, and even if the balloon was hit, the 'cold shot' would merely puncture the fabric rather than cause the inflammable gas inside to catch fire. Once incendiary ammunition became available (e.g. magnesium tracer bullets) shortly before the outbreak of the First World War, however, military balloons became anachronistic. The Union Balloon Corps came to an end in 1863. Apart from a brief dabble with aerial photography from balloons in the 1890s, the next time that the US would undertake military aeronautics it would do so with aeroplanes.

Military ballooning was not entirely extinguished with the end of the Civil War. Brazil's king, Dom Pedro II, hired two Civil War veterans, James and Ezra Allen, to help form a balloon corps within the Brazilian army. This corps helped Brazil and its allies, Argentina and Uruguay, to defeat Paraguay during the War of the Triple Alliance (1864–70). Similarly, a German military observer with the Union Army had a fortuitous encounter with a veteran of its Balloon Corps, and thereafter returned to Germany, with a new-found passion for ballooning and a desire to create rigid-framed and fully navigable airships powered by internal combustion engines. His name was Count Ferdinand von Zeppelin. When the First World War began in 1914, Zeppelin's fleet of dirigible airships would be used not only for reconnaissance, but also for bombing (Evans, 2002). There is a certain irony that the first real taste of 'terror from the air' should be delivered over London from airships previously used to speed Europe's elite around the continent in state-of-the-art luxury. 'From 1909 to 1914, Zeppelin ships made about 1,600 flights in Europe, carrying over 37,000 passengers without accident' (Evans, 2002: 302). The Zeppelin is a perfect example of a dual-use technology: in one context it is entirely genteel; while in another it is truly frightful. Even the British military was sufficiently impressed by the Union Army Balloon Corps to create its own Royal Balloon Detachment in the 1870s, for reconnaissance and 'pacification' work in some of its more troublesome African colonies. The mere sight of balloons in the sky was supposedly sufficient to frighten natives into submission.

In 1849, Austria invented an unmanned bomb-carrying balloon, and launched a few hundred of them against Venice during the First Italian War of Independence (1848–9). Although they were ineffective, they were arguably the first occurrence of aerial bombing (Tanaka, 2009). Within a few years of the Wright Brothers successfully flying the first motorized aircraft in 1903, aeroplanes were being tested for their ability to drop bombs. In 1911, Italy deployed nine aeroplanes and two airships to bomb a Turkish encampment near Tripoli, while in the same year France started bombing rebels in Morocco. 'In the Balkan wars of 1912 and 1913, Bulgarian forces hired French and British pilots to bomb their enemies' (Tanaka, 2009: 11). Early on in the First World War, Zeppelins raided London with very limited impact: barely a few dozen were killed or injured. By the end of 1916, once the British Royal Flying Corps – the forerunner of the Royal Air Force (RAF) – had been equipped with incendiary bullets that could shoot down the highly flammable airships, the Zeppelins were rapidly phased out of military use and replaced by the much more effective Gotha and Giant aeroplanes. Nevertheless, the Zeppelin fleet enjoyed a long and illustrious post-war career transporting civilian passengers around the world, until the infamous *Hindenburg* disaster on 6 May 1937 destroyed the airship's reputation. Newsreels filmed the hydrogen-filled airship catch fire and crash to the ground, killing 35 of the 97 people on board, as it attempted to dock in Manchester Township, New Jersey.

The first Hague peace conference in 1899 had anticipated the emergence of aerial bombardment, from balloons at that time, and considered permanently prohibiting their use, but in the event the 'Declaration on the Launching of Projectiles from Balloons' was only adopted for five years. When the Declaration was reintroduced in 1907, it was ratified by 15 countries, but not by some of the emerging air powers, such as France, Germany, Italy, Japan, and Russia. Many argued that the 'precision' of aerial bombing made it a uniquely powerful weapon, potentially enabling future wars to be accomplished more swiftly and with much less suffering. Bombing from the air was said to be supremely effective and essentially humane. Ever since, however, aerial bombing has been more like 'terror from the air' (Sloterdijk, 2009) – air frightfulness, *blitzkrieg*, terror bombing, area bombing, carpet bombing, shock and awe, and so on and so forth. And yet the mythology of its precision and cleanliness continues: surgical strikes, smart bombs, etc. Accordingly, such 'terror from the air' merits closer attention.

9

Atmospheric Terrorism

Exterminatory Air Conditioning

Here, even the sky is dead.

William Sharpe, quoted in Goldsmith, 2015: 845

The weaponization of gas and air since the 1790s, exemplified by the advent of military ballooning, the rise of gas warfare, and the construction of death factories fitted out with gas chambers and crematoria, is part of a wider ensemble that Peter Sloterdijk (2009) calls 'atmospheric terrorism' and 'black meteorology' – the application of weaponized science and military technology to the explication (unfolding) of lethal environments. Sloterdijk only traces this explication of 'environmental terrorism' back to the entrenched battle-fields of the First World War, and specifically to 22 April 1915, when the newly formed German gas regiment released chlorine gas on the Franco–Canadian infantry positions near Ypres, and in so doing transformed the atmosphere itself from a life-support system into a killing apparatus. One can immediately see the appeal of this killing operation in the context of trenches, tunnels, and bunkers, all of which render bullets and shells less and less effective. When chemical weapons penetrate these enclosed environments, however, they render them unliveable, necessitating the introduction of defensive measures to prevent the internal atmosphere from becoming lethal. For Sloterdijk, then, the key killing innovation of the twentieth century was the tendency to target not the body of the enemy directly, but his or her environment. This, he says, is the critical insight of terrorism, which is at root a kind of 'atmospheric terrorism' or 'atmos-terrorism' – the exploration of the environment from the perspective of its destructibility, the precursors of which we have mentioned in preceding chapters, such as poisoning watercourses and smoking-out besieged structures.

The fallout from the worldwide advent of 'atmospheric terrorism' is particularly apparent in the transformation of the landscape through bunker architecture – those 'cathedrals of artillery', as Friedrich Tamms referred to them – during the Second World War and the Cold War, from the modesty of pillboxes to the majesty of the Atlantic Wall, and its quotidian expression in the concrete Brutalism that cemented cities and fortified life in the shadow of nuclear war.

Consider how far air power has been explicated (unfolded) by science and technology since the small steps taken in 1806, by Francis Beaufort, a ship's commander in Britain's Royal Navy, who solved the seemingly intractable problem of creating an exact wind-scale for sea-going vessels by adapting a technique that had been developed for the sails of windmills. The force of the wind could be inferred from the physical state of the sail: from the zero-degree of complete calm to the limit of what a sail could withstand in a storm. In so doing, the sails of a fully rigged frigate became a precise instrument for recording wind intensity. The use of the eponymous 'Beaufort scale' became mandatory for every vessel in the Royal Navy in 1838. By replacing the vagaries of inexact descriptive terminology with precise measurements that allowed little if any interpretative discretion, thousands of logbooks from across the world were suddenly rendered commensurable, thereby enabling the Admiralty to interrogate the conduct of its captains, particularly with respect to the pursuit of enemy vessels. 'A captain who allowed the enemy to outrun him ... was soon going to find himself in trouble' (Hamblyn, 2001: 200). Meteorological logbooks that incorporated the Beaufort scale allowed the Admiralty to discipline errant captains as never before, much like verbatim transcripts of Inquisitorial investigations sourced from across the Holy Roman Empire enabled the authorities in Rome to control wayward Inquisitors, especially with respect to the misuse of torture. 'Beaufort's wind scale, in describing precisely the state of a ship under sail, and thus the exact power of the prevailing wind, was so useful to naval prosecutors that it might have been expressly designed to offer material evidence to the courts' (Hamblyn, 2001: 200). Most of the meteorological innovations of the nineteenth and twentieth centuries have been the result of military explication, from its observation and measurement to its modelling and simulation.

A century or two after Beaufort's scale, the techno-scientific explication of air power has moved well beyond weather observation to weather modification, such as cloud, precipitation, and storm enhancement through chemical seeding, and even environmental modification using chemical weapons in the form of pesticides, insecticides, herbicides, and defoliants, and other more or less hubristic geo-engineering 'solutions' to catastrophic climatic change, such as 'ocean fertilization', 'cloud brightening', and 'space sunshades'. For instance, in the Second World War's Pacific theatre, lice and mosquitoes were arguably more deleterious to American military personnel than enemy troops. Consequently, the US Army's Chemical Warfare Service (CWS), and Office for

Scientific Research and Development, coordinated the work of the military's chemical warfare laboratories and civilian pest-control laboratories to create pesticides and insecticides to combat mosquitoes and lice, such as pyrethrum-based aerosol bombs and louse powder. However, with supplies of pyrethrum curtailed by war, an alternative pesticide was urgently required. It came in the guise of dichlorodiphenyltrichloroethane (DDT), which made 'one of the more dazzling debuts in public health history' in December 1943, as part of a pro-gramme of 'dusting over a million civilians in Naples with louse powder' to curtail a typhus epidemic (Russell, 2001: 127). Chemical warfare equipment, such as backpacks, trucks, boats, helicopters, and aeroplanes, was easily repur-posed for spraying DDT from both the air and at ground level. However, there was always a risk that during deployment it could be mistaken for a poison-gas attack. This occurred at Iwo Jima, when US aeroplanes spraying DDT inadver-tently flew into Japanese-held territory. DDT also killed much more than lice and mosquitoes. Indeed, DDT was sometimes sprayed in such enormous quan-tities that it killed nearly all of the plant, bird, and animal life in an area, as happened on the Japanese island of Saipan. In the decades after the Second World War, DDT was redeployed for use in peacetime, especially for pest control in agriculture and cities. However, it was revealed to pose significant risks to ecosystems as well as to human health, not least through the transmission of toxins through the food chain, becoming a cause célèbre for the nascent envi-ronmental movement, following the publication of Rachel Carson's *Silent Spring* in 1962.

During the First Indochina War (1946–54), the French discovered '[t]he effec-tiveness of napalm for burning woods and crops' (SIPRI, 1975: 43). In the early 1950s, during the Malayan 'Anti-British National Liberation War' (1948–60) – or 'Malayan Emergency', as the British called it (since the term 'emergency', rather than 'war', enabled losses incurred by British plantation and mining interests in the colony to be recovered from their London-based insurers) – the British military concluded that incendiary weapons such as napalm were inef-fective for igniting sodden tropical rainforest. Consequently, in order to clear the roadside vegetation from which Malayan guerrillas launched their ambushes, Britain was the first country to use herbicides and defoliants as weapons. In conjunction with its American ally, Britain developed 'Agent Orange' to clear tropical vegetation, using modified fire engines to spray the herbicide. Agent Orange was also sprayed on crops from helicopters in an attempt to destroy the guerrillas' food supply. It was during the Vietnam War (1955–75), however, which spanned Cambodia and Laos, as well as Vietnam, that the US military used herbicides and defoliants, most notably Agent Orange, to eliminate vegeta-tion cover and to destroy crops on a vast scale. Between 1961 and 1972, at least 75 million litres were sprayed over 4.5 million acres of Vietnam, leaving in its wake not only environmental devastation but also serious health problems for the human population, which ranged from birth defects to cancer. Taken together, napalm and Agent Orange allowed 'terror from the air' to cast its dominion over the countryside, the jungle, and forests alike (Shaw, 2016). Napalm became synonymous with air power. For instance, it was used extensively during the Korean War (1950–3) and the Algerian War (1954–62).

After the US unilaterally renounced the hostile use of environmental modification techniques in 1972, and subsequently called for an international agreement 'prohibiting the use of any environmental or geophysical modification activity as a weapon of war', the US and USSR held bilateral discussions in 1974 and 1975. This led to the UN *Convention on the Prohibition of Military or Any Other Hostile Use of Environmental Modification Techniques*, which came into force in 1978. It prohibits the 'hostile use of environmental modification techniques having widespread, long-lasting or severe effects as the means of destruction, damage or injury to any other State Party' (Article 1). Under this Convention, the phrase environmental modification techniques 'refers to any technique for changing – through the deliberate manipulation of natural processes – the dynamics, composition or structure of the Earth, including its biota, lithosphere, hydrosphere and atmosphere, or of outer space' (Article 2). The Convention's Consultative Committee of Experts listed illustrative examples of phenomena that could be caused by the use of such techniques: 'earthquakes; tsunamis; an upset in the ecological balance of a region; changes in weather patterns ...; changes in climate patterns; changes in ocean currents; changes in the state of the ozone layer; and changes in the state of the ionosphere'. The Convention does not prohibit the 'peaceful' use of environmental modification techniques, nor the military or hostile use of techniques that are not widespread, or long lasting, or severely harmful, such as most pesticides, insecticides, herbicides, and defoliants. Moreover, for all of the efforts to 'weaponize the weather', warfare remains stubbornly subject to its contingencies.

If the explication (unfolding) of 'environmental terrorism' emerged from the gas-drenched trenches of the First World War, and reached its zenith in the 'atmospheric terrorism' of the nuclear explosions over Hiroshima and Nagasaki in the Second World War, then it is worth interpolating two other kinds of entrenched killing into this state-driven trajectory. The first of these occurs in the urban fabric of the modern metropolis, which has proven itself to be a perfect environment for acts of atmospheric terror: from tear gas and water cannons to improvised explosive devices and suicide bombers (Bargu, 2014; Mahajan, 2016; Merriman, 2016). The quintessential act of atmospheric terror in the city is the car and truck bomb. One of the first exploded on 16 September 1920, on the corner of Wall Street in New York, adjacent to the Assay Office and opposite J. P. Morgan & Co., one of the world's most powerful financial institutions at the time. The bomb killed 38 people and injured hundreds. It was treated as a national emergency, with 100 soldiers deployed to guard Wall Street. The bomb was actually a horse-drawn wagon filled with explosives and cast-iron bars, and detonated using a timer. The bomber is believed to have been an Italian immigrant, Mario Buda, who struck in retaliation for the imprisonment of his anarchist comrades: 'a poor immigrant with some stolen dynamite, a pile of scrap metal, and an old horse had managed to bring unprecedented terror to the inner sanctum of American capitalism' (Davis, 2007a: 3).

Buda's exploding horse-drawn cart was arguably 'the prototype car bomb: the first modern use of an inconspicuous vehicle ... to transport large quantities of high explosives into precise range of a high-value target' (Davis, 2007a: 4). His innovation built on the *fin-de-siècle* experience of explosive justice practised by anarchist and revolutionary organizations the world over. For example, the People's Will (1878–81), a Russian revolutionary group, was one of the first to use bombs to accomplish popular justice and revolutionary transformation: precisely targeted political assassinations intended to precipitate the collapse of the Tsarist regime. 'Its greatest success was on 1 March 1881, when the carriage of Alexander II was blown up, killing the tsar' (Fotion, Kashnikov, and Lekea, 2007: 26). The group was quickly liquidated by the police, however. The Socialist Revolutionary Party (1901–18), a successor organization, was much more effective, employing assassination to devastating effect: 'during a one-year period beginning in October 1905, 3,611 government officials of all ranks were killed and wounded throughout the empire. ... Between 1894 and 1916, close to 17,000 individuals became victims of revolutionary terrorists' (Fotion, Kashnikov, and Lekea, 2007: 27). Those killed were not only leading figures in the Tsarist regime, and its front-line operatives, such as police officers and military personnel, but also its bureaucratic functionaries, as well as ostensibly 'innocent' civilians.

The culpability of supposedly 'good people' is well illustrated by the fate of anti-communist intellectuals expelled from Russia in 1922, on a boat dubbed '*The Philosophy Steamer*' (Chamberlain, 2006). One of those expelled was Nikolai Lossky, a thoroughly kind and decent gentleman, who 'had enjoyed with his family the comfortable life of the haute bourgeoisie' (Žižek, 2009: 8). In the wake of the Bolshevik Revolution in October 1917, Lossky 'simply couldn't understand who would want to destroy his way of life' (Chamberlain, 2006: 23). To which Slavoj Žižek (2009: 8) replies: 'such an attitude betrays a breathtaking insensitivity to the *systemic* violence that had to go on for such a comfortable life to be possible'. Bertolt Brecht put it beautifully in *The Interrogation of the Good*: 'Step forward: we hear / That you are a good man. ... / This is why we shall / Now put you in front of a wall. But in consideration of your merits and good qualities. / We shall put you in front of a good wall and shoot you / With a good bullet from a good gun and bury you / With a good shovel in the good earth' (translated by Žižek, 2009: 32–3).

Vehicular bombs gradually emerged as an ideal weapon for clandestine yet spectacular urban warfare, with notable car and truck bombings in cities such as Haifa (1947), Saigon (1952 and 1964–6), Algiers (1962), Palermo (1963), Madison (1970), Belfast (1972), Beirut (1983), London (1992–6), Oklahoma City (1995), and New York (1993), with the latter inflicting damage to the

World Trade Center in Manhattan that amounted to hundreds of millions of dollars, but at a cost to the bombers of less than $4,000, one of whom was arrested when he tried in vain to retrieve the $400 deposit on the rental truck used in the attack. Indistinguishable from regular traffic, vehicular bombs are 'cheap to fabricate and astonishingly powerful: they elevated urban terrorism from the artisan to the industrial level and made possible sustained blitzes against entire city centers' (Davis, 2007a: 5). Such campaigns were rarely undertaken by lone bombers or small cells, but mostly by states and quasi-state agencies: the military, secret services, and guerrilla forces. 'Ironically the classical "weapon of the weak" is also the most popular clandestine instruments of terror employed by strong governments and superpowers' (Davis, 2007a: 11).

Car and truck bombs have been employed as semi-strategic weapons comparable to air power: a kind of 'poor man's air force' (Davis, 2007a: 4), just as radioactive material looks likely to become the poor man's nuclear weapon (so-called 'dirty bombs' or radiological dispersal devices). Car and truck bombs are 'stealth weapons of surprising power and destructive efficiency' (Davis (2007a: 8). Moreover, since they are so inexpensive and simple to deploy, they have enabled the military and political 'enfranchisement of marginal actors in modern history' (Davis, 2007a: 11). The four hijacked civilian aeroplanes that were used in the 11 September 2001 al-Qaeda attacks on the World Trade Center's 'Twin Towers' in Manhattan (both destroyed), the Pentagon in Arlington, Virginia (partially destroyed), and either the Capitol Building or the White House in Washington (this part of the attack was foiled when the aeroplane was brought down over Somerset County, Pennsylvania), literalized the metaphor of a 'poor man's air force' to devastating effect. The attacks precipitated a chain reaction of wealth destruction that may well have amounted to several trillion dollars once all of the costs associated with the loss of life, property, infrastructure, jobs, stock-market capitalization, and suchlike are taken into account. They also precipitated a chain reaction of societal destruction. First and foremost, consider the worldwide 'War on Terror', which includes disastrous wars in Afghanistan, Iraq, and Syria (Operation Enduring Freedom, Operation Iraqi Freedom, Operation Inherent Resolve, etc.), and US drone strikes in Pakistan, Somalia, and Yemen, especially 'signature' assassinations based on 'patterns of behaviour' (literally 'guilt by association' – killing those who resemble the traits of a certain class of target) rather than on the actual identity of those killed (who are summarily executed for being who they are). Second, consider the post-Cold War revival of geopolitical paranoia, which has sustained a seemingly endless 'state of emergency' that is being ruthlessly exploited by an ever-expanding 'disaster capitalism' complex (as distinct from the much more narrow notion of a 'military–industrial' complex) that is profiting from the increasingly lucrative business of disaster, emergency, catastrophe, and apocalypse, some of which are still rather quaintly dubbed 'natural disasters', such as earthquakes and tsunamis, and some of which are self-evidently cultivated by the evil demon of humanity, such as nuclear accidents, financial crises, and civil wars (Klein, 2008; Loewenstein, 2015; Parenti, 2011; Virilio, 2012). Finally, consider the transmogrification of warfare into international military policing (Neocleous, 2014) and humanitarian warfare (Weizman, 2008), which is exemplified by the extrajudicial killings and targeted assassinations accomplished by the now iconic rich man's car bomb – the lethal versions of those remotely piloted or unmanned aerial vehicles (RPAVs and UAVs) that are commonly referred to as 'drones' (Benjamin, 2013; Cohn, 2015; Chamayou, 2015; Gregory, 2014; Medea, 2013). The Israel Defense Force (IDF) 'employs the sanitizing term "focused obstruction" or "focused preemption" to describe these assassinations' (Weizman, 2008: 334).

The second kind of entrenched killing that should be interpolated between the battlefields of the First World War and the nuclear deathscapes of the Second is the fumigation industry, which overcame stiff agricultural and consumer resistance (Allen, 2008) to expand rapidly in the closing decades of the nineteenth century and the opening decades of the twentieth to combat pests in the city and the countryside: bed bugs, cockroaches, fleas, lice, rats, ticks, and other pestilent life-forms – 'the much-unloved wildlife that has so triumphantly colonized the domestic territories of human habitation' (William Cronon, in Biehler, 2013: x). This was a civilian precursor to the chemical warfare unleashed against mosquitoes and lice by the US Army's CWS in the 1940s, primarily using insecticides such as DDT, and a successor to the chemical warfare waged against the bacterial contamination of meat, primarily using salt, smoke, and ice. From the 1890s, structures such as warehouses, ships' holds, grain silos, and storerooms were simply sealed and fumigated, while open areas, such as orchards, were covered ('tented') to create an enclosed environment that could be made lethal (Biehler, 2013). The fumigation of infested houses and apartments in high-density and impoverished inner-city neighbourhoods was especially challenging for early fumigators. Given the absence of regulation, the novelty of the fumigation techniques, and the concentration of city-dwellers in poor-quality housing, a great many people were accidentally killed or injured by toxic chemicals.

Bed bugs, which European colonists had inadvertently brought with them to the New World (along with religious fundamentalism, smallpox, and a host of other lethal viruses), were essentially ineradicable from the late nineteenth-century American city-centre home. None of the early pesticides and fumigants was entirely successful in eliminating bed bugs (arsenic-based paint, mercuric chloride, sulphur candles, or naphtha), and so the war waged against them was not really a 'war of extermination', but rather a war of containment, suppression, and attrition. Such an unwinnable conflict required continual labour (washing, cleaning, scrubbing, disinfecting, etc.) and continual expense (on all manner of commercially available pesticides, cleaning aids, and associated gadgets, such as the Flit spray pump, famously advertised in the 1920s and 1930s with illustrations by the future Dr Seuss), both of which dramatically exacerbated the social injustice of living with domestic infestation. Moreover, the responsibility for day-to-day combat in defence of so-called 'public' health was put firmly in the hands of 'private' citizens and individual households, and housing codes increasingly placed obligations on individual landlords, such as calling upon the services of commercial pest-control firms in the event of an infestation. 'Wealthy households reduced their burden of bedbugs through the assiduous labor of their housekeeping staff, setting a trend that middle-class and low-income families tried to meet with their own sweat' (Biehler, 2013: 80). The poor, who invariably lived in the most infested housing due to the malign neglect of landlords, had little chance of even short-term success. Even the advent of motorized vacuum cleaners, in conjunction with metal-framed beds that had far fewer crevices than timber-framed beds, made relatively little headway against the bed bug in the opening decades of the twentieth century, not least because central heating and increased mobility favoured the bugs.

From the 1900s, some American domestic fumigators began to advertise themselves as 'exterminators', and they soon had access to the technology and the pesticides to live up to the hyperbole. What revolutionized the domestic pest-control industry was the adoption of hydrogen cyanide or 'prussic acid' (HCN) as their fumigant of choice: an extremely poisonous, colourless, and almost odourless liquid that turns to gas above 26°C. HCN was first used as an experimental pesticide in 1887, when the US Department of Agriculture (USDA) and University of California used it to fumigate citrus orchards infested with scale insects. HCN was so effective that it was soon being used in the 1890s to fumigate everything from greenhouses to factories – but rarely to fumigate homes, until the USDA started promoting such a use at the dawn of the twentieth century. 'HCN stood apart from existing bedbug poisons because a single fumigation filled every nook and cranny in the home, killing every adult and nymph, and even extinguishing tough bug eggs. Between 1901 and the 1910s, USDA released instructions for HCN fumigation for a variety of room sizes and pests' (Biehler, 2013: 67).

With the adoption of HCN urban pest-control firms gradually transformed their collective public persona from glorified rat-catchers to a profession delivering a modern public-health service that was sanitary, scientific, and humane. HCN was a very powerful fumigant, however, which inadvertently killed and injured many people as its unregulated use in crowded cities burgeoned. In the 1920s and 1930s, local regulations evolved slowly, unevenly, and inconsistently, usually in response to the vagaries of particular accidents vying for public and political attention. 'Many required exterminators to obtain insurance policies ... for damages, injuries, and deaths that might result from a botched job', as well as 'minimum airing-out times, evacuation of buildings, and use of sentinels and warning placards' (Biehler, 2013: 70 and 71, respectively). The pest-control industry, however, invariably resisted almost all attempts to regulate its domestic fumigations – with the exception of training and licencing requirements, since these tended to legitimate the trade in the eyes of the paying public, and served as barriers to entry for new and opportunistic firms trying to join such a lucrative market. Moreover, in impoverished inner-city residential districts 'few families could afford to hire a private exterminator, much less one that could comply with local HCN ordinances' (Biehler, 2013: 73). Treating this kind of environment effectively had to wait until the 1940s, using groundbreaking communal 'disinfestation' regimes developed for the newly created public housing in cities such as Chicago (although the cost remained the responsibility of each household rather than public housing authorities). These regimes relied upon HCN until DDT became available in 1945, in yet another instance of some toxic military fallout being mistaken for a peacetime miracle.

So, while the gas regiments of the First World War took weaponized chemicals into the trenches (chlorine, phosgene, and sulphur 'mustard' gas), the pest-control industry in the interwar period took them back into civilian spaces in an enormous urban-sanitation campaign that presented itself as a war of extermination, frequently of biblical and apocalyptic proportions (Biehler, 2013; Russell, 2001). Atmospheric terrorism was rehabilitated for its 'peaceful' use of exterminating everything from ants to weevils. Between 1917 and 1920, around 20 million cubic metres of the built environment had been gassed in Germany alone: boats, barracks, schools, hospitals, windmills, silos, and suchlike. Moreover, the 'delousing' with pesticides of groups of people on the move became increasingly common in a wide range of settings, including prisons, barracks, and encampments. An article from the *New York Times* on 17 July 1921, concerning a new 'delousing plant' on Hoffman Island for newly arriving immigrants selected for quarantine, is a salutary example. The article was written in the context of what the newspaper referred to as 'the typhus invasion' brought to America by European immigrants, which the Surgeon General characterized as a 'national emergency'.

> The immigrants who are to go through the process of delousing enter a room capable of accommodating groups of seventy-five to one hundred at a time. They are asked to remove their clothes. ... The bags full of clothing are put through two chambers, where they are treated with cyanide gas ... or with steam under pressure. ... Immigrants then pass into a series of shower baths where they are treated with a certain mixture of soap and oil or acetic acid, of which the principle is that the vermin are suffocated. The men's hair is cut off and the women's hair is thoroughly treated with oil. ... [T]his process is calculated to maintain, as much as is compatible with thoroughness and efficiency, the dignity and pride of the individual. Immigrants can be handled at the rate of 100 an hour, and ... are absolutely sterilized so far as carrying typhus is concerned.

The intertwining of wartime and peacetime fumigation is well illustrated by Professor Fritz Haber, the Nobel Prize-winning brains behind Germany's First

World War gas-warfare programme. He also perfectly illustrates the academic complicity in the unfolding of enlightened killing and atmospheric terrorism. In '1919, Haber's institute developed a cyanide-based gas, Zyklon-A, actually for use in pest control. ... [O]thers would modify it to produce Zyklon-B, thereafter used extensively against insects. Ultimately, however, it was the main gas used in the holocaust gas chambers' (Preston, 2015: 272). Despite his wartime service, Haber was a Jew, and went into exile in 1933, dying shortly thereafter. The pest-control product branded Zyklon A was a significant innovation for the fumigation industry because it was an HCN product that could be smelt by humans, thus making it much safer to use. Patented in 1926, a revolutionary new HCN product, branded Zyklon B, came in a solid form (canned pellets), making it much easier and safer to store, transport, and use than HCN in liquid or gaseous form. An eye irritant was added to Zyklon B as a precautionary measure against inadvertent exposure: 'tear gas' would alert the person to the co-presence of 'poison gas'. When cans of Zyklon B were opened up to warm air, the pellets inside released the lethal HCN gas. It was widely used for disinfecting clothing, warehouses, cargo holds, and similar structures. As the Nazis embarked on their biopolitical and necropolitical 'Final Solution' to their ill-conceived 'Jewish Question', using 'extraordinary means' and 'special treatment', they literalized their pseudo-scientific characterization of Jews as 'the lice of civilized humanity', as Goebbels' diary entry for 2 November 1941 chillingly put it, and their hyperbolic discourse of an 'anti-parasite struggle' against the Jews – and also against the so-called 'Gypsy Plague' of 'asocials' and 'workshy' pests with 'alien blood', which resulted in the 'murder of between one-quarter and one-half million Roma and Sinti' (Milton, 1997: 171). The SS established gas chambers in their extermination camps not to grant a 'mercy death' to lives unworthy of life, but rather to fumigate the rapidly expanding 'living space' (*Lebensraum*) of the Reich. 'Antisemitism is exactly the same as delousing', declared Himmler. 'Getting rid of lice is not a question of ideology. It is a matter of cleanliness', he insisted. 'We shall soon be deloused. We have only 20,000 lice left, and then the matter is finished within the whole of Germany' (speech to SS officers in April 1943, quoted in Raffles, 2011: 141).

Having learnt from the *Aktion 14f13* programme, which as we have already noted employed *Aktion T-4* medical expertise and facilities to kill concentration-camp inmates using carbon monoxide (diesel engine exhaust fumes), the SS turned their murderous attention to Soviet POWs, whom they envisaged coming into the KL system in their hundreds of thousands, if not millions. Under the codename *Aktion 14f14*, across the KL system the 'SS experimented with different killing methods. The most fateful trials took place in Auschwitz in early September 1941: inspired by the "euthanasia" killings, the local SS began to use gas ... to kill hundreds of these Soviet "commissars"' (Wachsmann, 2010: 29). As the anticipated influx of Soviet POWs failed to materialize, and as the programme of systematically exterminating European Jewry gathered momentum in 1941 and 1942, Zyklon B would displace both shooting and carbon-monoxide gassing as the principal way to accomplish the so-called 'Final Solution', and it would be used in purpose-built fumigation chambers working alongside crematoria at two of the six death camps: Auschwitz–Birkenau and Majdanek. (Belzec, Chelmno, Sobibor, and Treblinka relied on carbon monoxide. Majdanek used both carbon monoxide and Zyklon B.)

A variant of Zyklon B, which did not include the cautionary eye irritant, was provided to the 'hygiene sections' (killing squads) at Auschwitz–Birkenau and Majdanek for the 'special treatment' of the Jews. In keeping with the 'delousing' ruse, the canisters arrived in faux medical vehicles, and were administered in sealed fumigation chambers mocked up to look like disinfecting showers with changing rooms. What set Auschwitz–Birkenau apart as a death factory was the fact that it grew to such a gigantic size and operated so relentlessly. It could hold over 100,000 prisoners at any one time, and could kill and cremate 20,000 a day when functioning at full capacity. Once the extermination process was in operation, most newly arriving Jews were 'selected' for immediate extermination, without being registered as KL prisoners or indeed tattooed (a practice unique to Auschwitz). Nevertheless, 'by August 1943, there were 224,000 registered prisoners in all SS concentration camps, of whom 74,000 were held in Auschwitz. Previously, concentration camps resembled small towns; Auschwitz turned into a metropolis' (Wachsmann, 2010: 31). When Himmler ordered the cessation of killing by gas in November 1944, at least 1,100,000 Jews had been murdered at Auschwitz, ample proof that 'the camps were much better at mass killing than production' (Wachsmann, 2010: 29). Of the 7,000 or so staff who worked at Auschwitz–Birkenau during its operation, fewer than 1,000 were punished.

Given that over 3 million people were killed in purpose-built gas chambers during the Second World War, it is peculiar to think that things were very different on the battlefield. 'That no side used gas in the Second World War is perhaps the first example of the effectiveness of mutual deterrence', suggests Diana Preston (2015: 273). However, this reluctance did not prevent them from continuing to develop such weapons. For example, in 1937, IG Farben discovered the first nerve gas, *Tabun*, whilst developing insecticides, and, a year later, an even more toxic nerve gas: *Sarin*. Unsurprisingly, the Germans recognized the military potential of these toxins and managed to weaponize them by 1942: 'there was enough tabun available to kill the whole population of London, and the Luftwaffe had nearly half a million gas bombs ... German engineers even produced warheads capable of carrying the bases on the V1 and V2 rockets launched against Britain' (Preston, 2015: 272). Moreover, far from being averse to using chemical weapons during the Second World War, both the Allies and the Axis powers did precisely that. Not in the form of gas clouds released from cylinders on an entrenched battlefield, which would have been an anachronism, but rather in the form of incendiary bombing. Most people killed by incendiaries died from asphyxiation rather than burning, not just because of the inhalation of smoke and toxic fumes, but also because incendiaries rapidly deoxygenate the air. It is to this scene of 'atmospheric terrorism' that we now turn, where air power explicated its capacity for creating fearsome 'airquakes' to an extraordinary degree.

(10)

Black Meteorology

Experimental Airquakes and Lethal Landscapes

Peter Sloterdijk rightly rejects the Romantic notion of aerial warfare as a chivalrous joust between daring aeronauts, such as Adolphe Pégoud, the original 'flying ace' (*l'as*), who is also credited with making the first parachute jump from a 'sacrifice aeroplane', or Manfred von Richthofen, the legendary 'Red Baron'. Rather, it is a form of 'terror from the air', an 'airquake'. Airquake is a word that has been in English usage since the 1740s (although earthquake and seaquake entered into English usage much earlier, during the fourteenth and seventeenth centuries, respectively). It has been used to denote a 'tremor felt in the air' – a 'sonic boom' – such as the sound that accompanies lightning. In the context of air power, and especially *blitzkrieg* (lightning war), Sloterdijk lends the word 'airquake' (*Luftbeben*) a new meaning and significance. 'If, in their history to date, humans could step out at will under any given stretch of sky ... and take for granted ... the possibility of breathing in the surrounding atmosphere, then ... they enjoyed a privilege of naivety which was withdrawn with the caesura of the 20th century' (Sloterdijk, 2009: 50). The explication (unfolding) of 'atmospheric terrorism' that spans the first half of the twentieth century, from the ephemeral airquakes of gas attacks to the durable airquakes of nuclear bombings, is only one portion of a much broader explication of air power that we have already unfolded through the airquakes of fumigating all manner of human and non-human 'pests' as well as the airquakes that carried air power itself aloft, starting with balloons, airships, and aeroplanes, and then missiles, satellites, and drones. Having considered gas and air, the time has finally come to consider wind and fire, since they form a pair of elemental axes around which air power revolves. Setting fire to the landscape dates back to Antiquity – recall, for example, Samson's incineration of the Philistines' crops using firebrands affixed to the tails of foxes – but the ascent of air power has explicated such a measly airquake to almost unimaginably grotesque proportions. The destruction caused by earthquakes and seaquakes (such as Lisbon in 1755, San Francisco in 1906, and Sumatra in 2004) is of a piece with the destruction caused by incendiary and nuclear airquakes (such as Dresden and Tokyo, and Hiroshima and Nagasaki, all in 1945). Yet one of the great ironies of incendiary airquakes is that while they may readily lay claim to vast material destruction, the one thing that they were designed to destroy (supposedly with great ease) appears to have consistently eluded them: the enemy's morale. This is another characteristic that air power shares with car and truck bombs, as the world rediscovered when three small airquakes struck the Twin Towers and Pentagon, leaving lethal vapour trails in their wake that stretched from New York and Washington to Afghanistan, Iraq, Pakistan, and beyond. Terror from the air came 'out of the blue' (Bernstein, 2002), and it continues to rain down its toxic ash clouds the world over.

In the dying days of the nineteenth century the ground was fortuitously opened up to the weaponry of the future: aerial bombardment. 'At the first Hague peace conference of 1899, a principle that had been enshrined in warfare since the Middle Ages, that only fortified towns might be attacked, was abandoned. ... In 1907, at the second conference, ... the bombardment from the sea of undefended towns was recognised as a permitted act of war' (Patterson, 2007: 93). Having inadvertently cleared the way for aerial bombardment, 'shortly before 1910, the military forces of each major European nation began purchasing planes and airships, and by the outbreak of World War I in 1914, Germany possessed 246 planes and 11 airships, England had 110 planes and 6 airships, France owned 169 planes and 4 airships, while Russia had 300 planes and 11 airships' (Tanaka, 2009: 9). Although small in number, the mere existence of military aircraft in 1914 was remarkable considering that the first powered aeroplane flight happened in 1903. From these humble beginnings the air forces of the Allied and Central powers grew dramatically over the course of the war. For example, an astonishing '100,000 warplanes were produced in France and England', notes Yuki Tanaka (2009: 12). The vast majority of these aeroplanes were destroyed during the conflict (mostly through obsolescence and crashing rather than from being shot down). By the time the war ended in November 1918, 'the British forces possessed almost 23,000 planes, having entered the war with only 110' (Tanaka, 2009: 12), while France ended up with around 4,500. Moreover, at the start of the war aeroplanes were crude, flimsy, and typically used for short-range reconnaissance, and bombing amounted to little more than dropping lightweight bombs by hand over the side of the aeroplane with woeful success. By the end of the war, aeroplanes were much more technologically sophisticated and functionally differentiated, including: observation balloons, reconnaissance aircraft equipped with cameras, highly manoeuvrable fighters, ground-attack planes, flying boats (seaplanes), heavily laden bombers with sighting equipment, and long-range bombers. Likewise, ground defences had become more sophisticated: anti-aircraft artillery, searchlights, air-raid sirens, air-raid shelters, blackouts, decoys, camouflage, barrage balloons, and barrage nets. Nevertheless, for all of this airborne firepower, aerial bombardment killed barely a few thousand people. 'Between 1915 and 1918, the Germans dropped 300 tons of bombs on London and English coastal towns, killing more than 1,400 people. ... In the final year of the war alone, various cities in western Germany were bombed 657 times by the Allied forces, who dropped a total of 8,000 bombs, which killed approximately 1,200 people' (Tanaka, 2009: 11–12). Like poison gas and military tractors (tanks), the deployment of aeroplanes to attack the world below was premature: they were at best a 'frightful' spectacle rather than a lethal weapon from the perspective of those on the ground; although they did prove highly lethal for the flight crews themselves.

So, although First World War bombing killed very few people on the ground, and hardly left an impression on military and civilian infrastructure, it did sustain a tit-for-tat escalation that spanned the full duration of the war. From the start, the Imperial German Air Service (*Die Fliegertruppe*) repeatedly attacked London and Paris, and other British and French cities, from bases in occupied Belgium: first by Zeppelin airships, and then by the absolute novelty of a bomber that could operate away from the front line and engage in the 'strategic' bombing of targets far into enemy territory – the 1916 Gotha G.IV and 1917 Gotha G.V (*c*.500 mile range and 500 kg payload); followed shortly thereafter by the 1917 Zeppelin-Staaken R.VI (*c*.500 mile range and 1,000–2,000 kg payload). Likewise, when the world's first independent air force was established by the British in April 1918, through the amalgamation of the Army's Royal Flying Corps (founded in 1912) and the Royal Naval Air Service (founded in 1914), the objective of this new 'Royal Air Force' was to bomb 'strategic' targets in Germany that were within range (*c*.150 miles) of its bases in France: railways, airfields, factories, ports, etc. Given the imprecision of bombing, however, even in broad daylight and fine weather, few targets requiring precision (e.g. specific structures in the built environment) were ever hit. Most RAF bombs ended up being scattered in open countryside. In an inspired move, however, which came as early as 1918, the RAF began exploiting imprecision by targeting something of strategic importance but with a diffuse geography: enemy morale. In practice, bombing 'morale' meant bombing residential areas, which was often rationalized in terms of targeting the war economy's industrial workforce.

The notion of bombing morale is credited to Giulio Douhet, who commanded Italy's first aviation unit: the Aeronautical Battalion. This was the first air force to undertake sustained aerial bombardment (of targets in Libya during Italy's war with Turkey, 1911–12). With the tit-for-tat escalation of aerial bombing during the First World War, along with the transvaluation of imprecise bombing into a strategic virtue, 'terror from the air' was already a reality. 'The seeds sown by the German Zeppelins and Gothas in 1917 had grown into a full-blown policy of indiscriminate destruction: "area bombing" had been born' (Lowe, 2007: 49). The end of the war in November 1918 curtailed the unfolding of this policy, which would be taken up again in earnest in the Second World War. In the meantime, the RAF would refine its 'area bombing' techniques in the rebellious parts of the British Empire, from Afghanistan to Yemen, and rebrand its indiscriminate killing as 'air policing', 'imperial defence', and 'pacification'.

We can already sense the emergence of a frightful 'black meteorology' that would find its full explication in the deadly serious war games rehearsed by the North Atlantic Treaty Organization (NATO) and the Warsaw Pact during the Cold War. The Third World War has already happened ad nauseam. By way of war games, re-enactments, and simulations, actual wars are themselves transmogrified into simulacra (Baudrillard, 1995). 'The very definition of the real becomes: *that of which it is possible to give an equivalent reproduction*', as Jean Baudrillard (1983: 146) famously put it. 'At the limit of this process of reproducibility, the real is not only what can be reproduced, but *that which is always already reproduced* (italics in original). The hyperreal.' War has been hyperreal for at least a century, ever since training areas and proving grounds became fully established, such as the Dugway Proving Ground in Utah and the White Sands Missile Range in New Mexico. Indeed, war games and simulations have a very long pedigree, such as the original tabletop 'war game', *Kriegsspiel* (*c*.1812), which was a component of the Prussian army's officer-training programme, as well as much older war games, such as draughts, chess, and *Go*. It is worth noting that war games have not only been instrumental for the unfolding of military capability, such as the pivotal role they played for the US Navy between the two world wars (Lillard, 2016). They have also been central to child's play since the inadvertent invention of childhood in the nineteenth century: everything from toy soldiers, scale models, and strategic board games, such as *Battleship*, *Colditz*, and *Risk*, to military fancy dress, replica weapons, and mass-media entertainment (Harrigan and Kirschenbaum, 2016; Huntemann and Payne, 2009; Payne, 2016; Thomas and Virchow, 2005). Indeed, the war-machine has been a childish affair for centuries. Just think of the military's own passion for fancy dress and costume jewellery, from fur and feathers to medallions and patches (Beifuss and Bellini, 2013; Paglen, 2010).

War as playful, simulacral, and hyperreal is not, then, a new phenomenon, least of all does it originate with the 'virtual reality' and 'tele-presence' technologies occasioned by the advent of powerful real-time computer simulation and visualization in the late twentieth century. Adopting Sun Tzu's ancient maxim from *The Art of War*, that 'speed is the essence of war', Virilio has explicated the fundamentally aesthetic character of all warfare: '*war consists of the organization of the field of perception*' (Virilio, 2001: 185, italics in original). Like the spectacle of exemplary punishment in the *ancien régime*, 'a war begins with the planning of its theatre ... the stage on which the scenario should be played out' (Virilio, 1990: 14) – if only to yield foresight and a speed-space advantage over the enemy through enhanced tele-vision (via hilltops, binoculars, aircraft, maps, simulations, etc.) or else through retarding the tele-vision of one's enemy by way of deception, dissimulation, and the general 'fog of war' (Virilio, 2006). War is frequently dramatic (spectacular and specular) and often tragicomic (*'first as tragedy, then as farce'*, as Marx famously glozed Hegel on the repetition of history, my italics), but it is invariably theatrical. War is, then, primarily a lethal game of appearances and disappearances, whether it takes solid, liquid, or gaseous form. As a hyperrealist work of art in the speed-space of mechanical reproduction, to purloin the phraseology of Baudrillard, Benjamin, and Virilio, modern war commences ahead of time and strikes pre-emptively. War is disseminated amongst an open-ended series of rehearsals, the most spectacular of which are performed in the garb of multi-media dress rehearsals for public consumption, such as the so-called 'Gulf War' and its on-going prequels in Afghanistan, Pakistan, Syria, and elsewhere (Baudrillard, 1995).

A wonderful example of this hyperrealist déjà vu happened in the wake of the 1925 *Geneva Protocol for the Prohibition of the Use in War of Asphyxiating, Poisonous or Other Gases, and of Bacteriological Methods of Warfare*, in much the same way that debt has been rebranded as credit. Britain's chemical and biological warfare research and development programmes conducted at Porton Down were transposed from the offensive to the defensive register. 'As a gesture, the Offensive Munitions Department at Porton changed its name back to "Technical Chemical Department" and in 1930 the term "Chemical Warfare" was expunged from official language and titles and "Chemical Defence" was substituted. Thereafter all offensive work was done under the heading "Study of chemical weapons against which defence is required"' (*A Brief History of the Chemical Defence Experimental Establishment Porton*, quoted in Harris and Paxman, 2002: 47). This reasoning by the strongest is impeccable: in order to be able to defend itself against newfangled chemical and biological weapons, Britain needed to research, develop, and produce them in the first place. This warped logic, which necessitated offensive research in order to sustain defensive research, further cemented the complicity of the academic and medical research communities in the development of chemical, biological, and radiological weapons. Meanwhile, America, Germany, Japan, and the Soviet Union, amongst others, were also researching, developing, mass producing, and stockpiling chemical and biological weapons in order to be able to defend themselves against an enemy attack, and – as with the demented logic of 'mutually assured destruction' in the thermonuclear age – the key to defence was the ability to strike back pre-emptively.

Especially during the Cold War, these ostensibly defensive research campaigns that led ever worstward left in their wake toxic landscapes and decimated environments of extraordinary extent (Goin, 1991; Lerner, 2010; Misrach, 1990, 1992; Peterson, 1993; Vanderbilt, 2010), which take their place alongside the more humdrum landscapes of pollution created by the agricultural, mining, manufacturing, energy, and transport activities of an ecocidal modernity (Feshbach and Friendly, 1991; Komarov, 1980). In the US, for example, 'the Pentagon's "national sacrifice zone" (the Great Basin of eastern California, Nevada and western Utah) and its "plutonium periphery" (the Columbia–Snake Plateau, the Wyoming Basin and the Colorado Plateau) have few landscape analogues anywhere else on earth', writes Mike Davis (1993: 58–60). During the Cold War these zones were sacrificed to biological, chemical, and radiological weapons, exposing millions of people and animals to life-threatening forms of contamination, often deliberately, as was the case with St George in Utah in the 1950s: 'this small Mormon city, due east of the Nevada test-site, has been shrouded in radiation debris from scores of atmospheric and accidentally "ventilated" underground blasts. Each lethal cloud ... contained more radiation than was released at Chernobyl' (Davis, 1993: 62). Although the Cold War is over, its lethal landscapes endure, unleashing an achingly 'slow violence ... of delayed destruction that is dispersed across time and space, an attritional violence that is typically not viewed as violence at all' (Nixon, 2011: 2). For instance, in the US, '500 to 1,000 (the total number is classified) "highly contaminated" sites pose incalculable hazards on sixteen military and Department of Energy facilities from Mercury to Dugway' (Davis, 1993: 73). But these are just a small fraction of the vast 'military sprawl' that once covered 'more than 30 million acres' (Vanderbilt, 2010: 104), and which extended all over the world, and in some of the most unlikely locations, such as Camp Century, excavated beneath the Greenland icesheet as part of the short-lived 'Project Iceworm' (1959–67), which hoped to establish a secret subglacial network of launch sites for hundreds of nuclear missiles trained on the Soviet Union.

The Cold War left an equivalent legacy of lethal landscapes in the former Soviet Union. There is 'environmental degradation of "irreparable, catastrophic proportions" in ... no less than 3.3 per cent of the surface area of the former USSR' (Davis, 1993: 50). Moreover, its chemical and biological warfare programmes were no less formidable than those of Britain, Japan, and the US. 'Over a twenty-year period that began, ironically, with Moscow's endorsement of the Biological Weapons Convention of 1972, the Soviet Union built the largest and most advanced biological warfare establishment in the world' (Alibek and Handelman, 2000: x). With around 30,000 staff at its peak, the Biopreparat 'pharmaceutical' company 'was the hub of a clandestine empire of research, testing, and manufacturing facilities spread out over more than forty sites in Russia and Kazakhstan' (Alibek and Handelman, 2000: x). Biopreparat sought to weaponize pathogens such as anthrax, bubonic plague, Ebola, smallpox, and the Machupo and Marburg viruses. Meanwhile, the nuclear-power industry has continued to make its own contribution to the proliferation of lethal landscapes and atmospheric terrorism, including the disasters at Three Mile Island in 1979,

Chernobyl in 1986, and Fukushima in 2011 (Hindmarsh, 2013; Krementschouk, 2011; Nancy, 2015; Walker, 2004). And even when nuclear power stations work without leaking and exploding, and nuclear weapons remain snug in their hibernatory vaults, radioactive waste nevertheless keeps accumulating, spawning new kinds of lethal landscape, including subterranean labyrinths that must remain undisturbed 'into eternity', as Michael Madsen (2010) puts it in his documentary film about Onkalo, the world's first deep geological spent-nuclear-fuel repository, where Finland's stockpile of high-level radioactive waste will be permanently entombed in the granite bedrock. Once sealed in the early twenty-second century, the site must remain undisturbed for 100,000 years. It is literally a Neanderthal undertaking. A similar final solution for transuranic waste is underway at the US Department of Energy's Waste Isolation Pilot Project at Carlsbad in New Mexico (Vanderbilt, 2010).

From the outset, air power was envisaged as a communicative and educative force, offering moral instruction through bombing. (The so-called 'Shock and Awe' bombing campaign that opened the US-led Operation Iraqi Freedom in 2003 is perhaps the most infamous example of this kind of expression.) The British were at the forefront of this edifying unfolding of air power, which envisaged bombing as a form of exemplary punishment. Between the two world wars the RAF undertook a great many 'air policing', 'imperial defence', and 'pacification' operations all over the British Empire, including Afghanistan, Darfur, Egypt, India, Mesopotamia (Iraq), Palestine, Somaliland, Sudan, and Yemen – although the line was drawn at using aerial bombing in Ireland and mainland Britain itself. Bombing was regarded as a labour-saving, cost-effective, and swift way to suppress rebels in the colonies, especially in remote areas that were otherwise hard to strike, such as mountainous regions and deserts. For example, bombs were 'dropped on the villages of mutinous tribesmen in Mesopotamia or India's North West Frontier during the 1920s so as to obviate the need to deploy large numbers of ground troops in messy counter-insurgency operations' (Burleigh, 2010: 484). Many argued that a swift bout of intense bombing was more humane than a protracted ground offensive or a long blockade that caused indiscriminate suffering and starvation. The dual assumption that air power was demoralizing and humane helped rationalize increasingly destructive bombing campaigns over the coming decades.

The British air campaign in Iraq in the 1920s 'was the first instance in which surveillance and punishment from above were intended as a permanent, everyday method of colonial administration' (Satia, 2013: 224). Bombing was becoming a routine instrument of colonial administration, and Britain led the way in Iraq. 'What was permissible only in wartime in advanced countries turned out to be *always* permissible in Iraq' (Satia, 2013: 233), and this routinization allowed the British to perfect its terror-bombing techniques. 'Between 1920 and 1924, the recently formed Royal Air Force regularly targeted Iraqi villages, often remote settlements, where the rebellious natives might try to find shelter, with the raids "carried on continuously by day and night, on houses, inhabitants, crops and cattle," according to ... one RAF Wing Commander' (Sontag, 2003: 28). In 1924, Arthur Harris, a young squadron leader in Iraq and future chief of the RAF's Bomber Command in the Second World War, famously described the air campaign to crush rebels in the following terms: 'The Arab and the Kurd ... now know that within forty-five minutes a full-sized village ... can be practically wiped out and a third of its inhabitants killed or injured by four or five machines which offer them no real target, no opportunity for glory as warriors, no effective means of escape' (quoted in Sontag, 2003: 60).

By the 1920s, the word that 'stood in for all the consequences of bombing and shooting civilians – blowing them up, maiming, wounding, disfiguring or bereaving them, killing their animals, and destroying their homes and livelihoods – was "frightfulness"' (Patterson, 2007: 98). Attempts were made to limit such frightfulness. 'In 1923, Air Warfare Rules ... specifically prohibited "aerial bombardment for the purpose of terrorising the civilian population, of destroying or damaging private property not of a military character, or of injuring non-combatants"' (Patterson, 2007: 94). Nevertheless, 'air policing', 'imperial defence', and 'pacification' through aerial bombardment continued unabated in the colonies. Indeed, the French took colonial pacification ever worstward during the Battle of Dien Bien Phu (1953–4), which was the climax of the First Indochina War (1946–54), delivering victory to the People's Army of Vietnam (Viet Minh) in its war of resistance against the occupying colonial power. When France made 'overtures to the USA for the loan of B-29 Superfortress strategic bombers' its request for 'a tactical nuclear bomb met with a flat refusal from President Eisenhower' (Winchester, 2010: 172).

When the ill-fated Geneva Disarmament Conference started in February 1932, 'Italy and Japan called for the outlawing of aerial bombardment. France wanted bombing to be forbidden beyond a radius of a given number of miles from the front lines. ... Both Britain and to a lesser extent France had far-flung empires, parts of which occasionally needed to be bombed in the interests of good order, so neither was keen on an outright ban' (Grayling, 2006: 146). In March 1933, a League of Nations peace conference came close to banning firebombing, but this was scuppered by the recently appointed German Chancellor, Adolf Hitler. In the late 1930s, 'the Japanese ruthlessly used incendiaries in their bombing of Chinese cities like Shanghai and Chungking' (Patterson, 2007: 164), and on 27 April 1937, during the Spanish Civil War, the Basque town of Guernica was almost completely destroyed by German high-explosive and incendiary bombs. A few weeks earlier, German and Italian aeroplanes had bombed another Basque town, Durango, targeting the civilian population. 'For the Luftwaffe, the Spanish Civil War was a laboratory in which to test its machines and techniques, ... using bombing to destroy both the military and the civilian morale of the enemy' (Patterson, 2007: 54). Like the RAF's bombing of villages in the rebellious colonies of the British Empire, the Germans and Italians bombed Durango and Guernica to demoralize them. After Guernica a new phrase came into existence: 'weapons of mass destruction'.

One of the most infamous acts of demoralization and mass destruction came on 1 August 1944, when Hitler and Himmler declared that 'Warsaw was to be razed to the ground – "*Glattraziert*" – so as to provide a terrifying example for the rest of Europe' (Richie, 2014: 3). The 'Order for Warsaw' read as follows: '1. Captured insurgents ought to be killed regardless of whether they are fighting in accordance with the Hague Convention or not. 2. The part of the population not fighting, women and children, should likewise be killed. 3. The whole town must be levelled to the ground' (quoted in Richie, 2014: 3). Hitler had desired the destruction of various cities, including Leningrad, Moscow, and Paris. Warsaw was the place where this exterminatory desire was fulfilled – despite the heroic uprising of the Polish Resistance Home Army. 'In the end the entire population, which before the war had numbered over 1.3 million people, was gone' (Richie, 2014: 14), and over 85 per cent of the city was destroyed. But the desire to annihilate various towns and cities was not limited to the sadistic fantasies of Hitler. For instance, the Allies had long prepared for the moment – dubbed 'Thunderclap' – when the German capital, Berlin, would be reduced to smouldering ruins. They 'expected the operation to kill or seriously injure about 275,000 persons and might even precipitate German collapse – or so it was hoped' (Schaffer, 2009: 40). However, as we shall see, consuming an entire city in an artificial firestorm was a fiendishly difficult feat to pull off. Moving ever worstward, the RAF would again relish leading the way.

11

Firestorms and Corpse Mines

The Optimism of Imprecision in Incinerated Cities

It was an amazing city, so far-flung, so beautiful, so dead.

Theodore Dreiser, quoted in Goldsmith, 2015: 845

There were hundreds of corpse mines.

Kurt Vonnegut, 2000: 157

We have already noted that airborne terror was initially launched from the ground rather than from the sky, and prior to the 1920s its most accomplished form was not poison-gas clouds but artillery shelling. Almost 1.5 billion shells were fired during the First World War, and at the start of the Battle of Berlin in April 1945, which pitched over 2 million Russian troops against 1 million German troops, the Soviet General Georgy Zhurkov 'opened his part of the offensive with an artillery barrage of ferocious power: with up to 295 guns per 1,000 yards of front, his gunners fired 7.1 million rounds of ammunition' (Winchester, 2010: 163). We have also mentioned that so-called 'chemical' weapons have undeservedly acquired a more frightful reputation than the apparent banality of incendiary weapons, even though incendiaries are also chemical weapons, and that many people are under the misapprehension that while chemical weapons were used frequently in the First World War, they were not used in the Second World War: 'chemical weapons killed about 90,000 people in World War I and 350,000 in World War II, plus the victims of Nazi gas chambers' (Russell, 2001: 3). The chemical weapon of choice in the First World War was poison gas, but in the Second it was incendiary bombs. Moreover, 'the main agent of civilian deaths in cities in World War II was fire, and chemical weapons (incendiaries) started most of those fires' (Russell, 2001: 8). However, most of those killed by incendiaries were not burnt to death. They were asphyxiated. In short, the Second World War gave terror from the air a double twist. The horizontal drift of gas clouds and the parabolic trajectory of artillery shells were supplemented and surpassed by the vertical drop of incendiary bombs that burnt and gassed. As pilots took to the skies in balloons, airships, and aeroplanes they discovered the awesome power of dropping incendiaries on highly flammable cities.

At the outset of the Second World War the American President, Franklin D. Roosevelt, had called upon both sides 'to renounce the "bombardment from the air of civilian populations and unfortified cities," and both sides had hastened to agree' (Lowe, 2007: 54). Nevertheless, both soon reneged following a tit-for-tat escalation of bombing civilians. Germany bombed Warsaw in 1939, and then Rotterdam in 1940. Britain retaliated by bombing railways and oil facilities in the Rhine, and the shipyards of Hamburg. 'So began Britain's strategic bombing campaign against Germany: a long-term systematic effort to destroy ... anything of military value' (Lowe, 2007: 55). From June 1940, Britain and Germany exchanged aerial attacks on 'strategic' targets, until, on 24 August 1940, the Luftwaffe mistakenly bombed central London, with Churchill launching retaliatory attacks on Berlin shortly thereafter. Hitler responded with a slow-motion Blitz against London: 71 major attacks spread over 267 days, which resulted in around 20,000 deaths, nearly all civilian, and over 1 million homes damaged or destroyed (Calder, 1992; Ziegler, 2002). He also launched a wider Blitz against British industrial and port cities that lasted from September 1940 until May 1941. Belfast, Birmingham, Bristol, Cardiff, Coventry, Glasgow, Liverpool, Portsmouth, Plymouth, Sheffield, Southampton, and Swansea were all attacked, claiming another 20,000 civilian lives. This 'Battle of Britain' was arguably the first major military campaign that was entirely aeronautical. Meanwhile, the RAF targeted German industrial cities with densely populated residential areas, ostensibly to disrupt the war economy by bombing both its productive infrastructure and the homes of industrial workers. Consequently, the 'strategic' bombing of specific war-economy targets, such as factories and refineries, which required a high degree of precision, was supplemented by a more diffuse practice of 'area' bombing, targeting inner-city, working-class neighbourhoods, which was much more tolerant of imprecision. While the terror bombing of civilians in rebellious colonies was euphemistically dubbed 'pacification', the terror bombing of civilians in German cities was euphemistically called 'de-housing'. Those who were killed or seriously injured were not so much discounted as 'collateral damage', but regarded as a deduction from the stock of useful labour available to the German war economy. Working-class neighbourhoods were arguably legitimate targets with military value. Moreover, those 'de-housed' would burden the authorities. Meanwhile, recourse to area bombing elevated strategic bombing to the moral high ground. Like the 'wet guillotine', the precision of strategic bombing seemed morally superior to the imprecision of area bombing, which was quickly dubbed 'carpet bombing', 'obliteration bombing', or 'terror attacks' (*Terrorangriffe*). However, while area bombing may have seemed frightful and immoral, its power was widely appreciated. 'Moral means were not necessarily useful, and useful means were not necessarily moral, but for the airmen, a measure of moral validity adhered to methods of war that achieved quick victory and minimized prolonged suffering' (Sherry, 1987: 58). From this perspective, precision bombing seemed promising, but so too did area bombing, not least because frightful attacks on residential areas might kill the morale of the enemy and break its will to fight.

The emergence and explication of incendiary bombing in the Second World War took time, as the RAF and US Army Air Forces (USAAF) experimented with different ways to bomb cities. Daylight raids made sighting targets easier but left the bombers more exposed to counter attack. Nighttime raids made targeting much more difficult but cloaked the bombers in protective darkness. The relative ease or difficulty of bombing also depended on the vagaries of the weather (especially cloud cover) and the phases of the moon: 'on moonlit nights Bomber Command would target oil installations, while on moonless nights cities were to be attacked. ... Specific targeting within a darkened city on a moonless night was a practical impossibility, and the bombers either had to bomb blind or return home with their bombs' (Burleigh, 2010: 487). The relative ease or difficulty of bombing also depended on the capability of sighting techniques employed by the aircrews: either a reliance on the naked eye or else newfangled forms of television that were beginning to become available, such as the radio-detection and ranging device (nicknamed 'radar'). Then as now, the apostles of air power emphasized the precision of aerial bombardment, which they claimed could strike at the heart of the enemy war-machine – its military and industrial infrastructure. In practice, however, precision eluded bombers. So, the British preference for area bombing was partly due to the RAF's inability to bomb with accuracy, even in favourable conditions: daylight and clear skies. 'In an exercise conducted in April 1939, 40 per cent of bombers failed to find their targets over friendly cities in daylight' (Strachan, 2006: 12). 'Britain did not mount a strategic bombing offensive in 1939 because it could not.' As the war gathered pace, exactitude continued to elude the RAF. 'Forty-nine per cent of the bombs dropped between May 1940 and May 1941 fell on unbuilt-up countryside' (Burleigh, 2010: 489). So, the RAF made a virtue out of inaccuracy by turning to area bombing. It 'hit cities because they were big targets, and it hit city centres because industries tended to be scattered on the cities' peripheries and were therefore hard to locate' (Strachan, 2006: 13). Nevertheless, rather than the RAF's pre-war estimate of 50 casualties per imperial ton of bombs dropped, which had garnered the massive investment in bombers and support for their use, the actual rate was barely one death per two imperial tons of bombs. The Luftwaffe fared little better, with the London Blitz barely achieving a rate of one death per imperial ton of bombs dropped.

Explosives were well suited to destroying specific structures, especially those built from robust materials such as iron, concrete, and stone, while incendiaries were better suited to destroying diffuse targets, especially those built from flammable materials such as wood, paper, and fabric. The advent of area bombing, then, brought the ancient art of incendiary warfare back into vogue (Sawyer, 2004), and placed it at the heart of the most modern industrialized war-machine: huge fleets of purpose-built bombers. The human slaughter industry had rediscovered incineration – urban 'terror bombing' recast as a quotidian 'holocaust' (from the Greek *holos* 'whole' and *kaustos* 'burnt') – and it had also rediscovered pyromania, but with a key diabolical twist: this new-fangled 'fire craze' was elevated from the individual mental pathology into which pyromania had sunk during the nineteenth century (the deranged arsonist) to an institutional obsession that rekindled the 'burning passions' of the Inquisition and the Revolution (Marder, 2015). It unleashed a new kind of 'urbicide' (Graham, 2004).

Incendiary bombs were critical to exploiting the destructive potential of imprecision. In 1915, the Germans had already attempted to set London ablaze with incendiaries, but failed so to do because the *Fliegertruppe* (the forerunner of the Luftwaffe) spread its incendiary bombs too thinly. Rather than increasing the concentration and intensity of incendiary bombing, the *Fliegertruppe* switched to high explosives instead, which did little more than pockmark the cityscape killing a few people here and there. In the Second World War, with orders of magnitude more firepower at its disposal, the RAF did not make this mistake. Area destruction is best accomplished by incendiaries, rather than by explosives, with the latter serving to blast open doors and windows to maximize the flow of air through the built-up area, and the former being sufficiently concentrated so that fire-fighters would be overwhelmed and the individual fires would coalesce into a huge conflagration or a self-sustaining firestorm with hurricane-force winds. As the Allies experimented with the combination of explosives and incendiaries to optimize city-centre conflagrations and firestorms, 'the proportion of incendiaries dropped on German cities was increased from 25 or 30 per cent to about 70 per cent' (SIPRI, 1975: 33). The RAF bombing campaign on German towns and cities began on 11 May 1940, when 37 Hampden and Whitley medium-bombers struck Mönchen- Gladbach, and ended on 3 May 1945, when 126 de Havilland long-range Mosquito fighter-bombers attacked Kiel. Across the five-year campaign, over 100 towns and cities were bombed, from Aachen, Andernach, and Anklam to Zuffenhausen, Zweibrücken, and Zwickau, many of which were largely destroyed (Grayling, 2006).

At this point it is worth distinguishing between three forms of urban fire that incendiary bombs can cultivate (SIPRI, 1975). First, isolated multiple fires occur when the incendiaries are spread too thinly or the urban structure contains firebreaks that prevent the fires from coalescing, such as canals, wide avenues, and parks. Berlin and Munich had this type of urban fabric. Second, when isolated multiple fires are able to coalesce, either in the absence of firebreaks or by overwhelming them, they become coalescing multiple fires. Such fires 'coalesce into an advancing front ... depositing firebrands which ignite combustible materials in its path' (SIPRI, 1975: 81). Finally, if the convection column is sufficiently powerful to sustain ground-level gale-force or hurricane-force winds, then these act like a bellows stoking a firestorm. While bombing with impression over a widespread area is easy, conjuring a firestorm is a difficult feat to pull off. 'The tactics of area bombing evolved from trial and error, while the total operational bomb lift of the RAF increased fortyfold', writes Michael Burleigh (2010: 495). 'It began with 520 tons of bombs delivered by twenty-three squadrons in 1940, rising to 10,000 tons of bombs, dropped by a hundred operational squadrons in 1944–5. The USAAF contribution, after January 1943 when it first bombed Germany, doubled the last total to 20,000 tons by the closing months of the war.' From 1943 until 1945, atmospheric terrorism was the order of the day: an unprecedented reign of terror from the air that asphyxiated and incinerated hundreds of thousands, and traumatized millions more.

The decisive shift from ostensibly precise strategic bombing to frightful area bombing occurred on 12 December 1940, when 'Winston Churchill ordered the bombing of Mannheim: for the first time the British had designated the city as a target, rather than anything specific within it' (Lowe, 2007: 57). The fiction that area bombing was targeting military assets, many of which were 'dual use' (bridges, railways, storage depots, communication centres), also fell away when it became clear that the primary target was enemy morale, and particularly the morale of industrial workers. When Germany switched its attention to the Eastern Front in 1941, the RAF spent a year and a half assembling 'the most formidable bomber force the world had yet seen' (Lowe, 2007: 58). One third of Britain's national output was devoted to the strategic air offensive. For the next three years, Bomber Command's commander-in-chief, Sir Arthur 'Bomber' Harris, 'would preside over the greatest, most systematic destruction of population centres the world has ever known' (Lowe, 2007: 58). Indeed, 'by early 1944 there was an average of a thousand bombers a day available to Bomber Command' (Patterson, 2007: 158). This enabled the relentless campaign of terror from the air to reach gargantuan proportions. For example, 'the eighth airfleet alone used a billion gallons of fuel, dropped seven hundred and thirty-two thousand tons of bombs, and lost almost nine thousand aircraft and fifty thousand men' (Sebald, 2002: 38). Meanwhile, the RAF 'dropped 1 million tons of bombs on enemy territory', writes W. G. Sebald (2003: 1). Moreover, 'it is true that of the 131 towns and cities attacked ... many were almost entirely flattened, that about 600,000 German civilians fell victim to the air raids and 3.5 million homes were destroyed, while at the end of the war 7.5 million people were left homeless', he continues; 'but we do not grasp what it all actually meant'. It meant the 'death by fire within a few hours of an entire city, with all its buildings and its trees, its inhabitants, its domestic pets, its fixtures and fittings of every kind' (Sebald, 2003: 26).

Everyday urban life – rather than the nefarious war economy – was typically consumed in the conflagrations and firestorms. Indeed, 'of the 2,638,000 tons of bombs dropped on Germany and German-held territory, 48,000 – less than 2 per cent – fell on war-related factories, while 640,000 tons landed on "industrial areas" – largely workers' homes. Indiscriminate terror strikes on residential areas accounted for most of the rest' (Ham, 2012: 53). Area bombing did little to disrupt the German war-machine. The US Strategic Bombing Survey Unit 'estimated that the percentage loss in total German production attributable to strategic bombing was 2.5 in 1942; 9.0 in 1943; 17.0 in 1944; and 6.5 in 1945 (January to April)' (SIPRI, 1975: 35, note 17). However, when one considers the impact on war production rather than total production, the British Bombing Survey Unit estimated that it 'was never reduced by more than 3.8 per cent' (SIPRI, 1975: 35, note 17).

The Allied bombing campaign was relentless. As it reached its zenith, German towns and cities were subjected to a combination of fearsome airquakes and earthquakes. 'In the final months of the war, specially adapted Lancasters carried 22,000-pound Grand Slam bombs, which ... were designed to bore deep into the ground before exploding to create an earthquake effect' (Burleigh, 2010: 479). When the Allies were looking for a suitable place for the post-war criminal trials of captured Nazi leaders, a report recommended Nuremberg – that once glittering stage for spectacular Nazi rallies that had been reduced to ruins by RAF bombing – because it was 'among the dead cities of Germany' (quoted in Grayling, 2006: 12). In fact, the intention had been to bomb the urban out of Germany. In 1942, the British War Cabinet decided 'to destroy all of Germany's cities with populations over 100,000', and planned to transform post-war Germany 'into a solely agricultural region' (Grayling, 2006: 22).

Accordingly, on 14 February 1942, the Air Staff issued a new directive to Bomber Command: 'The *primary object* of your operations should now be focused on *the morale of the enemy civil population*, and in particular on the industrial workers' (quoted in Grayling, 2006: 50, italics in original). German towns and cities with a preponderance of timber buildings were chosen for the first experiments in area bombing: Essen on the night of 8–9 March 1942, Lübeck on 28–29 March, and then Rostock on three occasions in April; followed shortly thereafter by Operation Millennium, the unprecedented 1,000-bomber attack planned for either Hamburg (preferred choice) or Cologne (reserve). 'The idea was that by massing 1,000 bombers over a city in the space of an hour and a half, the defences of the city – its fire-fighters and medical services as well as its anti-aircraft batteries – would be overwhelmed, and the concentration of explosive and incendiary power would lay it to waste' (Grayling, 2006: 52). To deal with the aerial congestion the bombers would be split into three streams with precise timings to guide each bomber. Just as the vagaries of the weather would spare Kokura from atomic bombing on 9 August 1945, they would also spare Hamburg from Operation Millennium. After several days of adverse weather the objective was issued – to destroy the city of Cologne. 'The likely weather over northern Europe ultimately determined which city was to be attacked' (Burleigh, 2010: 495). On 30–31 May 1942, a fleet of 900 bombers dropped 915 imperial tons of incendiaries and 840 tons of explosives onto Cologne, and they were sufficiently concentrated to destroy over 600 acres of the city. 'More damage was done on the city on this one night than all the previous air raids on it put together' (Grayling, 2006: 53), of which there had been more than 50.

The second and third 1,000-bomber raids were on Essen and Bremen, in June 1942, neither of which was very successful: the bombing was too diffuse in the case of the former, and foiled by untoward weather in the case of the latter. Firestorms were proving to be just as fickle as gas clouds, but whereas the British had quickly abandoned the cultivation of the latter on the entrenched battlefields of the First World War, they persevered with the manufacture of the former in the heady atmosphere of the Second World War. Meanwhile, in the wake of the destruction of Lübeck, the German Luftwaffe retaliated with the so-called 'Baedeker raids' on some of England's iconic tourist cities: Bath, Canterbury, Exeter, Norwich, and York; interspersed with raids on more conventional war-economy targets, such as Grimsby and Hull.

The Allies had to wait until 1943, four years into the war, for the RAF to 'have the resources and equipment to bomb on a scale and in a manner required by the philosophy of "area bombing," the official term for attacks aimed at civilian populations' (Grayling, 2006: 21). The long-awaited firestorm that would consume a city was finally conjured by the Allies in July 1943. 'Operation Gomorrah consisted of five major and several minor attacks on Hamburg on the nights of 24–5, 27–8, 29–30 July and 2–3 August, and in the daylight hours of 25 and 26 July' (Grayling, 2006: 16). The daylight attacks were undertaken by the USAAF, and, following its doctrine of precision bombing, its bombers aimed to destroy Hamburg's shipyards and engineering plants. The nighttime attacks were undertaken by the RAF, and, following its doctrine of area bombing, it aimed to destroy German morale. 'The American raids did not much affect the citizens of Hamburg in their residential areas and city centre, whereas the raids by the RAF most certainly did; these latter had as their aiming point Hamburg's most central point, the *Altstadt* – the old city' (Grayling, 2006: 17). On the first night of the operation, 718 RAF bombers dropped 2,396 imperial tons of bombs, most of which were incendiaries, including magnesium, phosphorus, and petroleum jelly bombs. On the second night, which was fortuitously blessed by optimum weather conditions for an incendiary attack (unusually hot and dry), 787 RAF bombers concentrated their bombing to such an extent that they conjured the world's first deliberate firestorm (*Feuersturm*). (The 'Great Fire of London' in 1666 was an inadvertent artificial firestorm.)

Within a few minutes huge fires were burning all over the target area, which covered some 20 square kilometres, and they merged so rapidly that only a quarter of an hour after the first bombs had dropped the whole airspace was a sea of flames. ... Flames ... rolled like a tidal wave through the streets at a speed of over 150 kilometres an hour. ... Residential districts with a street length of 200 kilometres in all were utterly destroyed. (Sebald, 2003: 27–8)

To put this in perspective, the Saffir–Simpson Hurricane Wind Scale classifies hurricanes into five categories according to their sustained wind speeds, from 74 m.p.h. (Category 1) to over 157 m.p.h. (Category 5). The Hamburg firestorm had wind speeds of at least 120 m.p.h., and possibly of 170 m.p.h., with street-level temperatures of 1,400°C, and indoor temperatures even higher (Lowe, 2007). 'The word *Flammenmeer*, "sea of flames," comes up again and again in accounts of the firestorm' (Lowe, 2007: 213). 'It is probable that as many as 70 per cent of those who died were killed by smoke or carbon monoxide poisoning' (Lowe, 2007: 230). But neither the British nor the Germans expected that carbon monoxide would be so lethal: 'to the extent that these attacks amounted to "chemical warfare," it was ... by default rather than by design' (SIPRI, 1975: 208).

The third and fourth nights of Operation Gomorrah were much less effective than the second, not only because dense smoke, thick cloud, and heavy rain blanketed Hamburg, but also because most of the city was already destroyed. After '3,000 sorties ... the RAF had dropped more than 9,000 tons of bombs', and 'at least 45,000 corpses lay among the smoking ruins. ... Half the city had been reduced to rubble' (Grayling, 2006: 19–20). Around a million people were 'de-housed' and people fled the city in droves. The firestorm 'devastated eight and a half square miles of the city, while high explosives produced fifty-six million cubic yards of rubble. ... It was after seeing film of the raid on Hamburg that Churchill exclaimed, "Are we beasts? Are we taking this too far?," although a few days later he was all for pummelling Berlin' (Burleigh, 2010: 499).

In February 1945, almost two years after the Hamburg firestorm, the Allies finally succeeded in conjuring a perfect firestorm. The unfortunate target for such a fearsome feat was Dresden, a 'millionaire city' with around 400,000 refugees fleeing the Red Army's advance. It would turn out to be 'the last major terror raid on Germany' (Patterson, 2007: 161), not least because most German towns and cities had already been burnt out. '"To burn and destroy an enemy industrial centre", read 5 Group's orders on February 13, 1945' (Taylor, 2004: 401); 'the point was to surround the city centre ... with a thick ring of high explosive- and firebombs and engulf the entire area inside it in an overall blast furnace effect' (Sloterdijk, 2009: 54). The Allies accomplished this with astonishing effectiveness. Their 'bombers reduced this treasure to crushed stone and embers; disemboweled her with high-explosives and cremated her with incendiaries', writes Vonnegut (2009: 36). He was an American POW held in Dresden at the time, and spent that hellish night 'in an underground meat locker in a slaughterhouse. We were lucky, for it was the best shelter in town' (Vonnegut, 2009: 37). In *Slaughterhouse-Five*, Vonnegut likened the incinerated city to a moonscape, and the work of digging holes in the lunar crust to corpse mining. 'Nobody talked much as the expedition crossed the moon', he laments. 'Absolutely everybody in the city was supposed to be dead' (Vonnegut, 2000: 131). For a while, countless bodies were disinterred from 'hundreds of corpse mines', but once active decay set in, the Germans simply resorted to unceremoniously cremating the corpses in situ with flamethrowers (Vonnegut, 2000: 157).

'In the British Ministry of Economic Warfare's 1943 "Guide to the Economic Importance of German Towns and Industries" (somewhat irreverently titled "The Bomber's Baedeker"), Dresden was ranked at number twenty' (Cox, 2006: 53). From the German perspective, however, it was not regarded as a primary target since it actually contributed little to the war effort. Consequently, Dresden had few air-raid shelters and limited air defences. On 7 February 1945, Dresden was placed second on a list of ten towns and cities selected by the Combined Strategic Targets Committee for targeting in an attempt to cause chaos near the Eastern Front and thereby assist the Red Army. This listing would seal Dresden's fate.

On the night of 13–14 February 1945, the RAF attacked Dresden in two waves. The first wave was sufficient to consume the city centre in a firestorm, making sighting for the second wave impossible. Rather than curtail the bombing, however, the decision was taken 'to abandon the designated aiming point, and bomb outside the already burning areas of the city, which turned the raid into a byword for slaughter' (Taylor, 2004: 284). All in all, over 1,000 RAF Lancasters and USAAF Flying Fortresses dropped more than 4,500 imperial tons of high explosives and incendiaries onto Dresden, which completely 'destroyed an area of thirteen square miles' (Addison and Crang, 2006: xi). 'The photo-interpreters ... calculated that 85 per cent of the fully built-up area of the city had been destroyed' (Cox, 2006: 57). Once again, however, this accomplishment was fortuitous. 'The night after the raids on Dresden, Bomber Command went to Chemnitz, which ... was again planned as a "double raid"' (Cox, 2006, page 52) – but this time the attack was ineffective: most of the RAF's bombs struck the surrounding countryside and the rest were too widely scattered to enable coalescence; and inauspicious weather frustrated the USAAF's planned contribution.

Arguably, 'the shockwave triggered by Dresden swept away what was left of the will to resist, as the Germans now feared that such a catastrophe could be repeated daily' (Bergander, quoted in Probert, 2003: 321). Perhaps air power had finally achieved that most elusive of goals: bombing morale to the point of surrender. Bearing in mind that Nazi Germany was a suicidal state, however, this seems unlikely. Recall that 'If the war is lost, may the nation perish', was Hitler's apocalyptic death-wish. And perish it almost did. More importantly, perhaps, is the fact that 'the history of applied horror had yielded no other example of "life-world" devastation covering an area almost as big as an entire city district by producing a sort of high-performance combustion chamber', argues Peter Sloterdijk (2009: 55). 'This production of a special atmosphere capable of burning, carbonizing, desiccating, and asphyxiating at least 35,000 people in the space of one night constituted a radical innovation in the domain of rapid, mass killing' (Sloterdijk, 2009: 55–6).

Although '[t]he incineration of Dresden was intended as an act of terror' (Schaffer, 2009: 42), its accomplishment gave the British and the Americans food for thought. 'For some reason, the [American] censors passed an Associated Press cable, based on a British press briefing that described the ... raid as the result of a decision "to adopt deliberate terror bombing of great German population centers"' (Schaffer, 2009: 42). This admission rocked America, but was censored in Britain. Nevertheless, on 28 March 1945, Churchill wrote to the Chiefs of Staff Committee:

> It seems to me that the moment has come when the question of bombing German cities simply for the sake of increasing the terror, though under other pretexts, should be reviewed. Otherwise we shall come into control of an utterly ruined land. ... I feel the need for more precise concentration upon military objectives rather than on mere acts of terror and wanton destruction, however impressive. (Quoted in Probert, 2003: 321)

While the British pioneered and perfected the cultivation of atmospheric terrorism and artificial firestorms in Germany, the Americans belatedly did the same in Japan, but with even more deadly effectiveness. The US Army's CWS had worked on incendiary weapons during the First World War, but suspended this line of research in order to focus on developing what then seemed much more promising: gas weapons. The champion of incendiaries within the CWS, J. Enrique Zanetti, thought that fire, not gas, 'posed the biggest danger to cities in wartime. Gas dropped on cities from airplanes would dissipate; fire, the "forgotten enemy," would propagate' (Russell, 2001: 101). It would not be until the early 1940s, however, that Zanetti's view would be acted upon. 'The service that had no incendiary bombs on hand in December 1941 had, by December 1945, obtained almost 255 million' (Russell, 2001: 102). Much of this incendiary arsenal was dropped on Japanese cities, which were obligingly constructed from earthquake resistant yet highly flammable materials: wood and paper. By the end of the war, 'more than 100 Japanese cities were destroyed by firebombing, and two by atomic bombing, causing one million casualties' (Tanaka and Young, 2009: 5).

It is worth noting that atomic bombs are primarily incendiary weapons. 'The ease and openness with which bombing Japan was mentioned and ethical considerations were disregarded had no equivalent in speculation about war against Germany or other western nations', argues Michael Sherry (1987: 60). As with the European 'pacification' of rebellious natives in their African, Middle Eastern, and Asian colonial possessions during the 1920s and 1930s, 'the humane rationale imbedded in the [USAAF] doctrine of precision bombing was frail and disposable' (Sherry, 1987: 60). American wartime leaders 'drew on a long tradition of casual racism which made contemplation of air war against Japan easy and shallow. … Americans presumed that Asians would panic or collapse in the face of bombing which Englishmen or Germans could endure' (Sherry, 1987: 114). This casual racism was applied not only to Japanese civilians, but also to Japan's armed forces. 'Doubts about Japanese military capabilities in the air often rested on explicitly racial distinctions', argues Sherry (1987: 60); 'the inferior eyes and ears of Asians supposedly made them poor fliers'. Given that Japan endured the incineration of city after city it is important to appreciate that many more atomic bombs were in production when the first ones were exploded over Hiroshima and Nagasaki on 6 and 9 August 1945, respectively (claiming over 300,000 lives in the process), and that Japan may not have surrendered on 15 August 1945, had the Soviet Union not declared war on Japan the night before the Nagasaki bombing (Ham, 2012).

In just a couple of years, weaponized fire progressed from localized burning to widespread incineration, but the primary target remained consistent: civilian populations resting at home.

> From the start, incendiary developers envisioned using fire on enemy houses. Tests of incendiaries at Huntsville Arsenal, Alabama, took place in June 1942 on 'rickety old abandoned farmhouses, barns, and settlers' shacks.' Another set of tests in July 1942 at Jefferson Proving Ground, Indiana, used 'substantial houses in village and farm groups.' These tests showed that napalm and other incendiaries produced 'beautiful fires.' … But would incendiaries work as well on German and Japanese homes? To answer this question, … model towns at military sites in Florida, Maryland, and Utah … enabled researchers to develop incendiary bombs suited to each nation's architecture. (Russell, 2001: 105)

Having developed suitable incendiary weapons, however, the CWS nevertheless faced considerable resistance from the Air Force, which retained a preference for explosives. So, when the CWS began shipping incendiary bombs to Europe in June 1942, the USAAF did not take to them. It was only in the summer of 1943 that the USAAF began to embrace them, when it was persuaded to 'experiment' with incendiaries on industrial targets in France, and to join the RAF in the 'area bombing' of Hamburg in July 1943. 'After the Hamburg raid, it "began to scream for incendiaries … and CWS was hard pressed to meet the demand." In July 1943, the Eighth Air Force dropped 250 tons of incendiaries. In 1944, it dropped more than 5,000 tons per month' (Russell, 2001: 131).

While the USAAF discovered its appetite for incendiaries in Europe, it was in the Pacific theatre that it demonstrated its newfound passion for chemical warfare: 'the American air force relied mainly on incendiaries in its spectacular campaign of urban annihilation against Japan in 1945' (Russell, 2001: 139).

This was partly because Japanese cities were more flammable than German cities, and partly because they were bombing from high altitude, which made precision difficult. What took the Allies years to accomplish in Germany, the Americans repeated in a matter of months – primarily with incendiaries, rather than with either explosives or nuclear bombs. 'Of the areas of Japanese cities destroyed by American bombers, atomic bombs accounted for only about 3 percent ... [although they] caused about a fourth of the casualties suffered by Japanese civilians' (Russell, 2001: 142). It was not only the Japanese Archipelago that endured American air-frightfulness. 'The US incendiary raids on Japan were preceded by bombing raids in Burma, Thailand, Indo-China, South China and throughout the Pacific' (SIPRI, 1975: 36). By the end of the war, the USAAF had 'dropped a total of 656,000 tons of bombs in the Pacific area, of which 160,800 tons were dropped on the Japanese home islands' (SIPRI, 1975: 36).

The Japanese Archipelago only came within range of American B-29 Superfortress bombers from November 1944, following the construction of airfields on the captured islands of Saipan and Tinian in the wake of the Mariana and Palau Islands campaign. 'It was only in the last nine months of the war that Japan itself was bombed. ... The first attempts were high-altitude daylight precision-bombing raids aimed at destroying Japanese aircraft and engine factories' (Patterson, 2007: 161–2), but strong winds, poor visibility, and the limitations of bombsights and radar meant that precise bombing was the exception rather than the rule. 'Orders were therefore given to change to area bombing, and raids were planned on Nagoya, Osaka, Kawasaki and Tokyo' (Patterson, 2007: 162–3).

The USAAF pursued its area bombing campaign against Japanese cities with two new weapons: a flammable gel nicknamed 'napalm', and primarily used to burn and terrorize troops; and atomic bombs, which originally came in two flavours: uranium and plutonium. Enhanced versions of these new weapons would cast a long shadow over the second half of the twentieth century. For instance, the Americans deployed over 30,000 imperial tons of napalm during the Korean War, and almost 400,000 tons of napalm, phosphorus, and other incendiaries during the Vietnam War, both of which dwarfed the mere 16,500 tons dropped on Japan in 1945. 'There is some irony in the fact that one of the first stimuli to rebuilding the Japanese economy should come from the production of napalm bombs to be used to destroy towns and industries (many of them built by the Japanese) in newly liberated Korea' (SIPRI, 1975: 42). Meanwhile, atomic bombs became triggers for huge arsenals of thermonuclear hydrogen bombs that promised an eternal balance of terror thanks to a suicide pact of mutually assured destruction in the Cold War.

In November 1943, a year before the establishment of airfields on Saipan and Tinian that brought the Japanese Archipelago within striking distance of America's B-29 bombers, the USAAF 'tested a new kind of incendiary weapon on a mock Japanese town built in the Dugway Proving Ground in Utah' – the 'napalm-based M69 incendiary bomb, which came on stream at the end of 1944' (Ham, 2012: 57). Buoyed up by the success of an experimental incendiary raid on Japanese-occupied Hankow, China, in December 1944, the USAAF expedited its plans for a 'massive proto-napalm (jellied petroleum) strike on the Japanese mainland' (Ham, 2012: 57). The first target was Tokyo, a city of 4.3 million people living in densely packed and highly flammable neighbourhoods. On 9 March 1945, General Curtis LeMay sent more than 300 B-29 bombers to attack Tokyo with a combined payload of almost half a million incendiary bombs. 'Weather conditions were perfect for igniting a paper city', writes Paul Ham (2012: 59). 'What followed was a firestorm more terrible than anything seen in Germany. The flat plain of Tokyo's downtown *shitamachi* residential area, where up to 84,000 people per square kilometre lived in a crush of little wood-and-paper dwellings, was the kindling for a hurricane of flames.' This firestorm consumed a quarter of the city (40 km^2) in less than six hours. Around 100,000 were killed and a million injured. 'In his memoirs, LeMay chose a biblical metaphor: "It was as though Tokyo had dropped through the floor of the world and into the mouth of Hell"' (Ham, 2012: 60). The Japanese called this 'slaughter bombing'. In the following months, the USAAF 'firebombed the urban areas of every major Japanese city, dropping almost five million incendiaries … [that burnt] more than two million properties. Tokyo, Nagoya, Yokohama, Osaka, Kobe and Kawasaki were the worst hit' (Ham, 2012: 61–2). By the end of the war, 'forty per cent of all the "urban structures" in Japan were burned, and some four hundred thousand civilians had been killed' (Patterson, 2007: 166).

With the advent of atomic bombing atmospheric terrorism completed its urban explication. Firestorms would no longer require the Herculean effort of hundreds of aircraft and thousands of incendiaries, but could now be accomplished by the detonation of a single device. On 20 May 1945, the Manhattan Project's Target Committee decided that aeroplanes carrying atomic bombs 'should avoid trying to pinpoint' specific installations and simply seek to place the 'gadget in [the] center of [the] selected city' (quoted in Ham, 2012: 151). The Committee also rejected the idea of demonstrating the power of the bomb to Japan and the wider world, arguing that a test detonation over the desert or the ocean would appear disappointing and unimpressive. On 30 May 1945, the US Secretary of War's Interim Committee 'agreed that the atomic bombs should be used: (1) as soon as possible; (2) without warning; and (3) on war plants surrounded by workers' homes or other buildings susceptible to damage, in order to make a spectacular impression "on as many inhabitants as possible"' (Ham, 2012: 159). Consideration was given to the simultaneous atomic bombing of several cities, but a series of bombings was deemed preferable given the experimental nature of the weapon. Consideration was also given to following up atomic bombing with incendiary bombing, but this was rejected since the latter would obscure the impact of the former, both in terms of experimental evidence and public spectacle, and heaping firestorm upon firestorm would be a redundant operation.

Just as the fluctuations of wind speed and wind direction determined the success or failure of gas attacks in the First World War, the vagaries of cloud cover on 6 August 1945 determined whether the already weather-delayed first-ever nuclear bombing of a city by the USAAF, using the uranium 'Little Boy' atomic bomb, would take place over Hiroshima, Kokura, Nagasaki or Niigata (primary targets) or even Amagasaki, Omuta or Osaka (secondary targets), and whether the second nuclear bombing by the USAAF, on 9 August 1945, using the plutonium 'Fat Man' atomic bomb (which was twice as powerful as the 'Little Boy', and equivalent to 22,000 imperial tons of trinitrotoluene (TNT)), would be on Kokura, Nagasaki, or Niigata. Hiroshima and Niigata (along with Kyoto) had been secretly excluded at an early stage (May 1945) from America's incendiary bombing campaign, which by July 1945 had targeted 66 Japanese cities, so that Japan's 'prompt and utter destruction' (as the Allies' Potsdam Proclamation of 26 July 1945 chillingly put it), hastened by the world's first nuclear bombings, could be showcased on a relatively pristine city of 'sentimental value to the Japanese', with 'some military significance', being 'mostly intact', and 'big enough for a weapon of the atomic bomb's magnitude' (secret meeting of the Manhattan Project's Target Committee, 27 April 1945, quoted in Ham, 2012: 148). Tokyo was already 'all bombed and burned out' and 'practically rubble', the Target Committee noted; and Kyoto, the Committee's preferred stage for the debut of 'the gadget', as the atomic bomb was affectionately known, was subsequently struck off the list of potential locations for atomic bombing by the US Secretary of War, Henry Stimson, although it nevertheless remained on the list of cities to be spared from the conventional firebombing campaign.

On 6 August 1945, the mushroom cloud that hung over Hiroshima after the detonation of the 'Little Boy' prevented the American photo-reconnaissance planes from capturing the totality of the destruction, forcing them to take oblique aerial photographs instead, thereby depriving the historic press conference at the White House in Washington of the incontrovertible visual evidence and apocalyptic spectacle of the fearsome power of the atomic bomb. This was also true of the even more destructive strategic bombing campaign. 'Only at war's end could low-level photography begin revealing for Americans the full extent of the damage' (Sherry, 1987, unpaginated). Meanwhile, on 9 August 1945, cloud and haze obstructed all three runs over the primary target for the 'Fat Man', the city of Kokura; the winds of destiny had conspired to spare it from annihilation; and the weather may have hampered the radar-directed attack over the 'Fat Man's' secondary target, Nagasaki, were it not for the fact that the clouds obligingly parted to reveal some of the cityscape at an opportune moment in the bombing run.

The Allied area-bombing campaigns against civilians in Germany and Japan were 'moral crimes' and 'moral atrocities', argues A. C. Grayling (2006: 274 and 279, respectively), because in each case 'the centre-piece is an attack on a civilian population aimed at causing maximum hurt, shock, disruption and terror' (Grayling, 2006: 279).

> If Operation Gomorrah was *unnecessary* and *disproportionate*, ... then how much more so were the attacks on Dresden, Hiroshima and Nagasaki – and indeed the firebombing of Tokyo and other Japanese cities, the bombing of Berlin, ... and so many other German towns indiscriminately bombed in the very last months of the war for no better reason than that they were unbombed, and that there were many bombers and bombs waiting to be used. (Grayling, 2006: 272, italics in original)

For Todorov there is a more profound problem than the fact that the nuclear attacks were arguably unnecessary, disproportionate, punitive, demonstrative, and spectacular. These weapons were 'a source of pride for those who made and dropped them' (Todorov, 2005: 236). Only the vanquished typically enjoy the opportunity of being liberated from their goodly illusions, while the victors invariably remain deluded (Olick, 2005; Schivelbusch, 2003).

Fortuitously, the fact that by the end of the war there were a great many bombers and other aircraft 'waiting to be used' allowed the RAF and USAAF to snatch a heartwarming denouement from the jaws of infamy. When, in June 1948, as the Cold War gathered pace, the Russians closed all road, rail, and canal access into West Berlin, they expected the West to abandon the partitioned city, since it was located 100 miles inside Soviet-controlled East Germany. For over a year, however, the Allies thwarted the blockade by recourse to military and civilian cargo planes, repurposed bombers, and flying boats. They used the three air corridors that remained open to them as an air bridge into the besieged city. The Berlin Airlift involved around 280,000 flights travelling over 100 million miles, delivering more than 2,300,000 imperial tons of cargo, almost two thirds of which was coal, and most of the rest was food. The improbable success of this air bridge led the Russians to lift the blockade in May 1949. During the course of the airlift some pilots took to dropping chocolate, candy, and chewing gum for the children scurrying below. They were affectionately nicknamed 'candy bombers' or 'raisin bombers' (*Rosinenbomber*), finally delivering pleasure rather than terror from the air.

12

Capital Punishment

A Race of Outcasts Reduced to the Status of Ordinary Men

It is in the soul of all good men to shudder at the sight of someone who murders his fellow man in cold blood.

Abbé Maury, 1789, quoted in Friedland, 2012: 224

States employ many killers – in their armed forces, secret services, police forces, and criminal justice systems; and many subcontract their proclivity for violence to private-sector providers of 'security' services, such as policing, protecting, guarding, and fighting. While some states continue to recruit many of their killers as children (such as Britain, which at least spares them from combat), and so-called 'child soldiers' remain a staple of conflicts the world over, those employed as public-sector killers are invariably cast as well-trained professionals, law-abiding citizens, and dispassionate public servants. Whilst at work, the state's killers are not savages, psychopaths, or sadists, but bona fide functionaries who dutifully deploy violence for their employers. The violence they unleash is best served cold: as a precisely calibrated instrument of calculated force. And now that the state's killers' passion for violence has been quelled, they can be recast as everything from a kindly environmental protectorate to a goodly humanitarian taskforce: witness how endangered species of flora and fauna flourish in landscapes reserved for military training, and how nimbly the war-machine can be deployed for peacekeeping, emergency assistance, and disaster relief.

The state employees who most clearly exemplify the dutiful civil servants who happen to kill for a living are executioners. They simply 'administer' the death penalty under judicial oversight and medical supervision: hanging, shooting, gassing, electrocution, lethal injection, etc. Such an executioner, however, is of recent vintage. His advent is contemporaneous with the invention of the guillotine in the 1790s. We have already considered the emergence of enlightened killing in the Machine Age, and here I want to focus on the emergence of the enlightened state killer who drove humanity ever 'worstward' into the 'utmost dim' and the 'dimmer still' – the state executioner.

In Europe, professional executioners, who execute justice for a living, date from the early thirteenth century. Before then punishment was performed by the victim's family, judges, or convicts. It was not yet self-evident that punishment should be undertaken at the state's expense, nor in a cold and dispassionate manner. Victims had a right to witness the guilty suffer, and often to make them suffer. For if 'the sight of suffering does one good', then 'the infliction of suffering does one more good' (Nietzsche, 2003b: 42). Such was the 'Law of Talion' (*Lex Talionis*). Victims were compensated through a legally authorized retaliation: 'an eye for an eye', 'a tooth for a tooth'. 'If you repay me not on such a day, in such a place, such sum or sums as are express'd in the condition, let the forfeit be nominated for an equal pound of your fair flesh, to be cut off and taken in what part of your body pleaseth me' (Shakespeare's *Merchant of Venice*, Act I, Scene 3). Retributive punishment formed a libidinal economy where victims were entitled to take pleasure in the guilty party's suffering. For example, Rome's Code of the Twelve Tables (*c*.450 BC) 'decreed that it was immaterial how much or how little the creditors … cut off' a debtor's body in recompense for default, writes Nietzsche (2003b: 40). For 'instead of an advantage directly compensatory of his injury (that is, instead of an equalisation in money, lands, or some kind of chattel), the creditor is granted by way of repayment and compensation a certain *sensation of satisfaction* – … the joy in sheer violence'. Nietzsche rightly emphasized the pleasure of punishment, which is neither sadistic nor masochistic, but majestic: 'the creditor participates in the rights of the masters. … [He] attains the edifying consciousness of being able to despise and ill-treat a creature – as an "inferior" – or at any rate of *seeing* him being despised and ill-treated, in case the actual power of punishment … has already become transferred to the "authorities"' (Nietzsche, 2003b: 40–1).

The cold calculation of made-to-measure punishments tailored to fit the proportions of the crime will never entirely eclipse the majestic libidinal economy upon which the law rests, even if those cold calculations are rationally and clinically calibrated. Indeed, pre-modern societies were replete with 'precise schemes of valuation, frequently horrible in the minuteness and meticulosity of their application, *legally* sanctioned schemes of valuation for individual limbs and parts of the body' (Nietzsche, 2003b: 40, italics in original). Nor will the contemporary aversion to 'cruel and unusual' punishments quell the pleasure of the law's execution, which is invariably enjoyed by the judicial machinery itself (Kafka, 2000). Hence the majestic ruse of the masochist's hyper-conformity to the execution of the law: 'by the closest adherence to it, and by zealously embracing it, we may hope to partake of its pleasures' (Deleuze, 1989: 88). For example:

'The masochist regards the law as a punitive process and therefore begins by having the punishment inflicted upon himself; once he has undergone the punishment, he feels that he is allowed or indeed commanded to experience the pleasure that the law was supposed to forbid' (Deleuze, 1989: 88). Such a delicious ruse should not be confused with things like the medieval trade in 'indulgences', underwritten by the 'Treasury of Merit', and its vulgar commercialization from the late Middle Ages onwards (purchasing indulgences), right through to the secular purchasing of intimacy (Illouz, 2007; Zelizer, 2005), and our current predilection for financially engineered 'solutions' to any problem whatsoever.

During the thirteenth and fourteenth centuries, when 'the staging of executions became more complex and more specifically geared to audiences' (Friedland, 2012: 71), primarily for edification (witnessing and deterrence) rather than pleasure, many places in northern and central Europe appointed professional executioners to deliver these spectacular performances. Meanwhile, a long and drawn out parallel process forcibly wrested violence out of the collective hands of common folk, and reserved it for the state's more or less exclusive enjoyment (the vestigial right to keep and bear arms, to hunt, to self-defence, etc. notwithstanding), typically fortified with the retrospective fantasy of an agreeable exchange between consenting adults: some personal liberty swapped for collective security. (The state has traded on this delusion ever since.) The state sequestered the right to violence through the creation of modern standing armies and police forces, and by imposing a slew of laws curtailing people's right to violence (from the possession of weapons to the enjoyment of blood sports), although popular justice and revolutionary justice have nevertheless continued to find their illicit 'mob expression', so to speak, down the centuries: from the American, Chinese, French, Haitian, and Russian Revolutions to the so-called 'Arab Spring', when those who ordinarily count for nothing – or even less than nothing – demand the impossible and momentarily count for all (Badiou, 2010; Buck-Morss, 2009; Cobb, 1972; Žižek, 2011, 2012); and more prosaically, those revenge attacks, immediate riots, and festive lootings that are invariably triggered by state brutality, or those occasions when a community immunizes itself against evildoers, often tragicomically (such as the apocryphal tales of motherly mobs mistaking paediatricians for paedophiles). Naturally, the state has often cultivated, orchestrated, and exploited mob violence for its own ends, twisting popular justice into an oppressive atmosphere and repressive apparatus, often to lethal effect, such as the 1907 'Anti-Oriental Riots' in Vancouver's Chinatown and Japantown, the 1938 *Kristallnacht*, and the 1994 Rwandan Tutsi genocide, during which half a million people were killed, mostly with machetes, clubs, axes, and knives (Gilbert, 2006; Hatzfeld, 2005; Lemarchand, 1997).

An executioner was not an anonymous cog in the vast machinery of the state apparatus. 'He was, rather, the central player on the penal stage, the one who coaxed meaning from the flesh of the condemned' (Friedland, 2012: 71). He was an extraordinary and fearsome being, rather than a mundane and anonymous functionary. Like the Jews, actors, prostitutes, and other outcasts of early modern Europe, executioners undertook socially necessary yet morally dubious work that others were precluded from undertaking, such as money-lending and Oriental trade. 'They did not, in fact, have to execute anyone in order to be despised and reviled: the children, the wives, the brothers, sisters, and cousins of executioners were all tainted' (Friedland, 2012: 73). Their mere existence was an existential threat to other people.

As outcasts and untouchables the everyday life of executioners was heavily regulated. They lived with their families in enforced seclusion and were compelled to wear distinctive patches or unique clothing so that all who encountered them would appreciate their unwholesome status. 'The exclusion of Executioners of justice is not founded upon prejudice', claimed Abbé Maury. 'It is in the soul of all good men to shudder at the sight of someone who murders his fellow man in cold blood' (quoted in Friedland, 2012: 224). Moreover, while executioners could 'attend church, receive communion, and be buried on consecrated ground', they 'were nevertheless cordoned off and isolated in special pews and in special sections of cemeteries for fear that their presence, whether alive or dead, would contaminate others' (Friedland, 2012: 72 and 81, respectively). Yet despite their infamy executioners enjoyed aristocratic privileges: 'they held their offices in largely hereditary dynasties that spanned the borders of several European countries; they had the exclusive right to seize specific goods from sellers in the public marketplace; and they were reputed to have the ability to cure certain diseases with their touch' (Friedland, 2012: 72). As with royal succession, children occasionally inherited the executioner's mantle.

Reviled and ostracized, yet feared and exulted, these dynasties of executioners – the Guillaume and Sanson families, for example – monopolized a craft that enabled them to accrue a wide range of rights and privileges that could make them wealthy, particularly in large towns and cities. For executioners did much more than administer punishment. They also undertook lucrative public hygiene and 'policing' tasks: maintaining sewers and latrines; applying ordinances against public urination, defecation, and blasphemy; administering local livestock regulations; managing stray dogs and disposing of dead animals; and overseeing lepers, prostitutes, and gambling. Many executioners also enjoyed the right (called 'havage') to seize a small proportion of certain goods – typically foodstuffs (eggs, grain, fruit, etc.) – from market traders (usually foreign or travelling merchants rather than local sellers). Executioners used special spoons to take their havage so that their vile touch would not defile the rest of the produce. The entitlements, which varied from place to place depending on custom and practice, were often the source of disputes between traders, the authorities, and executioners. Moreover, havage often formed the bulk of an executioner's income, and as commercial trade dramatically increased over the course of the seventeenth and eighteenth centuries, the wealth of many dynasties of executioners accumulated magnificently.

Executioners, then, were often powerful figures in places where they exercised their duties and privileges. 'With respect to the citizens of the town, he was a kind of policeman, enforcing ordinances of moral and physical hygiene. With respect to outcasts and foreigners, his function was not unlike that of a *seigneur* [feudal lord], [extracting] tribute and enforcing order' (Friedland, 2012: 78). As market trading expanded, and local sellers got drawn into the system of *havage*, this way of financing official executioners became untenable. The execution of justice could not come at the retailers' expense indefinitely. Some towns and regions replaced *havage* with a system of fees for the exercise of various penal functions, which again varied from place to place (for instance, executioners were paid 90 *livres* to burn someone at the stake and dispose of their ashes in Paris, but only 20 *livres* in Bordeaux), while some other areas replaced *havage* with an annual salary. *Havage* as a whole was effectively ended in France by a 1775 decree that abolished all grain duties to forestall food riots. Those executioners who had not already relinquished their right to *havage* for set fees or an annual salary were left in a precarious position, with many of them losing the bulk of their income as a consequence. In 1789, the National Assembly abolished all remaining feudal privileges, which stripped executioners of all sources of income other than their annual salary or piece-rates for discharging their penal functions. Worse still, the new Revolutionary penal code of 1791 abolished most forms of spectacular punishment and promulgated incarceration instead. Consequently, the residual penal work that executioners had enjoyed in the *ancien régime* also dried up, from amputation to branding, and 'executioners, who for centuries had derived an income from the communities in which they lived, now effectively became wards of the state, entirely dependent on administrators for support' (Friedland, 2012: 87).

Stripped of their privileges, the bulk of their income, and their fearsome and exalted civil status, executioners were suddenly on the verge of becoming anachronistic figures in the Age of Reason. 'The advent of the guillotine, and the mechanization of the death penalty, spelled the end of a craft that had involved a kind of sculpting of flesh, and of a spectacle that had been more about the process than the final product' (Friedland, 2012: 264). Like so many other artisans in the industrial age, executioners were eclipsed by machinery. 'In the illustration shipped off with each guillotine to departments throughout France … the condemned stands facing the machine, ready to be executed, with no executioner in sight, almost as if the machine could perform the task without any help' (Friedland, 2012: 262). Here as elsewhere, the modern object appears to come alive – not simply as an automaton (a self-propelled mechanical device), but as an artificial life (an independent spirit). For a time, 'the guillotine achieved an almost cult-like status in certain circles. Innumerable images and ornamental objects were produced commemorating noteworthy executions' (Friedland, 2012: 252), especially those of the dethroned Louis and Marie Antoinette. Such souvenirs offered a foretaste of the 'fetishism of commodities' that would engulf the world in the nineteenth century via the arcades, department stores, and the other phantasmagoric 'dream-houses' of consumer culture (Benjamin, 2002; Buck-Morss, 1991). The quintessential commodity fetish was the 'snow globe' or 'blizzard-weight', which produced a snowstorm effect when shaken. These 'dream spheres' – as Ludwig II, King of Bavaria, called them – first appeared at the 1878 *Exposition Universelle* in Paris, and thereafter sold in their hundreds of thousands, becoming the archetypical travel souvenir. From spurting blood to swirling snow, the 'kitsch experience', as Celeste Olalquiaga (1999) calls it, has dogged the formation of the 'society of the spectacle' (Debord, 2010).

As capital punishment moved closer to becoming 'the simple deprivation of life', as Louis-Michel Lepeletier, the author of the new penal code of 1791, phrased it, the executioner became recast as an ordinary citizen. 'The headsman could not become the mere executioner – as the bureaucracy now referred to him – until he ceased to be held in awe; he was now to be a man like any other, and only his professional functions were to be other than ordinary' (Arasse, 1991: 120). The guillotine would facilitate this transformation. 'The good executioner had become an accomplished butcher, and thereby lost some of the prestige of the *carnifex* [the Roman executioner], but gained the great advantage of ordinariness: he had become a full citizen, almost a civil servant like any other' (Arasse, 1991: 121). His fall from grace would soon be complete. Killing in cold blood would be officially banal. The 'banality of evil', as Hannah Arendt (1977) called it, had already trod the blood-soaked cobblestones of the European heartland long before the Holocaust. The head of a French military tribunal held in 1794 put it rather starkly when he lambasted an incompetent executioner, Jean-Denis Peyrussan: 'Under the *ancien régime* the august function that you exercise had become odious, and one had to be a savage to perform it! This is no longer the case today; in every employment, one can show oneself humane and sensitive. ... You should thank the Lord for the Revolution, which has restored your position in society and made honourable citizens of you' (quoted in Arasse, 1991: 121).

Since we have already dwelt at length on the role of the guillotine in the advent of enlightened killing, suffice to recall here that 'it was the medical profession that proposed, invented and, in the last analysis, exonerated a machine for decapitating people', says Daniel Arasse (1991: 2). 'The medical science of the Enlightenment created in the guillotine one of its most accomplished products, and in so doing revealed its true nature as an art of death. Yet it should not be forgotten that the medical profession resolved upon the guillotine out of humanitarian considerations.' It was a crucial apparatus for setting the act of killing at a discreet distance from the executioner himself. For while execution using a 'sword or axe rendered the headsman's attentions personal', the guillotine 'spared the executioner his guilt of blood' (Arasse, 1991: 2). The guillotine would perform the act of killing, while the executioner would attend to the machine. Infamy and prestige would now accrue to the apparatus itself, while the executioner and his entourage were left to clean up the operational mess of implacable corpse production, and to make the most of a truncated spectacle: the often tortuous procession to the scaffold through the streets of Paris; and the postmortem brandishing of the severed head to the crowd. (The latter swiftly became the iconic image of the guillotine in action.) It is symptomatic of the machine's accrual of infamy that Tobias Schmidt – the German piano-maker who built the prototype guillotine in Paris in April 1792, and who was also awarded the contract for building the 83 other guillotines that were destined for each *département* in France – was refused a patent for the device: 'Humanity is repelled by the idea of granting a patent for an invention of this kind' (Letter from the Minister of the Interior, 24 July 1792, quoted in Arasse, 1991: 24). The apparatus would be held in common. It belonged to the people. It was one of them. In fact, it was in many respects the perfect citizen.

The guillotine, then, 'was perceived from the first as barbaric, for it brought together two virtually incompatible characteristics: a cold technical precision, and the savagery of physical mutilation' (Arasse, 1991: 2). In addition to precipitating the fall from grace of the executioner, rendering him and his ilk mere appendages to the machine, the guillotine also precipitated the profanation of its victim, who was now killed in the presence of a cold machine, rather than in the presence of a just God. 'The ordeal of traditional forms of execution was in some sense a supplication to the Almighty, and the torment endured, which was perceived as an appeal for divine mercy, might redeem the sin committed' (Arasse, 1991: 29). A slow and painstaking execution allowed sufficient time for the condemned person to make amends with God, while the crowd of witnesses could scrutinize the person's face for signs of His grace. For example, although the execution of Damiens in 1757 was botched, it was nevertheless an edifying experience for the attentive witness: 'though he was always a great swearer, no blasphemy escaped his lips; but the excessive pain made him utter horrible cries, and he often repeated: "My God, have pity on me! Jesus help me!"' (quoted in Foucault, 1979: 3). Or again: Georges Bataille (1989: 207) famously claimed that he had witnessed 'the identity of these perfect contraries, divine ecstasy and its opposite, extreme horror' in a *c.*1905 photograph of Fou-Tchou-Li's 'death by a thousand cuts' (*leng t'che*). The 'divine violence' of religious eroticism 'elevates the victim above the humdrum world where men live out their calculated lives' (Bataille, 1986: 82). Sexuality and death both enjoy 'the boundless wastage of nature's resources as opposed to the urge to live on characteristic of every living creature' (Bataille, 1986: 61). Mechanical execution leaves no room for either spiritual edification or religious eroticism. There is just killing. And always more killing. So it goes. *Worstward Ho!*

The speed of the guillotine did away with the figure of the dying patient, and with it the sacred relationship between execution, spirituality, edification, and eroticism. The 'dying patient' is essentially sacred, whereas the person who is merely alive or dead is profane. Accordingly, 'the decapitation machine had brought into being a "secular commonplace"' (Arasse, 1991: 30). Rather than a *transition* from life to death, a *passage* from this world to the next, the guillotine's 'simple deprivation of life' was an instantaneous jump-cut from life to death: 'in a flash he was lying face down, his severed head and fully clothed body tossed into a huge tumbril where everything was swimming in blood. ... What butchery!' (quoted in Arasse, 1991: 121). Whether it was one execution or many made not a jot of difference to this inglorious act of profanation. For all of the bloodletting, the Terror was essentially dull and grey. 'The batch executions were by no means a frenzied outburst of killing; they were a colourless processing, a regular production of death, in which the reliability of the machine was placed at the service of industrialized capital punishment that could execute identically and indefinitely' (Arasse, 1991: 109).

Following the advent of the guillotine, then, executioners, patients, and witnesses – perpetrators, victims, and bystanders – all lost their aura and prestige, and even the apparatus itself was degraded through endless repetition. Or to put it another way, by the time the Reign of Terror was curtailed in the summer of 1794, the aura of the art of killing in the Age of Mechanical Decapitation had already waned, to purloin a beautiful expression from Walter Benjamin (1985). Naturally, this profanation was a slow, gradual, and uneven process. Some parts of Europe were still gripped by witch hunts and witch trials, after all, and even in France, enlightened killing did not reach far beyond the Parisian scaffolds. For example, as late as 1803, one executioner was still bitterly complaining about having being sent to Grenoble in 1796:

> I was put in an isolated house, one league from town, and since execution-ers in this region before my arrival had been criminals whom judges had plucked from jail to exercise these duties, I was regarded as a wretched individual. ... So there I was, confused with the vilest of [people], and ever since then, insulted, scorned and constantly threatened. I live in fear, and I cry into my dinner. I beg of you, dear citizen minister, have pity on me. I can no longer survive in this monstrous region. (Letter to the Minister of Justice in Paris, 1803, quoted in Friedland, 2012: 264)

Over the course of the nineteenth century capital punishment in France was well and truly on the wane, both quantitatively and qualitatively, and judicial killing became an increasingly lonely and dreary affair. Executions would become scarce and simple, and executioners would eventually become redundant. In 1832, the number of executioners was halved; then, in 1848, it was reduced to just 28; and finally, in 1870, a solitary executioner based in Paris served the entire nation, taking a mobile guillotine and a couple of assistants with him by railway. France's last public execution by guillotine occurred in 1939, after which they were confined to a prison, with the final one happening in 1977. The death penalty was abolished in 1981, and the last exponent of the guillotine 'lost his part-time executioner's job' (Opie, 2003: 176). In the meantime, incarcera-tion filled the penal space vacated by corporal and capital punishment, where a new cast of characters eagerly set about sculpting the prisoner's psyche and soul, much like their Inquisitorial forebears: psychologists, counsellors, educators, and chaplains.

13

The Business of Genocide

Desk Murderers and Calculated Killers

We no longer believe in wild men in the forests, but we have discovered the beast in man.

Tzvetan Todorov, 1992: 248–9

If the transformation of the fearsome executioner into an ordinary citizen has not grabbed the limelight as much as it should have, then this is certainly not the case for the recasting of seemingly ordinary folk into fearsome mass killers, especially in the case of women (Lower, 2013; Mayer, 2000). 'How safe and comfortable, cosy and friendly the world would feel if it were monsters and only monsters who perpetrated monstrous deeds. Against monsters we are fairly well protected' (Bauman and Donskis, 2013: 22). But what haunts our disenchanted world, now that the light of reason has spirited away superstition and magic (or rather: nibbled at it, nudged it, obscured it – if only a little bit, if at all), is 'the mystery of monstrous deeds without monsters, and of evil deeds committed in the name of noble purposes' (Bauman and Donskis, 2013: 21). Faced with fearsome mass murders, such as the Armenian genocide or the Shoah, notions like sadism, monstrousness, bestiality, and fanaticism are all inadequate. Arthur Seyss-Inquart, the Nazi governor of Austria and then Holland, expressed it starkly: 'there is a limit to the number of people you can kill out of hatred or a lust for slaughter, but there is no limit to the number that you can kill in the cold, systematic manner of the military "categorical imperative"' (quoted in Todorov, 1996: 125). The subtitle of Hannah Arendt's famous account of the 1961 trial in Jerusalem of Adolf Eichmann, the SS officer and bureaucrat who oversaw the transportation of hundreds of thousands of Jews to the death camps for extermination, says it all: *A Report on the Banality of Evil* (Arendt, 1977). Eichmann is the quintessential 'desk killer' or 'desk murderer' (*Schreibtischtäter*). Desk killers simply do their work, their job – diligently, effectively, and efficiently. Or rather, it is sufficient for them simply to do their work and their job. Desk killers work with pens and reams of paper, telephones and memoranda, files and folders, calculators and clocks, invoices and accounts, rules and regulations, etc. Their more or less humdrum work takes place within a detailed and extensive social and technical division of labour that sustains the machinery of destruction: others will work with chemicals and containers; with rolling stock and timetables; with whistles and dogs; with batons and whips; with pistols and rifles; with food and nutrition; with clothes and hair-clippers; with syringes and scalpels; with buildings and landscapes; and with trees and shrubs, etc. Consider, for instance, the work involved in the *Aktion T-4* forced-euthanasia programme, which killed tens of thousands of patients in Nazi Germany's hospitals and asylums between 1939 and 1941. Personal responsibility for the decision to kill was not only 'adiaphorized' (offloaded onto a higher authority; disavowed as someone else's concern), as Bauman (1989) astutely argued, but also dissolved in the division of labour: a semi-automatic stepwise bureaucratic process that led from the ward to the gas chamber. 'There was no single point of responsibility – no place in the procedure at which it was possible to say, here is where the patient receives his death warrant; no point where it could be said, *this* physician is responsible for this patient's death' (Gallagher, 1997: 213).

When all is said and done, then, it is primarily the division of labour that enables killing on a vast scale to be accomplished, and as with all work-forces, the individual is essentially a personification – a place-holder and role-holder – even in those instances where individuals are enjoined or permitted or cajoled to project themselves into their performance at work. Executioners, torturers, desk killers, and all of the others in the division of labour not only perform at work, but also perform emotional and affective labour at work: such as cold-heartedness or hot-headedness; pleasure or displeasure; strain and relaxation, etc. For example, consider Eichmann's recollection of the time he spent with Reinhard Heydrich – one of the principal architects of the Holocaust – following the so-called 'Wannsee Conference' that discussed the 'Final Solution to the Jewish Question': 'Heydrich, Muller and my humble self settled down comfortably by the fire-place ... and I was thinking: today Heydrich is smoking. ... And he drinks cognac. ... And after this Wannsee Conference we were sitting together peacefully, and not in order to talk shop, but in order to relax after the long hours of strain' (quoted in Roseman, 2003: 99). Following the assassination of Heydrich by the Czech Resistance in June 1942, the plan to exterminate more than 2 million Jews in occupied Poland was lent the codename *Aktion Reinhard*. Three purpose-built death factories had been under construction since the autumn of 1941: Belzec, located on the Lublin–Lvov railway;

Sobibor, located 50 miles from Lublin; and Treblinka, located 50 miles from Warsaw. Hundreds of thousands of Jews were killed in these camps, brought from their Polish hinterlands by rail – around 1.5 million in total. By 1944, the camps had been decommissioned, dismantled, and effaced.

In the case of the Nazi regime's genocidal state, the work of extermination was indeed fearsome, but the jobs were often mundane: over 11 million were killed, including 6 million Jews (two thirds of Europe's pre-war Jewish population), 3 million of whom were Polish Jews (nine tenths of Poland's pre-war Jewish population). Of these 6 million, more than half were gassed in the *Aktion Reinhard* and KL death camps, more than a quarter were shot, and the remainder were killed by other means: starvation, disease, lethal labour, death marches, etc. (Hilberg, 2003). Around 42,500 facilities across occupied Europe were used to confine and kill Jews, and somewhere between 100,000 and 500,000 people participated either directly or indirectly in the killings, with hundreds of thousands more having some awareness of the killing operations as bystanders and witnesses (Hilberg, 1993).

It is no coincidence that the Final Solution and *Aktion Reinhard* were led from the RSHA, by a small complement of 600 or so staff drawn from over 50,000 RSHA employees. For the surveillance, regulation, rounding up, and transportation of the Jews to the death camps were essentially policing tasks, largely undertaken by the secret police (Gestapo) and criminal police (Kripo), which together formed the 'security police' (SiPo). 'The extermination of the Jews could be so methodical and deadly only because it was conceived and carried out as a police operation' (Agamben, 2000: 106). Just as those who run banks are much more dangerous than those who rob them, to echo Bertolt Brecht ('What is the robbing of a bank compared to the founding of a bank?' he asked rhetorically in *The Threepenny Opera*, 1928; a question that remains as timely as ever given the violence of finance, from personal debt and microcredit to structural adjustment and systemic financial crises), 'what the crimes of the Nazis teach is that those who enforce the law are more dangerous than those who break it', claims Todorov (1996: 123). 'If only the guards had given themselves over to their instincts!' he adds sardonically. 'Unfortunately, they followed the rules.' Like finance and commerce, the law is invariably an apparatus of violence: a trialectic of law-making, law-preserving, and law-destroying violence (Benjamin, 1986).

Christopher Browning (2001) focuses on one group of policemen: Reserve Police Battalion 101. These men were not zealous Nazi anti-Semites, or hardened SS men, or remote 'desk killers'. They were a few hundred seemingly 'ordinary' Germans, mostly middle-aged family men drawn from the working class and lower-middle class, who became accustomed to killing atrociously. Indeed, most seem to have had an aptitude for such killing, and some seem to have acquired a taste for it. The precise nature of the police work that they were required to perform is evident in this order issued on 11 July 1941, at the start of the systematic mass murder:

Confidential! I. ... all male Jews between the ages of 17 and 45 convicted
as plunderers are to be shot according to martial law. The shootings are to
take place away from cities, villages, and thoroughfares. The graves are to be
leveled in such a way that no pilgrimage site can arise. ... 2. The battalion
and company commanders are especially to provide for the spiritual care
of the men who participate in this action. The impressions of the day are to
be blotted out through the holding of social events in the evenings. (Quoted
in Browning, 2001: 13–14).

Of course, no one would be 'convicted' of anything. All male Jews that could be
found would simply be rounded up and shot. Regarding them *as if* they were
convicted plunderers provided a simulation of legality, and the 'Shooting Order'
issued in October 1941 helped in this regard. (Such a ruse remains all too familiar in the contemporary context of US drone strikes in places such as Afghanistan,
Pakistan, Sudan, and Yemen, where all military-aged men in a strike zone are
presumed to be legitimate targets, unless it can be posthumously proved otherwise.) There were concerns that the reservist policemen would not take to this
kind of police work, but most were soon habituated to it, and some – perhaps
most – became ardent killers.

Operating in occupied Poland from mid-1942 until the end of 1943, the men
of Reserve Police Battalion 101 shot dead at least 38,000 Jews, and deported
at least 45,000 to Treblinka (Browning, 2001: 225–6). Becoming accustomed
to killing is not unusual, as Joshua Oppenheimer's extraordinary film, *The Act
of Killing* (2012), so chillingly explores. Reflecting on his role in the 1994
Rwandan genocide, Jean-Baptise, for instance, says that while he was reluc-
tantly coaxed into killing someone with a machete to demonstrate his loyalty
to a baying crowd, things soon became easier: 'Later on we got used to killing
without so much dodging around' (quoted in Hatzfeld, 2005: 23). Some regard
such zealousness as evidence that these were no 'ordinary' men. 'To the very
end, the ordinary Germans who perpetrated the Holocaust willfully, faithfully,
and zealously slaughtered Jews. They did so even when they were risking their
own capture. They did so even when they had received a command from no
less a personage than Himmler that they desist' (Goldhagen, 1997: 380).
Rather than a mere personification of the 'banality of evil', then, these not-so-
ordinary policemen were in fact *willing* anti-Semitic eliminationists, who
eagerly rounded up, brutalized, terrorized, and killed Jews. Hannah Arendt
accounted for this volte-face with respect to the supposed 'animal pity by
which all normal men are affected in the presence of physical suffering' in the
following way: 'it consisted in turning these instincts around. ... So that instead
of saying: What horrible things I did to people!, the murderers would be able
to say: What horrible things I had to watch in the pursuance of my duties, how
heavily the task weighed upon my shoulders!' (Arendt, 2005: 46). This is certainly how Himmler expressed it in a speech in October 1943: 'We have carried
out this most difficult task for the love of our people. And we have suffered no

defect within us, in our soul, or in our character.' Such a sensibility echoes down the centuries, as we have seen, from the joy of crusading via the horror of guillotining to the indifference of slaughter factories.

The policemen were certainly required to carry out some extraordinarily odious tasks. Consider, for instance, this extract from a police captain's report regarding 'Jewish resettlement actions' undertaken by his unit (Regiment 24 of Reserve Police Battalion 133):

> The total number sent to Belzec on the resettlement train of September 10 amounted to 8,205. ... The slow journey was time and again used by the strongest Jews to press themselves through the holes they had forced open and to seek their safety in flight. ... Shortly beyond Lemberg the commando had already shot off the ammunition they had with them and also used up a further 200 rounds that they had received from army soldiers, so that for the rest of the journey they had to resort to stones while the train was moving and to fixed bayonets when the train was stopped. The ever greater panic spreading among the Jews due to the great heat, overloading of the train cars, and stink of dead bodies – when unloading the train cars some 2,000 Jews were found dead in the train – made the transport almost unworkable. ... In the actions themselves for the period of September 7–10, 1942, no special incidents occurred. (Quoted in Browning, 2001: 31–5)

The closing phrase speaks volumes. One way or another, the area had been made 'clean' of Jews. And the detail of the report may have helped ensure that subsequent actions went more smoothly. Only instrumental rationality remains operative: the imperative is to ensure that the work is done well, rather than to ensure that the work itself merits being done at all. The latter either evaporates in the face of the work to be accomplished or is displaced – 'adiaphorized' – onto others. The refinement of the murderous 'gas vans' used at Chelmno to kill around 80 Jews at a time is a perfect example of the instrumental rationality that was at work in the extermination of the Jews. These standard, mass-produced commercial vans that would ordinarily have trundled around delivering widgets, groceries, carpets, and other merchandise were modified and customized so that the rear compartment could be filled with exhaust fumes, thereby enabling those sealed inside to be killed. In June 1942, Willy Just, an SS mechanic, wrote to Walter Rauff, an RSHA official, demanding 'technical changes' to the Chelmno gas vans, which had already killed 97,000 people since coming into operation in December 1941:

> 1. The vans' normal load is usually nine per square yard. In Saurer vehicles, which are very spacious, maximum use of space is impossible, not because of any possible overload, but because loading to full capacity would affect the vehicle's stability. So reduction of the load space seems necessary. It must absolutely be reduced by a yard, instead of trying to

solve the problem, as hitherto, by reducing the number of pieces loaded. Besides, this extends the operating time, as the empty void must be filled with carbon monoxide. On the other hand, if the load space is reduced, and the vehicle is packed solid, the operating time can be considerably shortened. The manufacturers told us during a discussion that reducing the size of the van's rear would throw it badly off balance. ... In fact, the balance is automatically restored, because the merchandise aboard displays during the operation a natural tendency to rush to the rear doors, and is mainly found lying there at the end of the operation. ...

2. ... The lamps must be enclosed in a steel grid to prevent their being damaged. ... Also, because of the alarming nature of darkness, screaming always occurs when the doors are closed. It would therefore be useful to light the lamp before and during the first moments of the operation.

3. For easy cleaning of the vehicle, there must be a sealed drain in the middle of the floor. The drainage hole's cover ... would be equipped with a slanting trap, so that fluid liquids can drain off during the operation. (Quoted in Lanzmann, 1995: 92–3)

Like the trope of the beautiful young woman who could watch impassively as humans and animals were slaughtered by lightning-quick killing machines, it seems incomprehensible that 'ordinary' men could refine the operation of gas vans to make them easier to clean or casually toss children alive into burning pits and crematoria ovens. Here as elsewhere, a gentle economic nudge may have helped them see sense. SS accountants calculated that by 'not gassing the children to death prior to cremation, the state could save two-fifths of a cent per child' (Lippman and Wilson, 2013: 72). Accordingly, 'the Nazis elected to burn the children alive'.

This instrumental and pragmatic approach to the explication of the art of mass murder is well illustrated by the work of Kurt Prüfer, 'the leading engineer and designer of the furnaces supplied by the Erfurt family business Topf und Söhne for use by the SS at Auschwitz and elsewhere', a man the SS regarded as 'a "magician" of cremation' (Levene, 2013b: 125).

Prüfer's big challenge was to calculate how bodies might be efficiently burnt in the crematoria without wasting coal. ... Prüfer's response was to experiment with different loads of bodies, and he came to the conclusion that as female corpses were more combustible than male, and younger ones more so than older ones, a scientific method of mixing the bodies was necessary. For good measure, body fat collected from funeral pyres might itself be recycled as fuel for the next round of efficient burnings. (Levene, 2013b: 125)

Indeed, economic rationality – or at least a bespectacled bookkeeper's rationality – informs much of the fearsome mass killing undertaken by the Nazis. The case of lethal labour is instructive. Like those entrepreneurial English jailers who took advantage of the 1717 *Transportation Act* that enabled minor offenders to 'be transported for seven years to America instead of being flogged and branded, while men on commuted capital sentences ... might be sent for fourteen', and so 'did excellent business by selling these luckless colonists to shipping contractors, who in turn sold ... the rights to their labour ... to plantation-owners in the Caribbean and America' (Hughes, 1987: 41), the SS turned the leasing of concentration-camp labour to German industrialists into a vast and lucrative enterprise. As well as leasing labour to other businesses, the SS also exploited concentration-camp labour itself: not only to build and maintain the camps, but also to work in SS-owned businesses. The SS began acquiring enterprises long before the war, such as a publisher in 1934 and a figurine manufacturer in 1936, as well as businesses producing 'mineral water, clothing, flower pots and other goods' (Jaskot, 2000: 14). By 1945, the SS had over 500 businesses, from lumbering and quarrying (which were ideal for lethal labour) to food processing and art restoration. The workers in these firms were initially drawn from the regular labour market as wage labourers, with the SS generating profits like any other good capitalist: through the vampiric extraction of surplus labour from its wage slaves (Harman, 2009). As the SS diversified into the production of building materials, construction work, and the armaments industry, however, it cannibalized its camps for slave labour. The war enabled the SS to mobilize vast numbers of workers for itself and the war economy more generally, drawing on a seemingly endless supply of POWs, political prisoners, 'asocials' and the 'workshy', and Jews. Dachau, for example, eventually encompassed over 120 sub-camps scattered across southern Germany and Austria, from Allach to Zangberg, most of which provided slave labourers for munitions factories.

'In 1942, revenue to the SS from the lease of slave labourers totalled 13.2 million Reichsmarks', equivalent to around US$5 million at the time (Lippman and Wilson, 2013: 71). 'Unlike ancient slaves who were given adequate food and housing as a means to protect their value to the slave owners', however, 'the prisoner slaves were not worth protecting. They became a disposable good. And a profitable one' (Lippman and Wilson, 2013: 70–1). And where there is leasing, income, and expenditure, and profits and losses, there are business-service professionals on hand to optimize the calculations. SS accountants in the Business Administration Main Office (WVHA) 'prepared statements to reflect the profit, and sometimes the violence, from the slave labour operations' (Lippman and Wilson, 2013: 71). Moreover, the tension between slave labour and lethal labour remained. 'Among the Nazi leadership there was some disagreement on whether ... the Poles working for the German war economy were to be treated as machinery – that is to be used as labour and given basic living conditions sufficient to maintain their productive capacity – or that, through the creation of extreme circumstances, their labour would become the instrument of their destruction' (Klemann and Kudryashov, 2012: 119).

For those who may be aghast at such a tension, it is worth noting that there is nothing new about accounting for slave and convict labour. It was a fearsome instrument of European colonial exploitation that arguably unleashed as much suffering, death, and destruction as almost any other colonial war-machine – gunboats, machine guns, and bombers included (Fleischman, Funnell and Walker, 2013). And just as the transformation of the idling prison population into a profitable workforce fuelled the growth of the prison populations in Georgian England and the Third Reich alike, so too did it fuel the explosion of the American and Soviet prison populations (Applebaum, 2004; Blackmon, 2008; Gilmore, 2007; Khlevniuk, 2004; Viola, 2007). Moreover, the Nazi regime's drive towards Jewish slave labour began in the 1930s, following the seizure of Jewish businesses and the expulsion of Jewish workers from most sectors of the economy, including the military, civil service, and universities. 'Having made Jews unemployed, they were given state welfare only on condition that they accepted employment in difficult and demeaning conditions that were designed to remove them from fellow Germans' (Black, 2011: 236). They were being transformed into an untouchable 'race of outcasts' reminiscent of their treatment before the Age of Enlightenment, but with none of the rights or privileges that such outcasts previously enjoyed.

With the gentlest of economic nudges, then, the 'banality of evil' transmogrifies into the 'rationality of evil'. This is a conjuring trick that the desk killer pulls off with the help of a little quantification and statistical extrapolation. It allows the age-old financial violence of 'subjecting people to the condition of being "priced"' (Valenze, 2006: 272) – from ancient forms of slavery and indenture to contemporary forms of wage slavery and 'debt servitude' (Graeber, 2011; Lazzarato, 2012, 2015; Marazzi, 2010) – to be twisted into something truly lethal. For example, consider a humdrum financial statement from Buchenwald, which coldly calculated the

> estimated revenue from the leasing of a single prisoner, less the costs to lease which were listed only as food and clothing amortization. Then, the net revenue per day is extrapolated for a period of nine months [which] represented the average life expectancy of a prisoner working in the factories. ... The statement included estimated revenue from the value of the deceased's belongings, including personal clothing, valuables and currency. Further, it included estimated revenue from the prisoner's body, including sales of gold extracted from teeth, hair, fat for soap and ashes for fertilizer; it deducted the cost of cremation. (Lippman and Wilson, 2013: 71)

Economic rationality and the tools of accountancy were pivotal forces in the genocidal universe of the Nazi regime. 'From the creation of lists of victims used to plan railway rolling stock needs and the timetabling of transports to the disposal of Jewish property left outside the gas chambers or near the shooting pits, accounting ... fulfilled an essential part at each step' (Funnell, 2013: 60).

Accountancy allowed the wealth plundered by the Nazis' genocidal universe to be laundered, after which the accursed share could be put into licit circulation: 'before any of the property could be available for use by the state it had to pass through rigorous accounting procedures. ... symbolic means of spiritual cleansing for those at the killing centres and directly engaged in the annihilation of the Jews' (Funnell, 2013: 59). Such money laundering was big business. The section of Auschwitz–Birkenau where the property of deportees was sorted and stored was nicknamed 'Canada' – that mythical land of plenty; the epicentre of the SS's Cargo Cult. Cash and valuables seized in the death camps, amounting to almost 180 million Reichsmarks (equivalent to around US$70 million at the time), were sent to the WVHA. This was only a small proportion of the wealth plundered from the Jews during the years of persecution and destruction (1933–45), estimated to be well in excess of 100 billion Reichsmarks.

Like all good fascists, the SS loved to count: 'in reports to Hitler and Himmler, ... the emphasis is on reporting the *number* of people who had been killed and the number yet to be killed' (Funnell, 2013: 63). They kept meticulous records of such numbers. Counting and accounting were their 'special deliriums', to purloin a phrase that Gilles Deleuze uses to characterize capitalism and its demented regime of money. Consider, for instance, a report written by the commander of the SS in Galicia in June 1943, which lists all of the property confiscated from the Galician Jews, including: '25.580 kg copper coins; 97.190 kg gold coins; 20.952 kg wedding rings; 11.730 kg gold teeth; 343.1 kg cigarette cases; ... and 7.495 kg fountain pens and propelling pencils' (Funnell, 2013: 66). The compulsion to count and list lends itself to another special delirium: the compulsion to visualize what counts – in tables, graphs, and maps (a compulsion that our society has amplified to the point of hysteria). It is instructive to note that at the heart of the so-called 'Wannsee Protocol' for the Final Solution to the Jewish Question is a list of 'approximately eleven million Jews' (the 'approximation' stemming from the fact that some 'foreign countries still do not have a definition of the term "Jew" according to racial principles', which clearly exasperated the Nazis), 'distributed' amongst 35 'individual countries', and that a key 'prerequisite for reaching an overall solution is finding an answer to the question of mixed marriages and persons of mixed blood' (quoted in Roseman, 2003: 111 and 114, respectively). Specifically, how should the Final Solution account for the half-Jew (first degree *Mischling*), the quarter-Jew (second degree *Mischling*), and other fractional Jews, as defined by the 'Nuremberg Laws' of 1935? Who, precisely, should be 'rounded up' as a 'Jew' – both figuratively (in the accounts) and literally (in the streets)? Who, precisely, should be hailed as a 'Jew'? Who should be forced to reply to the Gestapo's call: 'Hey, you there!' as Louis Althusser (1971) succinctly expressed it in his famous essay on ideological state apparatuses and the interpellation of the subject. Lyotard was acutely aware of the difficulty when he considered 'the jews' (sic). 'I use lower case to indicate that I am not thinking of a nation. I make it plural to signify that it is neither a figure nor a political (Zionism), religious (Judaism), or philosophical (Jewish philosophy) subject. ... I use quotation marks to avoid confusing these "jews" with real Jews' (Lyotard, 1990b: 3). This frightful tailoring that cuts the baggy Real to fit the unforgiving proportions of the Imaginary applies not only to 'the jews', of course, but also to many others: from 'armenians' and 'bosniaks' to 'enemy aliens' and 'the undeserving poor', and – naturally – it also applies to *You*. Everyone is caught in nets of arbitrary classification (Perec, 1999), all of which are good for enforcing identity and strangling difference.

During the course of Claude Lanzmann's seminal documentary film, *Shoah* (1985), Raul Hilberg points out an astonishing fact: 'You have to remember one basic principle', he explains. 'There was no budget for destruction' (Hilberg, in Lanzmann, 1995: 134). 'This was a self-financing principle', he adds. 'The SS or the military would confiscate Jewish property and with the proceeds, especially from bank deposits, would pay for transports.' And as we noted above, from the start of the Nazi regime, during the 'years of persecution' (1933–9), as Saul Friedländer (2007a) calls them, the Nazis confiscated Jewish property and assets to finance emigration. For example, within two months of the annexation (*Anschluss*) of Austria in March 1938, a Property Transfer Office had been established and was 'actively promoting the Aryanization of Jewish economic assets' (Friedländer, 2007a: 242). The confiscated assets were used to 'compensate' Nazi fighters and support 'the pauperized Jewish population that was unable to emigrate' (Friedländer, 2007a: 242). By mid-1939, all 33,000 Jewish-owned businesses had disappeared from Vienna: 5,000 were 'Aryanized' and the rest 'liquidated in an orderly way' (Friedländer, 2007a: 242). Legalized persecution, including the seizure of property, was not a Nazi invention. The Armenian genocide, for instance, was enabled by a *Temporary Law of Deportation* and a *Temporary Law of Expropriation and Confiscation* (May and September 1915, respectively). Armenians were obliged to abandon their property ahead of deportation, which thereby defaulted to the state. Similarly, during the Second World War, the Canadian government created a 'protection zone' along the Pacific Coast from which all Japanese Canadians – dubbed 'enemy aliens' – were forcibly relocated to internment camps in the interior, and their property confiscated – ostensibly to be 'held in trust' by the state, but actually liquidated in fire-sales. The Americans did likewise.

In the 'years of persecution', the 'solution' to the Third Reich's 'Jewish question' was emigration. The annexation of Austria, which brought with it an additional 180,000 Jews, and around a quarter of a million half- and quarter-Jews, gave emigration a newfound urgency for the Nazis. (Around 70,000 Jews had emigrated prior to the annexation.) Eichmann 'was among the first SS men to arrive in Austria after the *Anschluss*' (Lozowick, 2002: 35). Based in Vienna, where the vast majority of Austrian Jews lived, Eichmann was tasked with overseeing their emigration. Against a background of escalating persecution that drove many Jews to seek emigration (much of which was at the hands of the law rather than at the hands of mobs and militia), there were two key problems that crippled emigration. First, most Jews were impoverished and so could not afford to emigrate. Second, even wealthy Jews struggled to emigrate. By the time they had traipsed around Vienna securing the necessary paperwork from the various agencies, some documents would have invariably expired. The solutions to both problems were straightforward for an accomplished bureaucrat like Eichmann. The emigration of poor Jews would be financed by the Jewish community itself: from confiscated Jewish property, a levy charged on Jewish emigrants, and relief funds secured from foreign Jewish organizations. As for the chaotic situation with respect to the issuance of paperwork, Eichmann established a 'Central Emigration Bureau, which was actually a building containing representatives of all the official bodies from whom a potential Jewish émigré needed documents. The bureau functioned like a conveyor belt of dispossession – a Jew would enter the building as a man of means and come out with nothing but an emigration permit' (Lozowick, 2002: 35). An echo of this accelerationist approach to emigration can be heard in the UK's recent 'Detained Fast Track and Non-Suspensive Appeals Process', which enabled asylum claims to be determined by the Home Office with (unlawful) expedition.

The success of Eichmann's 'assembly line' emigration system 'was spectacular: in eight months, forty five thousand Jews left Austria, whereas no more than nineteen thousand left Germany in the same period; in less than eighteen months, Austria was "cleansed" of close to a hundred and fifty thousand people, roughly sixty per cent of its Jewish population, all of whom left the country "legally"' (Arendt, 2005: 12–13). It would not be long before the volume of forced Jewish emigration would turn into a major international refugee crisis as countries increasingly refused them entry. The fate of the MS *St. Louis*, a German transatlantic liner that sailed from Hamburg in May 1939, became a worldwide cause célèbre at the time. With around 900 Jewish émigrés on board, most of whom were seeking refuge in the United States via Cuba, the liner found itself refused by Cuba, the US, and Canada, until eventually various European countries (Belgium, Britain, France, and the Netherlands) each begrudgingly accepted a portion of the émigrés after much diplomatic negotiation. Moreover, from the outset, Jewish émigrés were often regarded with suspicion by the countries that gave them refuge. The Soviet Union, for example, had even sought to curtail the influx of political émigrés from fraternal communist parties as early as 1936, fearing that spies and saboteurs were hidden amongst them. 'The 1930s in the USSR were a decade of mounting suspicion of foreigners, spy mania, and xenophobia, which reached their peak in 1937–1938 with the mass arrest of foreigners and Soviet citizens accused of participating in hostile conspiracies, often allegedly directed from abroad' (Chase, 2001: 5).

Once war commenced in 1939, mass Jewish emigration became untenable, and the Nazi regime's 'Final Solution' to the 'Jewish Question' became extermination. 'Instead of emigration, the new solution has emerged, after prior approval by the Führer, of evacuating Jews to the east' (Wannsee Protocol, 20 January 1942, quoted in Roseman, 2003: 111). The persistence of the discourse of 'evacuation' and 'resettlement' – this time to the nebulous East – was not only to dissimulate the plans for mass murder, but also because the Jews were soon required to fund the cost of deportation themselves.

> The Gestapo ... was charged the third-class *one-way* fare of 4 pfenning per track kilometre for each adult carried. A fare of 2 pfenning was charged for children under ten, while children under four travelled free. A discount of half the normal third-class fare was offered for groups of four hundred or more. ... As the scale of the deportations grew, however, the Gestapo found it more difficult to meet the costs of transportation out of their budget. To deal with this problem a charge was levied on the Jewish community for each person deported. (Funnell, 2013: 64, italics in original)

In a perfect example of the banality of evil, not only did the Jews pay for their own 'evacuation' and 'resettlement' to the East, but Eichmann's department (Sub-Department IV-B4 of the Office for the Suppression of Opposition within the RSHA) made the arrangements through an ordinary travel agent more accustomed to tourist bookings: the Central European Travel Agency (*Mitteleuropäisches Reisebüro*, or MER). Hence the seemingly incongruous group savings and family friendly child discounts. The MER 'would ship people to the gas chambers or they will ship vacationers to their favorite resort, and that was basically the same office and the same operation, the same procedure, the same billing. ... As a matter of course, everybody would do that job as if it were the most normal thing to do' (Hilberg, in Lanzmann, 1995: 133). And therein lies the essence of the banality of evil. The bulk of the *work* that went into the Holocaust was quotidian, even humdrum, at the heart of which was the state bureaucracy and its legion of pen-pushing bureaucrats weighed down with forms and files, accounts and reports, and rules and regulations: 'bureaucracy made the Holocaust. And it made it in its own image' (Bauman, 1989: 105). Indeed, although 'administrative massacres organized by the state apparatus' (Arendt, 2005: 124) have taken place for hundreds of years, from crusading and Inquisition to colonial pacification and strike breaking, the Holocaust 'could be committed only by a giant bureaucracy using the resources of government' (Arendt, 2005: 116). Bureaucracy, with its extensive and hierarchical division of labour, and its promulgation of instrumental rationality, tends to absolve individuals of both moral responsibility and ethical concern – even for those who directly administer and perform the state's violence. Everything can be 'adiaphorized', exempted 'from the realm of moral evaluation' (Bauman and Donskis, 2013: 15). 'Kill them all. For the Lord knoweth them that are His', so to speak. Everything can be recast as 'just working' – with any moral and ethical considerations disavowed as someone else's responsibility. Eichmann was famously proud of his role in the extermination of millions of Jews. But he always maintained that he was simply doing his duty as a law-abiding citizen and a 'humble' cog in a vast machine. The banality of evil boils down to sheer 'diligence' and 'thoughtlessness', concludes Arendt (2005: 114 and 115, respectively).

The true horror of Eichmann and his ilk, then, is that they performed their work exceptionally well. So, although it may 'have been very comforting indeed to believe that Eichmann was a monster', says Arendt (2005: 103), 'the trouble with Eichmann was precisely that so many were like him, and that the many were neither perverted nor sadistic, that they were, and still are, terribly and terrifyingly normal'. Bauman puts it even more bluntly: 'The truth is that every "ingredient" of the Holocaust – all those many things that rendered it possible – was normal; ... fully in keeping with everything we know about our civilization, its guiding spirit, its priorities, its immanent vision of the world' (Bauman, 1989: 8). Worse still: '*In the years leading to the Final Solution the most trusted of the safeguards had been put to a test. They all failed – one by one, and all together*' (Bauman, 1989: 108, italics in original). Everything failed to stop the Holocaust, including the law, the church, the media, civil society, and the international community; indeed, they all enabled the Holocaust. Not to *make* it happen, but to *let* it happen. And that is why Bauman insists that the Holocaust is not far removed from 'our' world. Rather, it remains coterminous with all that we do. 'Hilberg ... repeated again and again that the Nazi machine of genocide did not differ in its structure from the "normal" organization of German society' (Bauman and Donskis, 2013, page 34).

Eichmann and his office played a key role in the implementation of the Final Solution, applying the 'normal' means available to modern societies to achieve 'extraordinary' ends. They organized the registration, expropriation, rounding up, and deportation of the remaining Jews of Austria, Belgium, France, Germany, Greece, Holland, Hungary, Italy, and Slovakia. In Budapest alone, Eichmann personally directed the deportation of 437,000 Jews in just eight weeks, most of whom were killed on arrival in Auschwitz–Birkenau.

> He quickly became an expert in 'forced evacuation,' as he had been an expert in 'forced emigration.' In country after country, the Jews had to register, were forced to wear the yellow badge for easy identification, were assembled and deported, the various shipments being directed to one or another of the extermination centres in the East, depending on their relative capacity at the moment. (Arendt, 2005: 57)

Between autumn 1941, and spring 1945, there were over 260 deportation trains from Austria, Germany, and Czechoslovakia to the death camps; around 450 deportation trains from Western and Southern Europe, mostly from France, Holland, and Hungary; and many thousands within Poland itself. The coordination of thousands of 'special passenger trains' (*Sonderzuge*), as the SS euphemistically referred to them, is an exemplary instance of the banality of evil. During Lanzmann's interview with Hilberg in *Shoah* (1985), Hilberg holds a sheet of paper in his hand and says: 'This is the *Fahrplananordnung 587*, which is typical for special trains. The number of the order goes to show you how many of them there were' (Hilberg, in Lanzmann, 1995: 129). This 587th order lists the itinerary for a train that made four round trips to Treblinka (numbered 9228 to 9232), from 13–29 September 1942. For example, the first 'exceptionally long' transport of 50 freight cars was scheduled to arrive in and depart from Treblinka on 14 September at 11:24 and 15:59, respectively, during which time it had to be unloaded, cleaned, and turned around. '[W]e may be talking about ten thousand dead Jews on this one *Fahrplananordnung*', exclaims Hilberg (in Lanzmann, 1995: 131).

However, while it may be tempting to characterize the coordination of these 'special passenger trains' by an assortment of bureaucratic functionaries – or 'desk killers' – as a manifestation of the banality of evil, as we have already seen with respect to the work of the Reserve Police Battalions, the transportations themselves were far from banal. For instance, the so-called Iasi 'Death Train', which departed from Iasi in Romania on 30 June 1941, exemplified the horror of transit. Romanian army, police, and SS units had rounded up around 5,000 Jews from the vicinity of Iasi in the preceding days, half of whom were massacred on the spot. The survivors were 'evacuated' on two trains, sealed inside the packed freight wagons in the usual way. The trains drifted aimlessly from place to place, leaving the Jews inside to die in the stifling July heat. The trains were occasionally halted, the wagons unsealed, and either Jews or Gypsies forced to unload the fresh corpses before resealing the wagons so that the trains could resume their lethal peregrination.

Once again, however, the Nazi regime was not the first to mobilize a railway system for mass murder. The Armenian genocide 'began in part in the cattle cars of the Anatolian and the Baghdad Railway. ... Crammed behind slatted bars, they were starving, in terror, and defecating on themselves', writes Peter Balakian (2005: 190–1). The sight of these trains, packed mostly with women, children, and the elderly, horrified other rail users. 'Most of the rail cars went south and east, most often to the city of Konia, where the deportees were often let out to continue on foot before they were robbed, raped, and murdered by the killing squads. Sometimes they were shipped all the way through to Aleppo, where those who survived arrived emaciated and near death, only to confront more massacres.' Tens of thousands were deported in this manner, alongside the hundreds of thousands deported on foot. In 'October 1915 alone, more than 30,000 Armenians were packed into livestock cars to be sent to their deaths in the Der Zor Desert' (Balakian, 2005: 191). With so many Armenians forcibly driven in the same direction, 'detention camps sprang up alongside the tracks and stations. From Konia south to the desert, the whole stretch appeared as one long, concentrated detention camp' (Balakian, 2005: 191). Some of the camps were vast. For example, one 'near Osmaniye ... held as many as 70,000' (Balakian, 2005: 192). Moreover, the Armenians, like the Jews, were often forced to pay for their deportation.

Finally, it is worth noting that the Berlin–Baghdad Railway Company was one of Germany's key foreign-development projects in the opening decades of the twentieth century. 'It is ironic that the Turks used the railway in ways that the Nazis would later, and that Germans in Turkey in 1915 were on site to testify' (Balakian, 2005: 190). For instance, Franz Gunther, the head of the Railway Company's office in Istanbul, and a representative of its financier, Deutsche Bank, vociferously reported the 'bestial cruelty' of the Turks to the Bank and the Germany Embassy.

Before closing, there is one last thing that I would like to consider. We have already seen how 'the killing centers were factories of death' (Berenbaum, 1993: 127). Indeed, Henry Feingold characterized Auschwitz–Birkenau as 'a mundane extension of the modern factory system. Rather than producing goods, the raw material was human beings and the end-product was death. ... The brilliantly organized railroad grid of modern Europe carried a new kind of raw material to the factories' (quoted in Bauman, 1989: 8). The 'death factories' were essentially little different to any other factory in the industrial age, all of which geared themselves up for the efficient and profitable mass production of something or other: pins, textiles, cars, pork products, urinals, armaments, corpses, or telephones. And like any factory, a 'death factory' needs to be staffed by a workforce – a labour force – rather than a group of sadists or psychopaths. 'Camp survivors seem to agree on the following point: only a small minority of guards, on the order of five to ten percent, could legitimately be called sadists' (Todorov, 1996: 122). Indeed, 'a systematic effort was made to weed out all those who derived physical pleasure from what they did' (Arendt, 2005: 45). This is not to say, however, that sadism was not employed in the camps. But it was employed instrumentally. 'Violence has been turned into a technique', insists Bauman (1989: 98), and, 'like all techniques, it is free from emotions and purely rational', and thereby ame-nable to optimization.

Now, the thing that is puzzling is why the Nazis did not simply kill the Jews, amongst others, with the same indifference that our society kills animals, insects, and weeds; why they choose 'the aggressive liquidation of difference (as opposed to a reserved indifference to difference)', as Peter Hallward (in Badiou, 2002: xvi) puts it. For the Holocaust was much more than just killing. Millions of people were systematically 'demolished' as human beings (Agamben, 1998; Cavarero, 2011; Sofsky, 1997). The dehumanization of people through the application of bureaucratic and instrumental rationality is insufficient to account for this shift from killing to demolition. Truth be told, people have never been unequivocally 'human' (Bourke, 2011; Derrida, 2011), a notion that leaks in all directions: towards the heavens and the earth, the vegetal and the animal. For example, can men be beasts and animals beastly? 'Once effectively dehumanized', argues Bauman (1989: 103), 'human objects of bureaucratic task-performance are viewed with ethical indifference, which soon turns into disapprobation and censure when their resistance, or lack of cooperation, slows down the smooth flow of bureaucratic routine' (Bauman, 1989: 103). This is a long way from what Adriana Cavarero (2011: 37) refers to as 'the methodical process of annihilation of the human being that has as its result "a hollow man"' – a 'walking corpse', a 'bare life', or a '*Muselmann*' (Levi, 1988). 'Before their deaths, persons were destroyed gradually. ... The production of "living skeletons" is one of the genuine inventions of the concentration camp' (Sofsky, 1997: 25). These were the 'walking dead' – human beings 'in the process of dissolution'.

During the 1930s, a similar process of dissolution ravaged prisoners of the Soviet Gulag, just as it had ravaged those offered British 'famine relief' during the Indian famines of 1876–9, and 1886–1902. Towards the end of the Great Terror (1936–8), which claimed as many as a million lives as the Soviet Union attempted to purge itself of internal enemies, Andrei Vyshinsky, who presided over the Moscow Show Trials, inspected some of the Gulag camps, and wrote a memorandum to Nikolai Yezhov, who, as head of the NKVD (People's Commissariat for Internal Affairs), was the driving force behind the Terror and responsible for the Gulag: 'Among the prisoners there are some so ragged and lice-ridden that they pose a sanitary danger to the rest. These prisoners have deteriorated to the point of losing any resemblance to human beings' (quoted in Brent, 2008: 12). Vyshinsky quoted the chief procurator of the Bamlag camp: 'They resemble humans or, more likely, savages, or people of the Stone Age. ... And new trainloads of people without clothes keep coming, and people go on the road barefoot, unclothed, and we have minus twenty to minus fifty degrees centigrade here' (quoted in Brent, 2008: 13).

With regard to the 'living dead', it is a moot point as to whether the Nazi death camps continued to operate as a regime of terror, since that would presume a subject capable of being terrorized. Since those who have been demolished are essentially incommunicado, Cavarero (2011: 35) argues that 'the regime ... was not one of terror but rather – as Levi attests – one of horror'. The camps excelled in *applied horror* – horror as a technique and an apparatus. (Cf. Claude Lanzmann's *Shoah*, and László Nemes's film, *Son of Saul* (2015).) At 'the apex of horrorism' (Cavarero, 2011: 33), one will undoubtedly find the gas chambers and crematoria of the death camps; and Auschwitz–Birkenau 'attained the pinnacle of the Jew-destruction machine' (Levene, 2013b: 124). One will also find on this exact same spot the epitome of evil's banality: a memorandum, dated 6 November 1943, sent from the Head of Auschwitz's Central Building Directorate to the Head of Auschwitz's Agricultural Services. 'Objective: to assemble the plants for the purpose of providing a border of greenery for the camp's Nos 1 and 2 crematorium ovens. ... 200 trees in leaf from three to five metres high; 100 tree shoots in leaf from a metre and a half to four metres high; lastly, 1,000 bushes for use as lining from one to two and a half metres high' (Perec, 1999: 90).

In my mind's eye, I cannot help but see a scattering of signs amongst the crematoria's verdant shrubbery, helpfully informing death-camp salarymen, demolished inmates, and legions of dark tourists alike: 'Keep Off the Grass' (*Rasen betreten verboten*), 'No Ball Games Allowed' (*Keine Ballspiele erlaubt*), and 'Work Sets You Free' (*Arbeit Macht Frei*). In a parallel universe that is also our own, this would undoubtedly make an ideal spot for a darkly touristic day trip or an illicit 'place-hack' (Garrett, 2013; Hooper and Lennon, 2017; Sion, 2014).

Still Dead Certain

The system is demented, yet works very well.

Gilles Deleuze, in Félix Guattari, 2009: 36

It is good to give materialist investigations a truncated ending.

Walter Benjamin, 2002: 473

With the lingering image of a discreet and delightful 'border of greenery' planted around the crematorium ovens at the Auschwitz–Birkenau death camp – which, incidentally, could serve as the perfect emblem for the disgusting notions of 'sustainable development' and 'resilience' that have been impressed upon us – suffice to say that at this very moment in the text myriad forms of violence unleashed by the very special deliriums of the Enlightenment, optimism, modernity, and capitalism are working themselves out unabated. In violence we continue to trust: law-making violence, law-preserving violence, law-destroying violence, quotidian violence, and even – on rare occasions – divine violence. You are entreated to enjoy the fruits of their collective labour whilst you still can, before the sun finally sets on the all-consuming adventure of capitalism that is surely basking in its golden hour. Hereinafter, we are sure to continue ever worstward, whilst killing space and killing time. 'So leastward on. So long as dim still. Dim undimmed. Or dimmed to dimmer still. To dimmost dim. Leastmost in dimmost dim. Utmost dim. Leastmost in utmost dim. Unworsenable worst' (Beckett, 2009: 108). *Worstward Ho!* indeed. Meanwhile, the zombies are enjoying the resplendent carnival of cannibalism that has been so very kindly laid on by the powers that be. '*Beautiful day!*' '*Certainly is!*' So, without further ado, let's eat. *Hey, you there! Treat yourself! Enjoy yourself! Eat yourself!* And, as the sun finally sets on these sublime geographies of violence, let's take the opportunity to catch a final glimpse of the constellation set against an ashen sky.

> As he watched, the stars began to slide about, to realign themselves upon the black canvas of the sky as though to spell out some message for him. … Whut do they say, oletimer? he asked. Whut do the stars say? … After a long silent time, the Indian said: They say the universe is mute. Only men speak. Though there is nothing to say. (Coover, 1998: 83)

References

Abbott, G. (2005) *Execution: A Guide to the Ultimate Penalty* (Summersdale, Chichester).

Ackroyd, P. (2011) *London Under* (Chatto and Windus, London).

Adalian, R. P. (1997) 'The Armenian genocide', in *Century of Genocide: Eyewitness Accounts and Critical Views*, eds S. Totten, W. S. Parson and I. W. Charny (Garland, New York), 41–77.

Addison, P. and Crang, J. A. (eds) (2006) *Firestorm: The Bombing of Dresden, 1945* (Pimlico, London).

Adey, P., Whitehead, M. and Williams, A. J. (eds) (2013) *From Above: War, Violence and Verticality* (Hurst, London).

Agamben, G. (1998) *Homo Sacer: Sovereign Power and Bare Life* (Stanford University Press, Stanford, CA).

Agamben, G. (2000) *Means Without Ends* (Minnesota University Press, Minneapolis, MN).

Agamben, G. (2005) *State of Exception* (Chicago University Press, Chicago, IL).

Alibek, K. and Handelman, S. (2000) *Biohazard* (Arrow, London).

Allen, W. (2008) *The War on Bugs* (Chelsea Green, White River Junction, VT).

Althusser, L. (1971) *Lenin and Philosophy and Other Essays* (Monthly Review, New York).

Andress, D. (2005) *The French Revolution and the People* (Hambledon, London).

Annas, G. J. and Grodin, M. A. (eds) (1992) *The Nazi Doctors and the Nuremberg Code: Human Rights in Human Experimentation* (Oxford University Press, Oxford).

Applebaum, A. (2004) *Gulag: A History of the Soviet Camps* (Penguin, London).

Arasse, D. (1991) *The Guillotine and the Terror* (Penguin, London).

Arendt, H. (1977) *Eichmann in Jerusalem: A Report on the Banality of Evil* (Penguin, New York).

Arendt, H. (2003) *Responsibility and Judgment* (Schocken, New York).

Arendt, H. (2005) *Eichmann and the Holocaust* [Excerpts from *Eichmann in Jerusalem*] (Penguin, London).

Asbridge, T. (2005) *The First Crusade: A New History* (Free Press, London).

Augé, M. (2009) *Non-Places: Introduction to an Anthropology of Supermodernity* (Verso, London).

Badiou, A. (2002) *Ethics: An Essay on the Understanding of Evil* (Verso, London).

Badiou, A. (2007) *The Century* (Polity, Cambridge).

Badiou, A. (2008) *The Meaning of Sarkozy* (Verso, London).

Badiou, A. (2010) *The Communist Hypothesis* (Verso, London).

Badiou, A. (2012) *The Rebirth of History* (Verso, London).

Baker, S. (2007) *Ancient Rome: The Rise and Fall of an Empire* (BBC, London).

Balakian, P. (2005) *The Burning Tigris: A History of the Armenian Genocide* (Pimlico, London).

Ballard, J. G. (1973) *Crash* (Jonathan Cape, London).

Baratay, E. and Hardouin-Fugier, E. (2002) *Zoo: A History of Zoological Gardens in the West* (Reaktion, London).

Barber, S. (2002) *Projected Cities: Cinema and Urban Space* (Reaktion, London).

Bargu, B. (2014) *Starve and Immolate: The Politics of Human Weapons* (Columbia University Press, New York).

Barthelme, D. (2003) *Sixty Stories* (Penguin, London).

Bartky, I. R. (2000) *Selling the True Time: Nineteenth-century Timekeeping in America* (Stanford University Press, Stanford, CA).

Bataille, G. (1986) *Eroticism: Death and Sensuality* (City Lights, San Francisco, CA).

Bataille, G. (1988a) *Guilty* (Lapis, Venice, CA).

Bataille, G. (1988b) *The Accursed Share: An Essay on General Economy* (Zone, New York).

Bataille, G. (1989) *The Tears of Eros* (City Lights, San Francisco, CA).

Baudrillard, J. (1983) *Simulations* (Semiotext(e), New York).

Baudrillard, J. (1993) *Fatal Strategies* (Pluto, London).

Baudrillard, J. (1995) *The Gulf War Did Not Take Place* (Indiana University Press, Bloomington, IN).

Baudrillard, J. (2010a) *The Agony of Power* (Semiotext(e), Los Angeles, CA).

Baudrillard, J. (2010b) *Carnival and Cannibal: Ventriloquous Evil* (Seagull, London).

Bauman, Z. (1988) *Freedom* (Minnesota University Press, Minneapolis, MN).

Bauman, Z. (1989) *Modernity and the Holocaust* (Polity, Cambridge).

Bauman, Z. (1992) *Mortality, Immortality and Other Life Strategies* (Polity, Cambridge).

Bauman, Z. and Donskis, L. (2013) *Moral Blindness: The Loss of Sensitivity in Liquid Modernity* (Polity, Cambridge).

Beauregard, R. A. (1993) *Voices of Decline: The Postwar Fate of US Cities* (Blackwell, Oxford).

Beckett, S. (2009) *Company, Ill Seen Ill Said, Worstward Ho, Stirrings Still* (Faber & Faber, London).

Beevor, A. (1998) *Stalingrad* (Viking, London).

Beevor, A. (2002) *Berlin: The Downfall 1945* (Viking, London).

Beifuss, A. and Bellini, F. T. (2013) *Branding Terror: The Logotypes and Iconography of Insurgent Groups and Terrorist Organizations* (Merrell, London).

Bell, D. A. (2008) *The First Total War: Napoleon's Europe and the Birth of Modern Warfare* (Bloomsbury, London).

Benjamin, M. (2013) *Drone Warfare: Killing by Remote Control* (Verso, London).

Benjamin, W. (1985) *Illuminations* (Schocken, New York).

Benjamin, W. (1986) *Reflections: Essays, Aphorisms, Autobiographical Writings* (Schocken, New York).

Benjamin, W. (2002) *The Arcades Project* (Harvard University Press, Cambridge, MA).

Berenbaum, M. (1993) *The World Must Know: The History of the Holocaust as Told in the United States Holocaust Memorial Museum* (Little, Brown, Boston, MA).

Berg, M. (2011) *Popular Justice: A History of Lynching in America* (Rowman and Littlefield, New York).

Bergson, H. (1999) *Duration and Simultaneity: Bergson and the Einsteinian Universe* (Clinamen, Manchester).

Berlant, L. (2011) *Cruel Optimism* (Duke University Press, Durham, NC).

Berman, M. (1983) *All That is Solid Melts into Air: Experience of Modernity* (Verso, London).

Berman, M. (1999) *Adventures in Marxism* (Verso, London).

Bernstein, R. (2002) *Out of the Blue: The Story of September 11, 2001. From Jihad to Ground Zero* (Times Books, New York).

Bernstein, R. J. (2013) *Violence: Thinking Without Banisters* (Polity, Cambridge).

Bessler, J. D. (1996) 'The "Midnight Assassination Law" and Minnesota's Anti-Death Penalty Movement, 1849–1911', *William Mitchell Law Review* 22(2): 577–730.

Bessler, J. D. (2003) *Legacy of Violence: Lynch Mobs and Executions in Minnesota* (Minnesota University Press, Minneapolis, MN).

Bessler, J. D. (2013) *Cruel and Unusual: The American Death Penalty and the Founders' Eighth Amendment* (Northeastern University Press, Lebanon, NH).

Biehler, D. D. (2013) *Pests in the City: Flies, Bedbugs, Cockroaches, and Rats* (Washington University Press, Seattle, WA).

Black, J. (2011) *Slavery: A New Global History* (Constable & Robinson, London).

Blackburn, R. (2002) *Banking on Death, or, Investing in Life: The History and Future of Pensions* (Verso, London).

Blackmon, D. A. (2008) *Slavery by Another Name: The Re-enslavement of Black Americans from the Civil war to World War II* (Doubleday, New York).

Blatman, D. (2010) 'The death marches and the final phase of Nazi genocide', in *Concentration Camps in Nazi Germany: The New Histories*, eds J. Caplan and N. Wachsmann (Routledge, London), 167–85.

Blatman, D. (2011) *The Death Marches: The Final Phase of Nazi Genocide* (Harvard University Press, Cambridge, MA).

Bloom, C. (2012) *Riot City: Protest and Rebellion in the Capital* (Palgrave Macmillan, Basingstoke).

Borges, J. L. (2000) *Labyrinths: Selected Stories and Other Writings* (Penguin, London).

Bourke, J. (2007) *Rape: A History from 1860 to the Present* (Virago, London).

Bourke, J. (2011) *What It Means to Be Human: Reflections from 1791 to the Present* (Virago, London).

Bourke, J. (2014) *Wounding the World: How Military Violence and War-play Invade Our Lives* (Virago, London).

Brent, J. (2008) *Inside the Stalin Archives: Discovering the New Russia* (Atlas, New York).

Brinkley, D. (2006) *The Great Deluge: Hurricane Katrina, New Orleans, and the Mississippi Gulf Coast* (HarperCollins, New York).

Browning, C. R. (2001) *Ordinary Men: Reserve Police Battalion 101 and the Final Solution in Poland* (Penguin, London).

Buck-Morss, S. (1991) *The Dialectics of Seeing: Walter Benjamin and the Arcades Project* (Massachusetts Institute of Technology, Cambridge, MA).

Buck-Morss, S. (2009) *Hegel, Haiti, and Universal History* (Pittsburgh University Press, Pittsburgh, PA).

Burleigh, M. (2010) *Moral Combat: A History of World War II* (Harper, London).

Burleigh, M. and Wippermann, W. (1991) *The Racial State: Germany 1933–1945* (Cambridge University Press, Cambridge).

Butler, J. (2004) *Precarious Life: The Power of Mourning and Violence* (Verso, London).

Butler, J. (2009) *Frames of War: When is Life Grievable?* (Verso, London).

Calder, A. (1992) *The Myth of the Blitz* (Pimlico, London).

Carey, J. W. (1992) *Communication as Culture: Essays on Media and Society* (Routledge, London).

Carson, R. (1962) *Silent Spring* (Houghton Mifflin, Boston, MA).

Carver, T. (1998) *The Postmodern Marx* (Manchester University Press, Manchester).

Cavarero, A. (2011) *Horrorism: Naming Contemporary Violence* (Columbia University Press, New York).

Caygill, H. (2013) *On Resistance: A Philosophy of Defiance* (Bloomsbury, London).

Cederström, C. and Fleming, P. (2012) *Dead Man Working* (Zero Books, Alresford).

Chamayou, G. (2012) *Manhunts: A Philosophical History* (Princeton University Press, Princeton, NJ).

Chamayou, G. (2015) *Drone Theory* (Penguin, London).

Chamberlain, L. (2006) *The Philosophy Steamer: Lenin and the Exile of the Intelligentsia* (Atlantic Books, London).

Chase, W. J. (2001) *Enemies Within the Gates? The Comintern and the Stalinist Repression, 1934–1939* (Yale University Press, New Haven, CT).

Chomsky, N. (1988) *Manufacturing Consent: The Political Economy of the Mass Media* (Pantheon, New York).

Chomsky, N. (2000) *Rogue States: The Rule of Force in World Affairs* (Pluto, London).

Cioran, E. M. (2012a) *The Trouble With Being Born* (Arcade, New York).

Cioran, E. M. (2012b) *The Temptation to Exist* (Arcade, New York).

Claflin, K. (2008) 'La Villette: City of Blood (1867–1914)', in *Meat, Modernity, and the Rise of the Slaughterhouse*, ed. P. Y. Lee (New Hampshire University Press, Lebanon NH), 27–45.

Clastres, P. (1989) *Society Against the State* (Zone, New York).

Clausewitz, C. von (1993) *On War* (Everyman's Library, London).

Cobb, M. (2009) *The Resistance: The French Fight Against the Nazis* (Simon & Schuster, New York).

Cobb, R. (1972) *The Police and the People: French Popular Protest, 1789–1820* (Oxford University Press, Oxford).

Cobb, R. (1987) *The People's Armies: The Armées Révolutionnaires: Instrument of the Terror in the Departments, April 1793 to Floréal Year II* (Yale University Press, New Haven, CT).

Cohn, M. (ed.) (2015) *Drones and Targeted Killing: Legal, Moral, and Geopolitical Issues* (Olive Branch, Northampton, MA).

Cole, T. (2003) *Holocaust City: The Making of a Jewish Ghetto* (Routledge, London).

Cole, T. (2011) *Traces of the Holocaust: Journeying in and out of the Ghettos* (Continuum, London).

Cole, T. and Giordano, A. (2014) 'Bringing the ghetto to the Jew: spatialities of ghettoization in Budapest', in *Geographies of the Holocaust*, eds A. K. Knowles, T. Cole and A. Giordano (Indiana University Press, Bloomington, IN), 120–57.

Conquest, R. (1986) *The Harvest of Sorrow: Soviet Collectivization and the Terror-Famine* (Oxford University Press, New York).

Cooper, C. and Block, R. (2006) *Disaster: Hurricane Katrina and the Failure of Homeland Security* (Times Books, New York).

Coover, R. (1998) *Ghost Town* (Henry Holt, New York).

Cox, S. (2006) 'The Dresden raids: why and how', in *Firestorm: The Bombing of Dresden, 1945*, eds P. Addison and J. A. Crang (Pimlico, London), 18–61.

Cronon, W. (1992) *Nature's Metropolis: Chicago and the Great West* (W. W. Norton, New York).

Da Mosto, F. (2004) *Francesco's Venice: The Dramatic History of the World's Most Beautiful City* (BBC, London).

Damisch, H. (2001) *Skyline: The Narcissistic City* (Stanford University Press, Stanford, CA).

Dams, C. and Stolle, M. (2014) *The Gestapo: Power and Terror in the Third Reich* (Oxford University Press, Oxford).

Darnton, R. (1979) *The Business of Enlightenment: A Publishing History of the Encyclopédie 1775–1800* (Belknap, Cambridge, MA).

Darnton, R. (1984) *The Great Cat Massacre and Other Episodes in French Cultural History* (Basic Books, New York).

Darnton, R. (1996) *The Forbidden Bestsellers of Pre-revolutionary France* (HarperCollins, London).

Darnton, R. (2003) *George Washington's False Teeth: An Unconventional Guide to the Eighteenth Century* (Norton, New York).

Darnton, R. (2010a) *Poetry and the Police: Communication Networks in Eighteenth-century Paris* (Belknap, Cambridge, MA).

Darnton, R. (2010b) *The Devil in the Holy Water, or the Art of Slander from Louis XIV to Napoleon* (Pennsylvania University Press, Philadelphia, PA).

Davis, M. (1993) 'Dead West: ecocide in Malboro country', *New Left Review* 200: 49–73.

Davis, M. (2002) *Late Victorian Holocausts: El Niño Famines and the Making of the Third World* (Verso, London).

Davis, M. (2007a) *Buda's Wagon: A Brief History of the Car Bomb* (Verso, London).

Davis, M. (2007b) *Planet of Slums* (Verso, London).

Davison, C. (1936) *Great Earthquakes* (Thomas Murby, London).

De León, J. (2015) *The Land of Open Graves: Living and Dying on the Migrant Trail* (California University Press, Oakland, CA).

Debord, G. (2010) *Society of the Spectacle* (Black & Red, Detroit, MI).

DeJean, J. (2014) *How Paris Became Paris: The Invention of the Modern City* (Bloomsbury, New York).

DeLanda, M. (1997) *A Thousand Years of Nonlinear History* (Zone, Brooklyn, NY).

Deleuze, G. (1989) *Masochism: Coldness and Cruelty* (Zone, New York).

Deleuze, G. (1992) 'Postscript on the societies of control', *October* 59: 3–7.

Deleuze, G. (1994) *Difference and Repetition* (Athlone, London).

Deleuze, G. (1997) *Essays Critical and Clinical* (Minnesota University Press, Minneapolis, MN).

Deleuze, G. and Guattari, F. (1988) *A Thousand Plateaus: Capitalism and Schizophrenia* (Minnesota University Press, Minneapolis, MN).

Derrida, J. (1986) *Glas* (Nebraska University Press, Lincoln, NE).

Derrida, J. (1994) *Specters of Marx: The State of the Debt, the Work of Mourning, and the New International* (Routledge, London).

Derrida, J. (1996) *The Gift of Death* (Chicago University Press, Chicago, IL).

Derrida, J. (2005) *Rogues: Two Essays on Reason* (Stanford University Press, Stanford, CA).

Derrida, J. (2011) *The Beast and the Sovereign: Volume 1* (Chicago University Press, Chicago, IL).

Derrida, J. (2014) *The Death Penalty: Volume 1* (Chicago University Press, Chicago, IL).

Des Pres, T. (1980) *The Survivor: An Anatomy of Life in the Death Camps* (Oxford University Press, Oxford).

Dikötter, F. (2011) *Mao's Great Famine: The History of China's Most Devastating Catastrophe, 1958–62* (Bloomsbury, London).

DuBois, P. (1990) *Torture and Truth* (Routledge, London).

Duhamel, G. (1931) *America the Menace: Scenes From the Life of the Future* (Allen & Unwin, London).

Duverger, C. (1989) 'The meaning of sacrifice', in *Fragments for a History of the Human Body: Volume 3*, ed. M. Feher (Zone, New York), 366–85.

Dyson, M. (2006) *Come Hell or High Water: Hurricane Katrina and the Color of Disaster* (Basic, New York).

Eck, W. (2003) *The Age of Augustus* (Blackwell, Oxford).

Elden, S. (2013) *The Birth of Territory* (Chicago University Press, Chicago, IL).

Elkins, C. (2005) *Imperial Reckoning: The Untold Story of Britain's Gulag in Kenya* (Henry Holt, New York).

Ericksen, R. P. (2012) *Complicity in the Holocaust: Churches and Universities in Nazi Germany* (Cambridge University Press, Cambridge).

Evans, C. M. (2002) *War of the Aeronauts: A History of Ballooning in the Civil War* (Stackpole, Machanicsburg, PA).

Ewing, W. A. (2016) *Edward Burtynsky: Essential Elements* (Thames & Hudson, London).

Fanon, F. (2008) *Concerning Violence* (Penguin, London).

Ferguson, N. (2008) *The Ascent of Money: A Financial History of the World* (Penguin, London).

Feshbach, M. and Friendly, A. (1992) *Ecocide in the USSR: Health and Nature Under Siege* (Aurum, London).

Fleischman, R. K., Funnell, W. and Walker, S. P. (eds) (2013) *Critical Histories of Accounting: Sinister Inscriptions in the Modern Era* (Routledge, Abingdon).

Flood, J. (2010) *The Fires* (Riverhead, New York).

Fotion, N., Kashnikov, B. and Lekea, J. K. (2007) *Terrorism: The New World Disorder* (Continuum, London).

Foucault, M. (1972) *The Archaeology of Knowledge* (Routledge, London).

Foucault, M. (1974) *The Order of Things: An Archaeology of the Human Sciences* (Tavistock, London).

Foucault, M. (1979) *Discipline and Punish: The Birth of the Prison* (Peregrine, London).

Foucault, M. (1989) *Foucault Live: Interviews, 1966–84* (Semiotext(e), New York).

Foucault, M. (2004) *Society Must Be Defended* (Penguin, London).

Friedland, P. (2012) *Seeing Justice Done: The Age of Spectacular Capital Punishment in France* (Oxford University Press, Oxford).

Friedlander, H. (1995) *The Origins of Nazi Genocide: From Euthanasia to the Final Solution* (North Carolina University Press, London).

Friedländer, S. (2007a) *The Years of Persecution: Nazi Germany and the Jews, 1933–1939* (Phoenix, London).

Friedländer, S. (2007b) *The Years of Extermination: Nazi Germany and the Jews, 1939–1945* (HarperCollins, New York).

Fukuyama, F. (1993) *The End of History and the Last Man* (Penguin, London).

Funnell, W. (2013) 'Accounting for the Holocaust', in *Critical Histories of Accounting: Sinister Inscriptions in the Modern Era*, eds R. K. Fleischman, W. Funnell and S. P. Walker (Routledge, Abingdon), 57–68.

Gallagher, H. G. (1997) 'Holocaust: disabled peoples', in *Century of Genocide: Eyewitness Accounts and Critical Views*, eds S. Totten, W. S. Parson and I. W. Charny (Garland, New York), 208–35.

Gallagher, J. (2010) *Reimagining Detroit: Opportunities for Redefining an American City* (Wayne State University Press, Detroit, MI).

Garrett, B. L. (2013) *Explore Everything: Place-hacking the City* (Verso, London).

Gaskill, M. (2010) *Witchcraft: A Very Short Introduction* (Oxford University Press, Oxford).

Geertz, C. (2005) 'Deep play: notes on the Balinese cockfight', *Dædalus* 134(4): 56–86.

Gergan, M. D. (2017) 'Living with earthquakes and angry deities at the Himalayan borderlands', *Annals of the Association of American Geographers* 107(2): 490–8.

Gerould, D. (1992) *Guillotine: Its Legend and Lore* (Blast, New York).

Getty, J. A. and Naumov, O. V. (2010) *The Road to Terror: Stalin and the Self-destruction of the Bolsheviks, 1932–1939* (Yale University Press, New Haven, CT).

Giaccaria, P. and Minca, C. (eds) (2016) *Hitler's Geographies: The Spatialities of the Third Reich* (Chicago University Press, Chicago, IL).

Gigliotti, S. (2010) *The Train Journey: Transit, Captivity, and Witnessing in the Holocaust* (Berghahn, Oxford).

Gilbert, M. (1995) *First World War* (HarperCollins, London).

Gilbert, M. (1997) *Holocaust Journey: Travelling in Search of the Past* (Weidenfeld & Nicolson, London).

Gilbert, M. (2006) *Kristallnacht: Prelude to Destruction* (HarperPress, London).

Gilmore, R. W. (2007) *Golden Gulag: Prisons, Surplus, Crisis, and Opposition in Globalizing California* (California University Press, Berkeley, CA).

Gilmore, R. W. and Gilmore, C. (2008) 'Restating the obvious', in *Indefensible Space: The Architecture of the National Insecurity State*, ed. M. Sorkin (Routledge, New York), 141–62.

Gilroy, P. (1993) *The Black Atlantic: Modernity and Double Consciousness* (Verso, London).

Ginzburg, C. (1992) *The Cheese and the Worms: The Cosmos of a Sixteenth-century Miller* (Routledge, London).

Giroux, H. A. (2006) *Stormy Weather: Hurricane Katrina and the Politics of Disposability* (Paradigm, Boulder CO).

Glennie, P. and Thrift, N. (2011) *Shaping the Day: A History of Timekeeping in England and Wales 1300–1800* (Oxford University Press, Oxford).

Goin, P. (1991) *Nuclear Landscapes* (Johns Hopkins University Press, Baltimore, MD).

Goldhagen, D. J. (1997) *Hitler's Willing Executioners: Ordinary Germans and the Holocaust* (Abacus, London).

Goldsmith, K. (2015) *New York, Capital of the Twentieth Century* (Verso, London).

Gracq, J. (2013) *A Dark Stranger* (Pushkin, London).

Graeber, D. (2011) *Debt: The First 5,000 Years* (Melville House, New York).

Graham, S. (ed.) (2004) *Cities, War, and Terrorism: Towards an Urban Geopolitics* (Blackwell, Oxford).

Grayling, A. C. (2006) *Among the Dead Cities: Was the Bombing of Civilians in WWII a Necessity or a Crime?* (Bloomsbury, London).

Green, T. (2007) *Inquisition: The Reign of Fear* (Macmillan, London).

Gregory, D. (2006) 'The black flag: Guantánamo Bay and the space of exception', *Geografiska Annaler* 88B(4): 405–27.

Gregory, D. (2007) 'Vanishing points: law, violence, and exception in the global war prison', in *Violent Geographies: Fear, Terror, and Political Violence*, eds D. Gregory and A. Pred (Routledge, London), 205–36.

Gregory, D. (2014) 'Drone geographies', *Radical Philosophy* 183: 7–19.

Gregory, D. and Pred, A. (eds) (2007) *Violent Geographies: Fear, Terror, and Political Violence* (Routledge, London).

Gruffudd, P. (2000) 'Biological cultivation: Lubetkin's modernism at London Zoo in the 1930s', in *Animal Spaces, Beastly Places: New Geographies of Human–Animal Relations*, eds C. Philo and C. Wilbert (Routledge, London), 222–42.

Guattari, F. (2009) *Chaosophy: Texts and Interviews, 1972–1977* (Semiotext(e), Los Angeles, CA).

Haddal, C. C. (2010) *Border Security: The Role of the U.S. Border Patrol* (Congressional Research Service, Washington, DC).

Ham, P. (2012) *Hiroshima Nagasaki: The Real Story of the Atomic Bombings and their Aftermath* (Doubleday, London).

Hamblyn, R. (2001) *The Invention of Clouds: How an Amateur Meteorologist Forged the Language of the Skies* (Picador, London).

Hamblyn, R. (2009) *Terra: Tales of the Earth: Four Events That Changed the World* (Picador, London).

Hampson, N. (1990) *The Enlightenment: An Evaluation of its Assumptions, Attitudes and Values* (Penguin, London).

Hardt, M. and Negri, A. (2001) *Empire* (Harvard University Press, Cambridge, MA).

Harman, C. (2009) *Zombie Capitalism: Global Crisis and the Relevance of Marx* (Bookmarks, London).

Harrigan, P. and Kirschenbaum, M. G. (eds) (2016) *Zones of Control: Perspectives on Wargaming* (Massachusetts Institute of Technology, Cambridge, MA).

Harris, R. and Paxman, J. (2002) *A Higher Form of Killing: The Secret History of Chemical and Biological Warfare* (Arrow, London).

Harvey, D. (2010) *The Enigma of Capital and the Crises of Capitalism* (Profile, London).

Harvey, D. (2014) *Seventeen Contradictions and the End of Capitalism* (Profile, London).

Hasegawa, G. R. (2015) *Villainous Compounds: Chemical Weapons and the American Civil War* (Southern Illinois University Press, Carbondale, IL).

Hatzfeld, J. (2005) *Machete Season: The Killers in Rwanda Speak* (Farrar, Straus & Giroux, New York).

Headrick, D. R. (1981) *The Tools of Empire: Technology and European Imperialism in the Nineteenth Century* (Oxford University Press, Oxford).

Hell, J. and Schönle, A. (eds) (2010) *Ruins of Modernity* (Duke University Press, Durham, NC).

Hilberg, R. (1993) *Perpetrators Victims Bystanders: The Jewish Catastrophe, 1933–1945* (HarperCollins, New York).

Hilberg, R. (2003) *The Destruction of the European Jews* (Yale University Press, New Haven, CT).

Hindmarsh, R. (ed.) (2013) *Atomic Accidents: A History of Nuclear Meltdowns and Disasters: from the Ozark Mountains to Fukushima* (Routledge, Abingdon).

Hobsbawm, E. (1962) *The Age of Revolution: Europe 1789–1848* (Weidenfeld & Nicolson, London).

Hobsbawm, E. (1994) *The Age of Empire: 1875–1914* (Abacus, London).

Hobsbawm, E. (1995) *The Age of Extremes: 1914–1991* (Abacus, London).

Hochschild, A. (2006) *King Leopold's Ghost: A Story of Greed, Terror and Heroism* (Pan, London).

Hooper, G. and Lennon, J. J. (eds) (2017) *Dark Tourism: Practice and Interpretation* (Routldge, Abingdon).

Horowitz, H. L. (1996) 'The national zoological park: "city of refuge" or zoo?', in *New Worlds, New Animals: From Menagerie to Zoological Park in the Nineteenth Century*, eds R. J. Hoage and W. A. Deiss (Johns Hopkins University Press, Baltimore, MD), 126–35.

Hudson, R. (ed.) (1993) *The Grand Tour: 1592–1796* (Folio Society, London).

Huet, M.-H. (1997) *Mourning Glory: The Will of the French Revolution* (Pennsylvania University Press, Philadelphia, PA).

Hughes, R. (1987) *The Fatal Shore: A History of the Transportation of Convicts to Australia, 1787–1868* (Collins Harvill, London).

Huhtamo, E. (2013) *Illusions in Motion: Media Archaeology of the Moving Panorama and Related Spectacles* (Massachusetts Institute of Technology, Cambridge, MA).

Huntemann, N. B. and Payne, M. T. (eds) (2009) *Joystick Soldiers: The Politics of Play in Military Video Games* (Routledge, Abingdon).

Ignatieff, M. (2004) *The Lesser Evil: Political Ethics in an Age of Terror* (Edinburgh University Press, Edinburgh).

Illouz, E. (2007) *Cold Intimacies: The Making of Emotional Capitalism* (Polity, Cambridge).

IOM (2014) *Fatal Journeys: Tracking Lives Lost During Migration* (International Organization for Migration, Geneva).

Jaskot, P. B. (2000) *The Architecture of Oppression: The SS, Forced Labor and the Nazi Monumental Building Economy* (Routledge, London).

Kafka, F. (1999) *The Complete Short Stories* (Vintage, London).

Kafka, F. (2000) *The Trial* (Penguin, London).

Kaplan, C. (2013) 'The balloon prospect: aerostatic observation and the emergence of militarised aeromobility', in *From Above: War, Violence and Verticality*, eds P. Adey, M. Whitehead and A. J. Williams (Hurst, London), 19–40.

Kern, S. (1983) *The Culture of Time and Space 1880–1918* (Harvard University Press, Cambridge, MA).

Khlevniuk, O. V. (2004) *The History of the Gulag: From Collectivization to the Great Terror* (Yale University Press, New Haven, CT).

Klein, N. (2002) *Fences and Windows: Dispatches from the Front Lines of the Globalization Debate* (Flamingo, London).

Klein, N. (2008) *The Shock Doctrine: The Rise of Disaster Capitalism* (Penguin, London).

Klemann, H. and Kudryashov, S. (2012) *Occupied Economies: An Economic History of Nazi-occupied Europe, 1939–1945* (Berg, London).

Komarov, B. (1980) *The Destruction of Nature in the Soviet Union* (Pluto, London).

Krell, A. (2002) *The Devil's Rope: A Cultural History of Barbed Wire* (Reaktion, London).

Krementschouk, A. (2011) *Chernobyl Zone* (Kehrer Verlag, Heidelberg).

Kyle, D. G. (2001) *Spectacles of Death in Ancient Rome* (Routledge, London).

Langbein, J. H. (2006) *Torture and the Law of Proof: Europe and England in the Ancien Régime* (Chicago University Press, Chicago, IL).

Lanzmann, C. (1995) *Shoah: The Complete Text of the Acclaimed Holocaust Film* (De Capo, New York).

Lapavitsas, C. (2013) *Profiting Without Producing: How Finance Exploits Us All* (Verso, London).

Lazzarato, M. (2012) *The Making of the Indebted Man: Essay on the Neoliberal Condition* (Semiotext(e), Los Angeles, CA).

Lazzarato, M. (2015) *Governing By Debt* (Semiotext(e), South Pasadena, CA).

LeDuff, C. (2013) *Detroit: An American Autopsy* (Penguin, New York).

Lee, P. Y. (2008) *Meat, Modernity, and the Rise of the Slaughterhouse* (New Hampshire University Press, Lebanon, NH).

Lefebvre, H. (1991) *The Production of Space* (Blackwell, Oxford).

Lefebvre, H. (2004) *Rhythmanalysis: Space, Time and Everyday Life* (Continuum, London).

Leibniz, G. W. (1985) *Theodicy: Essays on the Goodness of God, the Freedom of Man and the Origin of Evil* (Open Court, La Salle, IL).

Leith, J. A. (1991) *Space and Revolution: Projects for Monuments, Squares, and Public Buildings in France, 1789–1799* (McGill-Queen's University Press, Montreal).

Lemarchand, R. (1997) 'The Rwandan genocide', in *Century of Genocide: Eyewitness Accounts and Critical Views*, eds S. Totten, W. S. Parson and I. W. Charny (Garland, New York), 408–23.

Lerner, S. (2010) *Sacrifice Zones: The Front Lines of Toxic Chemical Exposure in the United States* (Massachusetts Institute of Technology, Cambridge, MA).

Le Roy Ladurie, E. (1990) *Montaillou: Cathars and Catholics in a French Village* (Penguin, London).

Leslie, R. (2013) *Stormbelt* (Dewi Lewis, Stockport).

Levene, M. (2013a) *The Crisis of Genocide: Volume 1. Devastation: The European Rimlands, 1912–1938* (Oxford University Press, Oxford).

Levene, M. (2013b) *The Crisis of Genocide: Volume 2. Annihilation: The European Rimlands, 1939–1953* (Oxford University Press, Oxford).

Levi, P. (1988) *The Drowned and the Saved* (Michael Joseph, London).

Lillard, J. M. (2016) *Playing War: Wargaming and U.S. Navy Preparations for World War II* (Nebraska University Press, Lincoln, NE).

Linderman, G. F. (1987) *Embattled Courage: The Experience of Combat in the American Civil War* (Free Press, New York).

Lippman, E. J. and Wilson, P. A. (2013) 'Accountants and the Holocaust', in *Critical Histories of Accounting: Sinister Inscriptions in the Modern Era*, eds R. K. Fleischman, W. Funnel and S. P. Walker (Routledge, Abingdon), 69–81.

Livingstone, D. (1992) *The Geographical Tradition: Episodes in a Contested Enterprise* (Blackwell, Oxford).

Loewenstein, A. (2015) *Disaster Capitalisn: Making a Killing out of Catastrophe* (Verso, London).

London, J. (1903) *The People of the Abyss* (Isbister, London).

Lordon, F. (2014) *Willing Slaves of Capital: Spinoza and Marx on Desire* (Verso, London).

Lowe, K. (2007) *Inferno: The Devastation of Hamburg, 1943* (Viking, London).

Lowe, K. (2013) *Savage Continent: Europe in the Aftermath of World War II* (Penguin, London).

Lower, W. (2013) *Hitler's Furies: German Women in the Nazi Killing Fields* (Chatto & Windus, London).

Lozowick, Y. (2002) *Hitler's Bureaucrats: The Nazi Security Police and the Banality of Evil* (Continuum, London).

Lyotard, J.-F. (1989a) *The Lyotard Reader* (Blackwell, Oxford).

Lyotard, J.-F. (1989b) *Pacific Wall* (Lapis, Venice, CA).

Lyotard, J.-F. (1990a) *Duchamp's Trans/formers* (Lapis, Venice, CA).

Lyotard, J.-F. (1990b) *Heidegger and 'the jews'* (Minnesota University Press, Minneapolis, MN).

Lyotard, J.-F. (1993) *Libidinal Economy* (Indiana University Press, Bloomington, IN).

Lyotard, J.-F. (1998) *The Assassination of Experience by Painting, Monory* (Black Dog, London).

Mahajan, K. (2016) *The Association of Small Bombs* (Viking, London).

Marazzi, C. (2010) *The Violence of Finance Capitalism* (Semiotext(e), Los Angeles, CA).

Marchand, Y. and Meffre, R. (2010) *Ruins of Detroit* (Steidl, Göttingen).

Marder, M. (2015) *Pyropolitics: When the World is Ablaze* (Rowman & Littlefield, London).

Martin, S. (2005) *The Cathars: The Most Successful Heresy of the Middle Ages* (Pocket Essentials, Harpenden).

Marx, K. and Engels, F. (1848) *Manifesto of the Communist Party* (Progress, Moscow).

Massumi, B. (2011) 'National enterprise emergency: steps towards an ecology of powers', in *Beyond Biopolitics: Essays on the Governance of Life and Death*, eds P. T. Clough and C. Willse (Duke University Press, Durham, NC), 19–45.

Maximoff, G. P. (1940) *The Guillotine at Work: Twenty Years of Terror in Russia. Part 1: The Leninist Counter-Revolution. Part 2: Data and Documents* (Alexander Berkman Fund, Chicago, IL).

Maxwell-Stuart, P. G. (2003) *Witch-hunters: Professional Prickers, Unwitchers and Witch Finders of the Renaissance* (Tempus, Stroud).

Mayer, A. J. (2000) *The Furies: Violence and Terror in the French and Russian Revolutions* (Princeton University Press, Princeton, NJ).

Mayer, A. J. (2012) *Why Did the Heavens Not Darken? The 'Final Solution' in History* (Verso, London).

Mazower, M. (2009) *Hitler's Empire: Nazi Rule in Occupied Europe* (Penguin, London).

Mbembe, A. (2003) 'Necropolitics', *Public Culture* 15(1): 11–40.

McAllister, P. (2003) *Death Defying: Dismantling the Execution Machinery in 21st Century U.S.A.* (Continuum, London).

McGlynn, S. (2015) *Kill Them All: Cathars and Carnage in the Albigensian Crusade* (History Press, Stroud).

McNeill, W. H. (1979) *Plagues and Peoples* (Penguin, Harmondsworth).

Medea, B. (2013) *Drone Warfare: Killing by Remote Control* (Verso, London).

Merriman, J. M. (2016) *The Dynamite Club: How a Bombing in Fin-de-Siècle Paris Ignited the Age of Modern Terror* (Yale University Press, New Haven, CT).

Michman, D. (2014) *The Emergence of Jewish Ghettos During the Holocaust* (Cambridge University Press, Cambridge).

Milligan, B. (1995) *Pleasures and Pains: Opium and the Orient in Nineteenth-century British Culture* (Virginia University Press, Charlottesville, VA).

Milton, S. (1997) 'Holocaust: the Gypsies', in *Century of Genocide: Eyewitness Accounts and Critical Views*, eds S. Totten, W. S. Parson and I. W. Charny (Garland, New York), 171–207.

Misrach, R. (1990) *Bravo 20: The Bombing of the American West* (Johns Hopkins University Press, Baltimore, MD).

Misrach, R. (1992) *Violent Legacies: Three Cantos* (Cornerhouse, New York).

Moore, A. (2010) *Detroit Disassembled* (Damiani, Bologna).

Moore, R. I. (1990) *The Formation of a Persecuting Society: Power and Deviance in Western Europe, 950–1250* (Blackwell, Oxford).

Murphy, C. (2013) *God's Jury: The Inquisition and the Making of the Modern World* (Penguin, London).

Nagorski, A. (2008) *The Greatest Battle: The Fight for Moscow 1941–42* (Aurum, London).

Nancy, J.-L. (2015) *After Fukushima: The Equivalence of Catastrophes* (Fordham University Press, New York).

Neiman, S. (2004) *Evil in Modern Thought: An Alternative History of Philosophy* (Princeton University Press, Princeton, NJ).

Neocleous, M. (2003) 'The political economy of the dead: Marx's vampires', *History of Political Thought* 24(4): 668–84.

Neocleous, M. (2014) *War Power, Police Power* (Edinburgh University Press, Edinburgh).

Netz, R. (2009) *Barbed Wire: An Ecology of Modernity* (Wesleyan University Press, Middletown, CT).

Nietzsche, F. (2003a) *Beyond Good and Evil: Prelude to a Philosophy of the Future* (Penguin, London).

Nietzsche, F. (2003b) *The Genealogy of Morals* (Dover, Mineola, NY).

Nixon, R. (2011) *Slow Violence and the Environmentalism of the Poor* (Harvard University Press, Cambridge, MA).

Noys, B. (2005) *The Culture of Death* (Berg, London).

O'Hara, K. (2010) *The Enlightenment: A Beginner's Guide* (Oneworld, Oxford).

O'Neil, R. (2008) *Belzec: Stepping Stone to Genocide* (JewishGen, New York).

O'Regan, P. (2013) 'Accounting for famine and empire', in *Critical Histories of Accounting: Sinister Inscriptions in the Modern Era*, eds R. K. Fleischman, W. Funnell and S. P. Walker (Routledge, Abingdon), 114–25.

O'Shea, S. (2001) *The Perfect Heresy: The Revolutionary Life and Death of the Medieval Cathars* (Profile, London).

Oettermann, S. (1997) *The Panorama: History of a Mass Medium* (Zone, New York).

Olalquiaga, C. (1999) *The Artificial Kingdom: A Treasury of the Kitsch Experience* (Bloomsbury, London).

Oldroyd, D., Fleischman, R. K. and Tyson, T. N. (2013) 'Somebody knows the trouble I've seen: moral issues of New World slavery and accounting practitioners', in *Critical Histories of Accounting: Sinister Inscriptions in the Modern Era*, eds R. K. Fleischman, W. Funnell and S. P. Walker (Routledge, Abingdon), 144–55.

Olick, J. K. (2005) *In the House of the Hangman: The Agonies of German Defeat, 1943–1949* (Chicago University Press, Chicago, IL).

Ophir, A., Givoni, M. and Hanafi, S. (eds) (2009) *The Power of Inclusive Exclusion: Anatomy of Israeli Rule in the Occupied Palestinian Territories* (Zone, New York).

Opie, R. F. (2003) *Guillotine: The Timbers of Justice* (Sutton, Stroud).

Orwell, G. (2000) *Nineteen Eighty-Four* (Penguin, London).

Osborne, M. A. (1995) 'Zoos in the family: the Geoffroy Saint-Hilaire clan and the three zoos of Paris', in *New Worlds, New Animals: From Menagerie to Zoological Park in the Nineteenth Century*, eds R. J. Hoage and W. A. Deiss (Johns Hopkins University Press, Baltimore, MD), 33–42.

Pacyga, D. A. (2008) 'Chicago: slaughterhouse to the world', in *Meat, Modernity, and the Rise of the Slaughterhouse*, ed. P. Y. Lee (New Hampshire University Press, Lebanon, NH), 153–66.

Pacyga, D. A. (2015) *Slaughterhouse: Chicago's Union Stock Yard and the World it Made* (Chicago University Press, Chicago, IL).

Paglen, T. (2010) *I Could Tell You But Then You Would Have to be Destroyed By Me: Emblems from the Pentagon's Black World* (Melville, New York).

Paice, E. (2008) *Wrath of God: The Great Lisbon Earthquake of 1755* (Quercus, London).

Pakenham, T. (1991a) *The Boer War* (Cardinal, London).

Pakenham, T. (1991b) *The Scramble for Africa, 1876–1912* (Weidenfeld & Nicholson, London).

Parenti, C. (2011) *Tropic of Chaos: Climate Change and the New Geography of Violence* (Nation, New York).

Patterson, I. (2007) *Guernica and Total War* (Profile, London).

Payne, M. T. (2016) *Playing War: Military Video Games After 9/11* (New York University Press, New York).

Perec, G. (1999) *Species of Spaces and Other Pieces* (Penguin, Harmondsworth).

Perrault, C. (2010) *The Complete Fairytales* (Oxford University Press, Oxford).

Peterson, D. J. (1993) *Troubled Lands: The Legacy of Soviet Environmental Destruction* (Westview, Boulder, CO).

Pfeifer, M. J. (2004) *Rough Justice: Lynching and American Society, 1874–1947* (Illinois University Press, Champaign, IL).

Phillips, J. (2009) *Holy Warriors: A Modern History of the Crusades* (Bodley Head, London).

Pick, D. (1993) *War Machine: The Rationalisation of Slaughter in the Modern Age* (Yale University Press, New Haven, CT).

Porter, R. (2002) *Madness: A Brief History* (Oxford University Press, Oxford).

Preston, D. (2015) *A Higher Form of Killing: Six Weeks in World War I That Forever Changed the Nature of Warfare* (Bloomsbury, New York).

Preston, P. (2012) *The Spanish Holocaust: Inquisition and Extermination in Twentieth-century Spain* (Harper, London).

Probert, H. (2003) *Bomber Harris: His Life and Times: The Biography of Marshall of the Royal Air Force Sir Arthur Harris, the Wartime Chief of Bomber Command* (Greenhill, London).

Raffles, H. (2011) *Insectopedia* (Pantheon, New York).

Rapport, M. (2013) *The Napoleonic Wars: A Very Short Introduction* (Oxford University Press, Oxford).

Razac, O. (2002) *Barbed Wire: A Political History* (New Press, New York).

Rediker, M. (2008) *The Slave Ship: A Human History* (John Murray, London).

Rees, S. (2001) *The Floating Brothel* (Headline, London).

Relph, E. (1976) *Place and Placelessness* (Pion, London).

Rhodes, R. (2002) *Masters of Death: The SS-Einsatzgruppen and the Invention of the Holocaust* (Alfred A. Knopf, New York).

Richie, A. (2014) *Warsaw 1944: Hitler, Himmler and the Crushing of a City* (William Collins, London).

Richter, D. (1994) *Chemical Soldiers: British Gas Warfare in World War I* (Leo Cooper, London).

Roach, M. (2004) *Stiff: The Curious Lives of Human Cadavers* (Penguin, London).

Roberts, J. (1990) *The Counter-revolution in France, 1787–1830* (Macmillan, London).

Robins, N. (2012) *The Corporation That Changed the World: How the East India Company Shaped the Modern Multinational* (Pluto, London).

Robinson, J. (2013) '"Concealing the crude": airmindedness and the camouflaging of Britain's oil installations, 1936–9', in *From Above: War, Violence and Verticality*, eds P. Adey, M. Whitehead and A. J. Williams (Hurst, London), 145–61.

Roseman, M. (2003) *The Villa, the Lake, the Meeting: Wannsee and the Final Solution* (Penguin, London).

Ross, A. (2012) *The Rest is Noise: Listening to the Twentieth Century* (Fourth Estate, London).

Ross, K. (1995) *Fast Cars, Clean Bodies: Decolonization and the Reordering of French Culture* (Massachusetts Institute of Technology, Cambridge, MA).

Ross, K. (2008) *The Emergence of Social Space: Rimbaud and the Paris Commune* (Verso, London).

Rotman, B. (1993) *Signifying Nothing: The Semiotics of Zero* (Stanford University Press, Stanford, CA).

Rubenstein, R. L. (2001) *The Cunning of History: The Holocaust and the American Future* (Perennial, New York).

Rubio-Goldsmith, R., Fernández, C., Finch, J. K. and Masterson-Algar, A. (eds) (2016) *Migrant Deaths in the Arizona Desert: La Vida No Vale Nada* (Arizona University Press, Tucson, AZ).

Russell, E. (2001) *War and Nature: Fighting Humans and Insects with Chemicals from World War I to Silent Spring* (Cambridge University Press, Cambridge).

Satia, P. (2013) 'The pain of love: the invention of aerial surveillance in British Iraq', in *From Above: War, Violence and Verticality*, eds P. Adey, M. Whitehead and A. J. Williams (Hurst, London), 223–45.

Sawyer, R. D. (2004) *Fire and Water: The Art of Incendiary and Aquatic Warfare in China* (Westview, Oxford).

Scahill, J. (2008) *Blackwater: The Rise of the World's Most Powerful Mercenary Army* (Serpent's Tail, London).

Scarre, G. and Callow, J. (2001) *Witchcraft and Magic in Sixteenth- and Seventeenth-century Europe* (Palgrave, Basingstoke).

Schaffer, R. (2009) 'The bombing campaigns in World War II: The European theatre', in *Bombing Civilians: A Twentieth-century History*, eds Y. Tanaka and M. B. Young (New Press, London), 30–45.

Schivelbusch, W. (1986) *The Railway Journey: The Industrialization of Space and Time in the Nineteenth Century* (California University Press, Berkeley, CA).

Schivelbusch, W. (1988) *Disenchanted Night: The Industrialisation of Light in the Nineteenth Century* (Berg, Oxford).

Schivelbusch, W. (1992) *Tastes of Paradise: A Social History of Spices, Stimulants, and Intoxicants* (Vintage, New York).

Schivelbusch, W. (2003) *The Culture of Defeat: On National Trauma, Mourning and Recovery* (Granta, London).

Schmitt, C. (2007) *Theory of the Partisan* (Telos, Candor, NY).

Schwartz, V. R. (1999) *Spectacular Realities: Early Mass Culture in Fin-de-Siècle Paris* (California University Press, Berkeley, CA).

Sebald, W. G. (2002) *The Rings of Saturn* (Vintage, London).

Sebald, W. G. (2003) *On the Natural History of Destruction* (Random House, New York).

Segal, R. and Weizman, E. (eds) (2003) *A Civilian Occupation: The Politics of Israeli Architecture* (Verso, London).

Sennett, R. (1996) *Flesh and Stone: The Body and the City in Western Civilization* (W. W. Norton, New York).

Shaw, I. G. R. (2016) 'Scorched atmospheres: the violent geographies of the Vietnam War and the rise of drone warfare', *Annals of the Association of American Geographers* 106(3): 688–704.

Shepard, W. (2015) *Ghost Cities of China: The Story of Cities Without People in the World's Most Populated Country* (Zed Books, London).

Sherry, M. S. (1987) *The Rise of American Air Power: The Creation of Armageddon* (Yale University Press, New Haven, CT).

Shoemaker, R. B. (2004) *The London Mob: Violence and Disorder in Eighteenth-century England* (Hambledon and London, London).

Shrady, N. (2009) *The Last Day: Wrath, Ruin and Reason in the Great Lisbon Earthquake of 1755* (Penguin, London).

Silverman, L. (2001) *Tortured Subjects: Pain, Truth and the Body in Early Modern France* (Chicago University Press, Chicago, IL).

Simmons, J. (1995) *The Victorian Railway* (Thames & Hudson, London).

Simon, L. (2005) *Dark Light: Electricity and Anxiety from the Telegraph to X-Ray* (Harcourt, Orlando, FL).

Sinclair, U. (2012) *The Jungle* (Stirling, New York).

Singer, P. W. (2008) *Corporate Warriors: The Rise of the Privatized Military Industry* (Cornell University Press, Ithaca, NY).

Sion, B. (ed.) (2014) *Death Tourism: Disaster Sites as Recreational Landscape* (Chicago University Press, Chicago, IL).

SIPRI (1975) *Incendiary Weapons* (Stockholm International Peace Research Institute, Almqvist and Wiksell, Stockholm).

Slack, P. (2012) *Plague: A Very Short Introduction* (Oxford University Press, Oxford).

Sloterdijk, P. (2009) *Terror from the Air* (Semiotext(e), Los Angeles, CA).

Sloterdijk, P. (2011) *Bubbles* (Semiotext(e), Los Angeles, CA).

Sloterdijk, P. (2014) *The World Interior of Capital: For a Philosophical Theory of Globalization* (Polity, Cambridge).

Sofsky, W. (1997) *The Order of Terror: The Concentration Camp* (Princeton University Press, Princeton, NJ).

Solnit, R. (2002) *Wanderlust: A History of Walking* (Verso, London).

Solnit, R. (2009) *A Paradise Built in Hell: The Extraordinary Communities that Arise in Disaster* (Viking, London).

Sontag, S. (2003) *Regarding the Pain of Others* (Hamish Hamilton, London).

Southern, P. (2001) *Augustus* (Routledge, London).

Stafford, B. M. (1994) *Artful Science: Enlightenment Entertainment and the Eclipse of Visual Education* (Massachusetts Institute of Technology, Cambridge, MA).

Standing, G. (2011) *The Precariat: The New Dangerous Class* (Bloomsbury, London).

Steinbacher, S. (2004) *Auschwitz: A History* (Penguin, London).

Steinweis, A. (2009) *Kristallnacht 1938* (Harvard University Press, Cambridge, MA).

Stone, D. (2015) *The Liberation of the Camps: The End of the Holocaust and Its Aftermath* (Yale University Press, New Haven, CT).

Strachan, H. (2006) 'Strategic bombing and the question of civilian casualties up to 1945', in *Firestorm: The Bombing of Dresden, 1945*, eds P. Addison and J. A. Crang (Pimlico, London), 1–17.

Sutherland, K. (2011) *Stupefaction: A Radical Anatomy of Phantoms* (Seagull, London).

Tanaka, Y. (2009) 'British "humane bombing" in Iraq during the interwar era', in *Bombing Civilians: A Twentieth-century History*, eds Y. Tanaka and M. B. Young (New Press, London), 8–29.

Tanaka, Y. and Young, M. B. (eds) (2009) *Bombing Civilians: A Twentieth-century History* (New Press, London).

Taylor, F. (2004) *Dresden: Tuesday 13 February 1945* (Bloomsbury, London).

Taylor, P. (1999) *Modernities: A Geohistorical Interpretation* (Polity, Cambridge).

Theweleit, K. (1987) *Male Fantasies: Volume 1. Women, Floods, Bodies, History* (Polity, Cambridge).

Theweleit, K. (1989) *Male Fantasies: Volume 2. Male Bodies: Psychoanalyzing the White Terror* (Polity, Cambridge).

Thomas, G. and Morgan Witts, M. (1971) *The San Francisco Earthquake* (Stein & Day, New York).

Thomas, H. (1997) *The Slave Trade: The History of the Atlantic Slave Trade: 1440–1870* (Picador, London).

Thomas, T. and Virchow, F. (2005) 'Banal militarism and the culture of war', in *Bring 'Em On: Media and Politics in the Iraq War*, eds L. Artz and Y. R. Kamalipour (Rowman & Littlefield, New York), 23–36.

Thomson, D. (1990) *Europe Since Napoleon* (Penguin, London).

Todorov, T. (1992) *The Conquest of America: The Question of the Other* (HarperPerennial, New York).

Todorov, T. (1996) *Facing the Extreme: Moral Life in the Concentration Camps* (Metropolitan, New York).

Todorov, T. (2005) *Hope and Memory: Reflections on the Twentieth Century* (Atlantic, London).

Totten, S., Parson, W. S. and Charny, I. W. (eds) (1997) *Century of Genocide: Eyewitness Accounts and Critical Views* (Garland, New York).

Tyerman, C. (2005) *The Crusades: A Very Short Introduction* (Oxford University Press, Oxford).

Tyerman, C. (2007) *God's War: A New History of the Crusades* (Penguin, London).

Tyler, I. (2013) *Revolting Subjects: Social Abjection and Resistance in Neoliberal Britain* (Zed Books, London).

Tyner, J. A. (2016) *Violence in Capitalism: Devaluing Life in an Age of Responsibility* (Nebraska University Press, Lincoln, NE).

Urry, J. (1990) *The Tourist Gaze: Leisure and Travel in Contemporary Societies* (Sage, London).

US DoD (1990) *Total Quality Management Guide* (Office of the Deputy Assistant Secretary of Defense for Total Quality Management, Washington, DC).

Valenze, D. M. (2006) *The Social Life of Money in the English Past* (Cambridge University Press, Cambridge).

Vanderbilt, T. (2010) *Survival City: Adventures Among the Ruins of Atomic America* (Chicago University Press, Chicago, IL).

Vaneigem, R. (1979) *The Revolution of Everyday Life* (Red & Black, London).

Veblen, T. (2007) *The Theory of the Leisure Class* (Oxford University Press, Oxford).

Vergara, C. J. (1999) *American Ruins* (Monacelli, New York).

Vidal-Naquet, P. (1996) *The Jews: History, Memory, and the Present* (Columbia University Press, New York).

Viola, I. (2007) *The Unknown Gulag: The Lost World of Stalin's Special Settlements* (Oxford University Press, Oxford).

Virilio, P. (1989) *War and Cinema: The Logistics of Perception* (Verso, London).

Virilio, P. (1990) *Popular Defense and Ecological Struggles* (Semiotext(e), New York).

Virilio, P. (2001) *Virilio Live: Selected Interviews* (Sage, London).

Virilio, P. (2006) *Speed and Politics* (Semiotext(e), Los Angeles, CA).

Virilio, P. (2012) *The Administration of Fear* (Semiotext(e), Los Angeles, CA).

Virilio, P. and Lotringer, S. (1997) *Pure War* (Semiotext(e), New York).

Voltaire (2005) *Candide, or Optimism* (Penguin, London).

Vonnegut, K. (2000) *Slaughterhouse-Five, or, The Children's Crusade* (Vintage, London).

Vonnegut, K. (2009) *Armageddon in Retrospect and Other New and Unpublished Writings on War and Peace* (Vintage, London).

Wachsmann, N. (2004) *Hitler's Prisons: Legal Terror in Nazi Germany* (Yale University Press, New Haven, CT).

Wachsmann, N. (2010) 'The dynamics of destruction: the development of the concentration camps, 1933–1945', in *Concentration Camps in Nazi Germany: The New Histories*, eds J. Caplan and N. Wachsmann (Routledge, London), 17–43.

Wachsmann, N. (2015) *KL: A History of the Nazi Concentration Camps* (Little, Brown, London).

Wagner, J.-C. (2010) 'Work and extermination in the concentration camps', in *Concentration Camps in Nazi Germany: The New Histories*, eds J. Caplan and N. Wachsmann (Routledge, London), 127–48.

Wahnich, S. (2012) *In Defence of the Terror: Liberty or Death in the French Revolution* (Verso, London).

Walker, J. S. (2004) *Three Mile Island: A Nuclear Crisis in Historical Perspective* (California University Press, Berkeley, CA).

Wall, T. (2014) 'Legal terror and the police dog', *Radical Philosophy* 188: 2–7.

Walvin, J. (2011) *The Zong: A Massacre, the Law and the End of Slavery* (Yale University Press, New Haven, CT).

Weindling, P. (2015) *Victims and Survivors of Nazi Human Experiments: Science and Suffering in the Holocaust* (Bloomsbury, Lodnon).

Weizman, E. (2007) *Hollow Land: Israel's Architecture of Occupation* (Verso, London).

Weizman, E. (2008) 'Thanatotactics', in *Indefensible Space: The Architecture of the National Insecurity State*, ed. M. Sorkin (Routledge, New York), 325–50.

Weizman, E. (2011a) *The Least of All Possible Evils: Humanitarian Violence from Arendt to Gaza* (Verso, London).

Weizman, E. (2011b) 'Thanato-tactics', in *Beyond Biopolitics: Essays on the Governance of Life and Death*, eds P. T. Clough and C. Willse (Duke University Press, Durham, NC), 177–210.

Weizman, E. (2012) *Forensic Architecture: Notes from Fields and Forums* (documenta and Museum Fridericianum, Kassel).

White, J. (2012) *London in the Eighteenth Century: A Great and Monstrous Thing* (Bodley Head, London).

Wilcken, P. (2004) *Empire Adrift: The Portuguese Court in Rio de Janeiro, 1808–1821* (Bloomsbury, London).

Wildt, M. (1995) 'Plurality of taste: food and consumption in West Germany during the 1950s', *History Workshop Journal* 39: 23–41.

Williams, P. and Wallace, D. (1990) *Unit 731: The Japanese Army's Secret of Secrets* (Grafton, London).

Winchester, C. (2010) *Total War: The Great Battles of the 20th Century* (Quercus, London).

Wood, A. L. (2009) *Lynching and Spectacle: Witnessing Racial Violence in America, 1890–1940* (North Carolina University Press, Chapel Hill, NC).

Wood, E. M. (2005) *Empire of Capital* (Verso, London).

Woods, L. (1993) *War and Architecture* (Princeton Architectural Press, New York).

Wytwycky, B. (1980) *The Other Holocaust: Many Circles of Hell* (Novak Report, Washington, DC).

Yarnell, J. (2011) *Barbed Wire Disease: British and German Prisoners of War, 1914–19* (History Press, Stroud).

Yolton, J. W., Porter, R., Rogers, P. and Stafford, B. M. (eds) (1995) *The Blackwell Companion to the Enlightenment* (Blackwell, Oxford).

Zamoyski, A. (2005) *1812: Napoleon's Fatal March on Moscow* (Harper Perennial, London).

Zamoyski, A. (2014) *Phantom Terror: The Threat of Revolution and the Repression of Liberty, 1789–1848* (William Collins, London).

Zelizer, V. A. (2005) *The Purchase of Intimacy* (Princeton University Press, Princeton, NJ).

Ziegler, P. (2002) *London at War, 1939–1945* (Pimlico, London).

Žižek, S. (2007) *Maximilien Robespierre: Virtue and Terror* (Verso, London).

Žižek, S. (2009) *Violence: Six Sideways Reflections* (Profile, London).

Žižek, S. (2011) *Revolution at the Gates: A Selection of Writings from February to October 1917: V.I. Lenin* (Verso, London).

Žižek, S. (2012) *The Year of Dreaming Dangerously* (Verso, London).

Žižek, S., Santner, E. L. and Reinhard, K. (2005) *The Neighbor: Three Inquiries in Political Theology* (Chicago University Press, Chicago, IL).

Zola, É. (2004) *Thérèse Raquin* (Penguin, London).

Index

punishment *cont.*
  retributive, 150
  spectacular, 36, 66, 153
  at the state's expense, 150, 153
  terror, 100
pyromania, 137

Qing (Manchu) dynasty, 33
Quaker guns, 110
quarantine, 61, 121

'race', 32, 100
'racial aliens', 54, 70
racial ideology, 62, 165
racial purgation, 12, 104
racial selection, and *Aktion 14f13*, 106
racism, casual, 144
radar (radio-detection and ranging device), 136, 145, 147
radiation, 84, 130
radioactive waste, 131
radiological dispersal devices ('dirty bombs'), 118
RAF. *See under* Britiain
railways
  and accident shock, 94
  age of, 73
  and animal slaughter, 29, 76, 79–83, 89
  and crashes, 89–90
  'Death Railway' (Thailand–Burma Railway), 40
  and death trains, 13, 170
  and democratization of travel, 90
  and deportation trains, 13, 100, 169–71
  and the end of war, 55–6, 89
  and genocide, 13, 54, 83, 98–100, 158–9, 161, 164, 169–72
  and guillotines, 156
  and manhunts, 59
  and military mobilization, 82, 93–4, 95, 97
  and porterage, 39–40
  and rail time, 91–2
  Railway Regulation Act, British (1844), 90
  and 'special passenger trains', 169–70
  and speed-space, 89–94, 129
  as strategic bombing targets, 127, 135, 138
  and time–space compression, 89–92
RAND Corporation, 16
rape, 13, 50–1. *See also* violence: sexual
Rapport, M., 49
Rath, E. E. vom (Nazi German diplomat), 103
Rauff, W. (Nazi RSHA official), 161
Rawlinson, Sir H. S. (British general), 59
Reagan, R. W., 16

Reason, Age of, 24, 153
reason,
  in bits and pieces, 21–2
  and courage, 5–7, 66–7
  and faith, 6–7, 16
  of the strongest, 18, 84, 103, 129
  and superstition, 21, 157
  and violence, 88–9
rebellions, 10, 28, 33, 38, 57, 60, 85, 111, 128, 131–2, 135, 143
recidivists, 53
reconcentration, of rural populations in cities, 60
Red Army, Soviet, 12, 87, 98–9, 134, 141, 142
'Red Baron' (Richthofen, M. von), 125
Rees, S., 23, 68
Reformation, 55, 56–7
refrigeration, 78–80
refuge, camps of, 60
refugees, 8, 60, 141, 167
Reich Main Security Office, RSHA (*Reichssicherheitshauptamt*), 51, 97, 159, 161, 168
Reich Ministry of Justice, 70
Reich Nuremberg Laws (Defence of German Blood and Honour; Reich Citizenship) (1935), 103, 165
Reichart, J. B. (executioner), 70
religious buildings, destruction of, 8, 35, 53, 103
religious fundamentalism, 17, 119
religious murder, 46. *See also* sacrifice (human)
remotely piloted aerial vehicles (RPAVs) *See* drones (military)
Renaissance, 78
'rendition, extraordinary', 45
reporters, 30–1, 65
Republic of Letters, 22
residential destruction, 87, 127, 135–48
resilience, delirium of, 2, 174
resistance
  Boer, 59
  Czech, 158
  Danish, 99
  French, 99
  gaseous, 57–8
  guerrilla, 58
  Jewish, 99, 101
  Malay, 115
  Mau Mau, 60
  Polish, 133
  Vietnamese, 132
Reval, 85